THE
SUPERNATURAL
SUBLIME

THE

SUPERNATURAL

SUBLIME

The Metaphysics of Terror
in Anglo-American Romanticism

Jack G. Voller

Northern

Illinois

University Press

DeKalb 1994

© 1994 by Northern Illinois University Press

Published by the Northern Illinois University Press,

DeKalb, Illinois 60115   ∞ ✺

Design by Julia Fauci

Part of chapter 1 appeared earlier as "Todorov among the
Gothics: Structuring the Supernatural Moment" and is
reprinted here by permission of Greenwood Publishing
Group, Inc., Westport, CT, from *Contours of the
Fantastic: Selected Essays from the Eighth International
Conference on the Fantastic in the Arts,* edited by
Michelle K. Langford. Copyright © 1990 by Michelle K.
Langford.

Library of Congress Cataloging-in-Publicaton Data
Voller, Jack G.
       The supernatural sublime : the metaphysics of
terror in Anglo-American romanticism / Jack G. Voller.
              p.   cm.
       Includes bibliographical references and index.
       ISBN-87580-194-3
       1. English literature—19th century—History and
criticism.   2. Horror tales, American—History and
criticism.   3. Horror tales, English—History and
criticism.   4. Sublime, The, in literature.
5. Supernatural in literature.   6. Romanticism—Great
Britain.   7. Romanticism—United States.   8. Terror in
literature.   I. Title.
PR457.V65   1994
820.9'145—dc20   94-9360
                     CIP

in memoriam

r.l.v.

Contents

P r e f a c e

The point of departure for this investigation of Gothic and Romantic supernaturalism was the observation that Gothic fiction arose in the same cultural moment when aesthetic discourse in Britain was acutely interested in the sublime. The prominence of an aesthetic of sublimity in Gothic and Romantic literature has long been recognized, but a fundamental question remains: how is the period's supernaturalism, with its powerful interest in the psychological, shaped by the aesthetic of the sublime? This study offers an answer to that question.

There is no doubt that Gothic fiction and Romantic supernaturalism are of a piece with the more academically valued projects of Romantic literary expression, but the full contribution of the sublime to Romantic supernaturalism, and hence to Romanticism itself, has yet to be determined. Attempts on the part of some critics to distance "High Romanticism" from the Gothic have, I think, made the assessment of Romantic and Gothic supernaturalism more difficult; the "major" Romantics did not spurn the Gothic so much as they responded to it, revised it, adapted it to their own purposes, not so much to domesticate it as to appropriate its emotional power and metaphoric capacity. Much of this adaptation was effected through the sublime, arguably the primary bridge between Romantic and Gothic authors. Foregrounding this aesthetic linkage, what this study establishes is that a particular adaptation of sublimity, what I call the supernatural sublime, was put into practice, consciously or otherwise, by the authors in question, and that it informed their work so fully that the concept may be used not only as a conceptual tool for the analysis of individual texts but also as the basis for a typology of Gothic (but not Romantic) supernaturalism.

For both of these applications it is the underlying structure of the sublime experience that proves most valuable. In this structure, the mind's normal emotional and cognitive state is violated by some overwhelming or traumatic experience, producing a moment of arrest or suspension that is immediately followed by recovery, a return to the pre-sublime state. In conventional understandings of sublimity, the experience usually is precipitated by a powerful natural experience; in the supernatural sublime the trauma takes the form of a supernatural encounter, whether truly so or only perceived as such. In conventional sublimity, recovery from the moment of suspension is effected through recognition of a gratifying aesthetic response or an intimation of transcendence, usually of a conventionally religious variety. Supernatural sublimity likewise has two paths or modes of recovery, but the intellectual distance between them is considerably greater. One mode, which I term the conservative, resolves its supernatural moment or moments in favor of received wisdom. The second mode, the radical, is far less certain of the efficacy of traditional consolations.

There is a very deep and direct connection between those domains of human intellection and cultural praxis generally labeled "metaphysics" and "ideology," and it is perhaps this connection that has led me to this terminology of "radical" and "conservative," but in the final analysis this is a study that concerns itself with the metaphysical implications of Gothic and Romantic supernaturalism. To trace these out in any detailed way into the worlds of social and political action was beyond the scope of this work.

While it is inevitable that the sharp focus of this study may slight certain aspects of Gothic fiction, such sacrifices are, I hope, a legitimate (and, I would argue, necessary) trade-off for those insights provided by the supernatural sublime. This model allows us not only to appreciate more fully the extent to which these texts participated in the aesthetic and theoretical debates of their time, but also to advance our understanding of them as documents in the course of our own intellectual history. Gothic fiction and Romantic supernaturalism— the latter being very much a reading of or reaction against the former—are intimately connected to the cultural and historical currents of their moment, which themselves are the direct ancestors of our own, and the concept of the supernatural sublime, by making explicit an important adaptation of sublimity by Romantic-era writers, may contribute not only to our understanding of that cultural moment but to how that moment continues to affect our own.

The development and anatomy of this supernatural sublime, including its four modes in Gothic fiction, forms the subject of the introductory chapter. This introduction, although it lays the groundwork for the entire study, is most directly linked with Part I, which examines four Gothic works, for Gothic fiction is the only literary form that makes unequivocal use of the supernatural sublime.

Part II, a study of the Romantic supernatural, examines texts whose supernaturalism is configured by engagement with and critique of Gothic supernaturalism, particularly its appropriation of sublimity in its deployment of the supernatural in English literature; the notoriety of Gothic novels ensured that they, even more than the theories of their underlying aesthetics or their precursors such as graveyard poetry and sentimental fiction, would become the objects of later scrutiny and response. This does not mean Romantic writers ignored these theories; some, such as Coleridge (and through him Wordsworth), were significantly influenced by Kantian aesthetics in their rejection of Gothic supernaturalism. But theories were not the point of contention. Practice was, particularly as embodied in the structure of suspension and the modes of recovery inherent in all understandings of sublime experience. Other elements are considered here, of course; narrative structure cannot neatly be isolated from imagery, language, theme. But supernatural sublimity is predicated on the narrative and psychological suspension that follows experience of the supernatural, and revisions of this suspension, both of its underlying psychology and its significance, most often constitute the Romantic revision or, in some cases, repudiation of Gothicism.

Acknowledgments

I used to think pages such as this in books such as this were little more than perfunctory gestures of obligation, but in travelling the road of this project I have been disabused of that piece of cynicism, and it is with genuine delight and sincere gratitude that I acknowledge the contributions of those who have helped this book be better than it otherwise would have been. To my early guides, especially Fred V. Randel and Roy Harvey Pearce, I owe much. A particular debt of gratitude is gladly paid—although in coin not sufficient—to Donald Wesling, patient mentor and valued teacher.

Closer to the journey's end are the contributions of my editor, Susan Bean, whose careful eye and thoughtful efforts have improved my work, and of Mary Lincoln, Director of NIU Press, whose support, encouragement, and patience have been more than any author has the right to expect.

Before, during, and after the journey, feelings of gratitude beyond words have been and will be sent to my mother for her support. At the point farthest beyond the failure of words lies the debt that is more than due my wife, Anne, who patiently bore those periods of scholarly widowhood—those dinners eaten alone even when we sat together at the same table—and whose support and love were a *sine qua non* of this journey—and of the larger one ongoing.

THE
SUPERNATURAL
SUBLIME

If the mind of man is naturally subject to secret terrors and apprehensions, if such beings as ghosts and witches are inevitable symbols of these fears, it is clearly difficult to pretend that the ghostly is interesting as a subject only at a distance, that it has to do only with the unsophisticated intelligence; for in fact it has profound significance—even if only symbolically—for *all* men.

—Patricia Meyer Spacks
The Insistence of Horror

But [Ajax] gave no reply, and turned away,
following other ghosts toward Erebos.
Who knows if in that darkness he might still
have spoken, and I answered?

—*The Odyssey* XI
Fitzgerald translation

Chapter One

The Supernatural Sublime

Aesthetic theories, like all cultural artifacts, are historically conditioned. This study concludes with an examination of Romantic texts because they are, largely, subsequent to Gothic fiction, commenting upon and critiquing Gothic supernaturalism and thereby furthering the evolution of an aesthetic of terror. By the same token, Gothic supernaturalism, while very much a response to the anxieties of its age and indebted to prior forms of literary supernaturalism, acquires much of its character in reaction to and elaboration upon a preexisting aesthetic of terror: the conventional sublime.

Commonly associated with the awe or terror produced by the more powerful manifestations of natural forces, conventional sublimity was given a major boost by the work of Edmund Burke and his many detractors and competitors, who spilled a great deal of ink in their efforts to explain why the agents of sublimity (about which there was general consensus) affected us as powerfully as they did. These explanations, it should be stated at the outset, are not particularly germane to this study, which instead proposes to follow the lead of the Gothic novelists by focusing on the agents of sublimity (that is, the cataracts, the earthquakes, the gloomy passageways), the emotional responses elicited by these agents, and their larger implications.[1]

Here, from Ann Radcliffe's *The Mysteries of Udolpho,* is a veritable textbook example of the natural strain of conventional sublimity—

"textbook" because Radcliffe was an ardent disciple of Burke's; her landscape descriptions and many of her heightened narrative moments closely followed Burkean theory, as Malcolm Ware and others have noted. In this passage, Emily and her guardian, Madame Montoni, cross the Alps into Italy:

> The solitary grandeur of the objects that immediately surrounded [Emily], the mountain-region towering above, the deep precipices that fell beneath, the waving blackness of the forests of pine and oak, which skirted their feet, or hung within their recesses, the headlong torrents that, dashing among their cliffs, sometimes appeared like a cloud of mist, at others like a sheet of ice—these were the features which received a higher character of sublimity from the reposing Italian landscape below. . . . Madame Montoni only shuddered as she looked down precipices near whose edge the chairmen trotted lightly and swiftly, almost, as the chamois bounded, and from which Emily too recoiled; but with her fears were mingled such various emotions of delight, such admiration, astonishment, and awe, as she had never experienced before. (164–66)

Radcliffe's description adheres strictly to the principles of the natural sublime, the moment of inspired astonishment that exists primarily for the sake of aesthetics, sentiment, or both. This sublime moment is centered on a sensual experience of delightful terror rather than on religious enthusiasm or devotion, although it is but a short step from "astonishment and awe" in the face of nature to the second variety of conventional sublimity, the religious sublime. Although it entered British cultural debate along with the natural sublime, the religious variety had a certain theological privilege: England's first theorist of the sublime, John Dennis, put "Gods," "Hell," and "Daemons" higher on his list of sublime agents than any natural phenomena. Except for the example that will be offered below, nonsupernatural employments of this religious sublime (and of the natural sublime) will receive little scrutiny in these pages.

These remarks should not be taken to imply that the distinction between natural and religious sublimity is absolute. We need only recall Thomas Gray's famous response to his 1739 trip across the Alps—"Not a torrent, not a cliff but is pregnant with religion and poetry. There are certain scenes that would awe an atheist into belief"—to know that the two are points on the same continuum.

It is the fundamental premise of this study that there exists a third point on this aesthetic spectrum: the supernatural sublime. While aestheticians since Dennis have suggested that intimations of the supernatural could precipitate the sublime experience and while much of the literary atmosphere associated with the supernatural, such as gloom, ruins, and shadow, have been treated by Burke and others, the supernatural sublime is justifiably regarded as a distinct aesthetic. Such a claim discovers its proof in the deliberateness with which Gothic writers appropriated sublimity. These writers sought to ground their supernaturalism, their literary praxis, in a theoretical matrix that linked them to mainstream literary culture; tapping the sublime allowed the artists to legitimate their experimental enterprise while their deep fascination with the tropes of supernaturalism produced a discretely different, if recognizably related, hybrid aesthetic.

Yet Gothic fiction's repeated deployment of agents of sublimity canonized since the first years of the eighteenth century is not what finally makes the supernatural sublime a rewarding object of critical study. Gothic novelists were hardly the only eighteenth-century writers to employ the supernatural. There was, however, a significant distance between the preeminent Gothic texts and the popular graveyard and elegiac poetry of the later eighteenth century. Writers of the latter forms sought not to interrogate the "supramundane," to use Rudolph Otto's term, as much as they wished to ponder "the inconstancy of all sublunary things" (Monk 88):

> As a rule, in neither the graveyard nor the descriptive poetry did the emotion exist for its own sake. In the poetry of death, the purpose of terror was to prepare the mind for whatever moralizing the poet might choose to indulge in; in the descriptive poetry, terrible aspects of nature helped to show the greatness of the Creator and the inscrutability of his way. (Monk 90)

Samuel Monk is here concerned with conventional terror, the sort promulgated by Dennis and Burke, and Monk has correctly identified its use. However, he only partially comprehends the supernaturalist project of the period when he claims that "The gothic novel exists almost purely for the sake of evoking pleasant terror" (90). Such titillation may account for its popular appeal—William Patrick Day is correct in his claim that "The Gothic came into existence and endured because it gave pleasure and satisfaction to its readers" (3)—but Gothic supernaturalism does more than thrill with what Nathan

Drake called "the most awful, yet the most delightful species of terror" (I: 141). Patricia Meyer Spacks, in her study of the supernaturalism of eighteenth-century poetry, noted that for the poets of the time "recognition of the fact that the mystery of death and the dead evokes an engulfing terror for which no substitute image is adequate" meant that "the genuine importance of the supernatural is in a sense denied by its relegation to imagery. As image it retains full potency . . . but once it is made a concomitant of purely psychological reality, its theological, and to a large extent its intellectual, significance is destroyed" (77). Gothic fiction's more considered employment of the supernatural in the form of the supernatural sublime, and the metaphysical implications of that sublime, rescue Gothic supernaturalism from the fate of its predecessor.

The essential value of the supernatural sublime arises from its origins in the confluence of powerful, indeed revolutionary currents of aesthetics and history. An aesthetic of transcendence (that is, an aesthetic useful in metaphysical speculation), plasticized by its wholesale appropriation by writers often more interested in events of earthly rather than transcendent import, ran full force into the turbulent energies of the French Revolution at a time when altered or heightened forms of (self-) consciousness were an increasingly consuming cultural subject. In this crucible of conflict and reaction, the aesthetic of the supernatural sublime became, at least *in posse,* a tool that allowed writers to probe the darkest heart of their age. We can begin to appreciate the value of this tool by considering for a moment the value of the conventional sublime, a value linked—as would become true for the supernatural sublime—to developments and events outside the realm of aesthetics.

The Enlightenment, perhaps in particular the implications of Copernican cosmology, forever undermined the sense, prevalent in earlier ages, that the physical universe betokened the possibility of direct access to intimations (at least) of transcendent possibility. By the close of the seventeenth century, there could be little doubt, as Ernest Tuveson explains, that "radically new conceptions of space and time" were necessary if Western civilization was to align its cosmology with scientific fact (20). One of the most brilliant of these new conceptions was the direct correlation of the apparently infinite universe with the power and majesty of God. Such a troping of the new universe, vast beyond human comprehension and crowded with planets and stars in overwhelming number and confusion, proved at first surprisingly responsive when theologians and writers sought to harmonize religious thought with newly acquired scientific knowledge. The expansion of the natural universe came to mean only that nature revealed more thoroughly the omnipotence of God. As a consequence of this shift in understanding, experience of the natural began to acquire Christian metaphysical implications: "The presentation of the universe as some kind of real image (not the opposite) of the infinite God helped to promote a 'this-worldly' trend in men's thinking. It encouraged a tendency to see in the physical universe the good and desirable expression of the spirit" (Tuveson 22–23).

One cannot dwell long on these matters without contemplating the effect of such a change on literary treatments of human self-perception, and with such contemplation we take another step closer to the metaphysical import of the textual sublime. The inseparability of the aesthetic and metaphysical implications of sublimity was inscribed into sublime theory from the moment of its first full expression in England. In *The Grounds of Criticism in Poetry*, published in 1704, John Dennis argues explicitly that "the greatest sublimity is to be deriv'd from Religious Ideas" (76); he finds the impelling emotion of this sublimity to be "Enthusiastick Terrour." As David Morris notes in his study of the religious sublime, for Dennis "the common bond between poetry and Christianity was their reliance upon passionate and suprarational persuasion and their similar design to restore the inner harmony disrupted by the Fall" (*Religious* 59–60). The original point of the literary sublime, in other words, was to bridge the gap caused by the retreat of God, to catch heaven in the net of the world.

Radcliffe again provides a representative example of the religious sublime, for while some eighteenth-century poets outdid her in the piety they extracted from the sublime, it is instructive to consider an example from a Gothic work. Early in *The Mysteries of Udolpho*, in passages heavily indebted, ironically, to Rousseau, Radcliffe details the education Emily was given by her wise and judiciously sensitive father. Taught to appreciate the natural, Emily has learned well the capacity of nature to intimate the divine:

> It was one of Emily's earliest pleasures to ramble among the scenes of nature; nor was it in the soft and glowing landscape that she most delighted; she loved more the wild wood-walks, that skirted the mountain; and still more the mountain's stupendous recesses, where the silence and grandeur of solitude impressed a sacred awe upon her heart, and lifted her thoughts to the GOD OF HEAVEN AND EARTH. (6)

Radcliffe was adept at harnessing the religious dimension of the sublime to the service of her didacticism, although passages such as this
are not as common as those represented by the example given at the
beginning of this chapter. Nonetheless, the presence of both types of
sublimity in a single novel (which itself employs one mode of the supernatural sublime) testifies to the fluidity and self-complementary
multivalence of the aesthetic.

Emily's experience of the religious sublime derives, at least in the
passage just quoted, from "the silence and grandeur of solitude" in a
raw montane setting. These landscape elements constituted, even by
Radcliffe's time, a stock cluster of associations in the sublime experience, but the passage also gestures at one other component of sublimity aesthetics, one of paramount value in tracing the evolutionary path
of the eighteenth-century sublime. The passage traces a rising motion,
lifting its gaze, as it were, from the soft rural landscape to the mountain skirt, then to its "stupendous recesses." Emily's next thought is
of God, but silently, implicitly present between the mountain and God
is the limitless expanse of the heavens. A significant element of most
sublimity theories, the infinite was of foundational value to most early
post-Ptolemaic efforts to apprehend, or at least respond meaningfully
to, the new universe. Infinity became, as Marjorie Hope Nicholson
explains, the key to the sublime as a trope of transcendence:

> In a vastly expanded universe, men . . . discovered new powers in the
> human soul, new expansion of the imagination. Into an infinite uni-
> verse, they read qualities of the Infinite who had created it, and in them-
> selves, made in the image of the Creator, they found capacities they had
> not known before. (140)

> [However,] it was less the metaphysics of infinity that liberated their
> imaginations than an aesthetic implicit in their response to grandeur,
> vastness, majesty, a gratification in the richness, fullness, vastness of a
> universe man might not intellectually comprehend, which yet satisfied
> his unquiet soul, fed his insatiability. In his divine discontent lay his
> greatness. He grew with what he attempted to comprehend. Mind and
> spirit released from finite bonds, he became in part the thing he sought.
> The basis of "The Aesthetics of the Infinite" was laid down by English-
> men who found themselves astounded yet enthralled by infinite space.
> (143)

The need for and value of an aesthetic of the infinite in what is essentially a religious experience is obvious, for experience of infinity serves

as the objective correlative of transcendence, the spatially or tempo-
rally enacted mental drama of the limited in search of that which is
beyond itself.

But the early emphasis upon and centrality of the infinite meant
also that it could not readily be discarded when the intellectual and
spiritual foundations of Western culture began to shift. The need for
infinity inscribed into aesthetic theory a privileging of the boundless,
the ungraspable, the indeterminate. Arguably the ultimate signifier, infinity can have only one of two signifieds (outside the sciences): the
divine or the void. While for the seventeenth and much of the eighteenth centuries the infinite was uncontested as an argument in favor
of God's existence, the later years of the eighteenth century began to
see the scale tip in the other direction. The early use of the boundless
universe to signify the infinite power of God was a brilliant aesthetic
and spiritual response to the troubling implications of seventeenth-
century scientific discoveries, but such an appropriation also created
a space that Western civilization's progressive secularization would
construe as a locus of terror, an empty crypt haunted by the ghosts of
spiritual entropy.[2]

The privileging of infinity set the stage for the development of the
darkest mode of the supernatural sublime even as conventional sublimity was being given its most definitive treatment. Edmund Burke's
*A Philosophical Enquiry into the Origin of our Ideas of the Sublime
and the Beautiful* (2nd ed. 1759), although it did not invent the correlation, established as incontestable the link between infinity and the
experience of terror: Burke found that infinity "has a tendency to fill
the mind with that sort of delightful horror, which is the most genuine,
and truest test of the sublime" (73). Such was the case for Burke and
many of his contemporaries, even for objects that merely intimated or
suggested infinity by virtue of indefinite boundaries:

> But let it be considered that hardly anything can strike the mind with its
> greatness, which does not make some sort of approach towards infinity;
> which nothing can do whilst we are able to perceive its bounds; but to
> see an object distinctly, and to perceive its bounds, is one and the same
> thing. (Burke 63)

Boundlessness, then, is the key to the sublime power of the infinite, a
power that in earlier theories of sublimity had always been the province of an omnipotent God. Burke does not deny this "almighty
Power," to be sure, but he does bracket off religious awe from the rest

of his theory, treating it as a minor adjunct of little interest. For Burke, God is not *necessarily* the source of infinity's sublime power, and this makes a crucial difference. Gothic authors will discover that ghosts and other supernatural agents, by virtue of the unknown laws that inform their existence, have as much to do with boundlessness as does God, for both reach well beyond any humanly perceptible metaphysical horizon.

Burke was not the only unwitting subverter of his own optimistic aesthetic. Elaborating a theory of aesthetics that is, at times, a vehemently polemical response to Burke's, Richard Payne Knight posits a sublime free from the secular terror and fear so fundamental in Burke. For Knight, "All sublime feelings are . . . feelings of exultation and expansion of the mind, tending to rapture and enthusiasm" (367–68). Knight disliked Gothic and supernatural fiction (384) and was referring, in the above passage from *An Analytical Inquiry into the Principles of Taste* (4th ed. 1808), to the conventional sublime. Yet despite, or perhaps because of, his efforts at countering Burke, Knight contributed significantly to a sublime of supernatural terror. Sublimity, for Knight, is induced by an absence that shapes the affective implications of natural phenomena. The mind's failure to apprehend these phenomena is due to the "negative existence" that defines such powerful agents of sublimity as "darkness, vacuity, [and] silence" in addition to infinity. All of these agents are defined by Knight in exclusively negative terms: they are, respectively, without light, substance, sound, or limit (369–70).

Knight's formulation is important because, in concert with Burke's linkage of terror and infinity, it marks an important shift in the capacity of the infinite to act as a signifier in the literary quest for transcendence. Although contemporaries of Knight such as Dugald Stewart still argued for infinity as a direct intimation of God's omnipotence (294), infinity—and, by extension and implication, the sublime—was no longer an exclusively positive construct. For Burke, sublimity was engendered by terror, not religious passion; even while finding "rapture and enthusiasm" to be the emotional core of sublimity, Knight uncovered a fundamental absence in the experience.

In the sublime experience the mind operates in an emotional and aesthetic realm which, in the historical period under consideration, increasingly came to be characterized by absence and negation, as Knight's definitions suggest. The sublime moment has always concerned itself profoundly with absence; its generative impulse, after all, was the attempt to fill the void caused by the retreat of God from the natural universe. Further, it was marked (paradoxically, for such a literary phenomenon) by ineffability: the sublime "consists in a kind of admiration and expansion of the mind; it raises the mind much above the ordinary state; and fills it with a degree of wonder and astonishment, which it cannot well express" (Blair, *Lectures* I: 46).

The primary absence with which the sublime is concerned, however, is what might be called an absence of self, the suspension of most cognitive, emotional, and sensory faculties. The point is especially crucial, for consideration of this suspension leads directly to the structure of the sublime moment and thence to the structures and function of the supernatural sublime.

The most famous expression of the concept of suspension is, not surprisingly, Burke's:

> The passion caused by the great and sublime in nature, when those causes operate most powerfully, is Astonishment; and Astonishment is that state of the soul, in which all its motions are suspended, with some degree of horror. In this case the mind is so entirely filled with its object, that it cannot entertain any other, nor by consequence reason on that object which employs it. Hence arises the great power of the sublime, that far from being produced by them, it anticipates our reasonings, and hurries us on by an irresistible force. (57)

Mary Arensberg points out that such an aesthetic foregrounds anxiety over the threat of absence and goes on to note that

> Concurrent with this positioning of anxiety as the central emotional response to the sublime by Burke, particularly, was the Lockean notion of anxiety elicited by the perception of absence. Locke, of course, was concerned with the absence of the soul, the empty vessel, which becomes, in more modern versions of the sublime, the nothingness of the self and the perceived loss of the Other. (5)

The Gothic supernatural sublime, I hope to show, is an early form of the modern sublime.

Understanding the basic structure of the sublime moment might best begin with a diagram chronologically mapping the experience (see figure 1).

The sublime experience begins with a normal state, in which emotional and intellectual energies are relatively calm (the horizontal arrow on the left). Impressed by some natural phenomenon, the mental faculties experience a brief moment of suspension or abeyance (marked by the asterisk), which is followed immediately by a sense of elevation or expansion that is an ultimately fruitless attempt to recognize or apprehend that power which gives the object of nature its capacity to move us so dramatically. In traditional formulations of the sublime, the moment of expansion is often associated with religious emotion. This ecstatic moment will inevitably be followed by a return to the normal state (the horizontal line at the right). It is deliberate

FIGURE 1

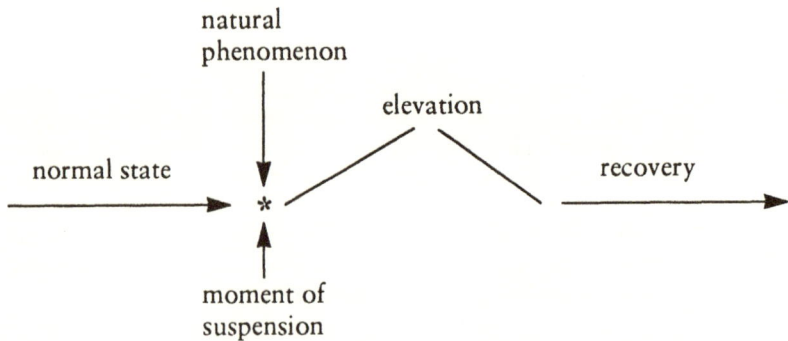

that, in the diagram, this line is at the same level as that on the left, for recovery from the natural or religious sublime is almost always a return to the presublime state. Such is certainly the case for the Christian sublime, in which the moment of expansion intimates a divine presence that was presupposed, indeed worshipped, prior to the sublime experience. The secular sublime of Burke is likewise conservative in this regard, for it is founded on physiological responses to terror that have nothing to do with human understandings of the universe.

It may at first seem paradoxical that such an affective structure may articulate human experience of the transcendent, for this structure insists upon a return to something very close to the subject's original state of knowledge and power. The conventional sublime, in other words, insists on limits, on a transcendent that genuinely and ineluctably resides beyond human ken:

> The sublime is not created by man's ratiocinative processes but rather serves to signal their limitations: it occurs at the moment when man is

overwhelmed by feelings of awe, wonder and terror on confronting aspects of the universe which go beyond his comprehension and which simultaneously reveal the grandeur of God and his own limited place in the divine scheme of things. (Morse 140)

At the same time, however, the sublime attempts to evade the recognition of these limits: following the initial moment of trauma in which the motions of the soul are suspended, the sublime appropriates for the self, indirectly, the power or grandeur of the arresting object. It effects this by foregrounding our self-conscious awareness of our failure; and the ability to recognize, even theorize about, our failure is taken as evidence of an innate, if not directly accessible, transcendent capacity.

In the early years of this century, A. C. Bradley noted the dialectical operation of these simultaneous gestures of limitation and liberation throughout and beyond the sublime moment. According to Bradley, sublimity causes us to "burst our own limits, go out to the sublime thing, identify ourselves ideally with it, and share its immense greatness. But if, and in so far as, we remain conscious of our differences from it, we still feel the insignificance of our actual selves, and our glory is mingled with awe or even with self-abasement" (52–53). A more recent formulation of the experience affirms the dual nature of the sublime's affective significance:

> The sublime is . . . not visionary per se but, rather, a visionary irony or a dramatic irony given a visionary turn. A circumstance of palpable physical subjection becomes, by an ironic logic of the worse the better, the means for the self to register the significance of an unseen world of spirit that nonetheless remains unseen. Its consequence is felt; its contents stay hidden. (Laurence 57)

The sublime as both construct and process is dialectically engaged with itself. If in its essential moment it gestures at transcendent liberation, it is also never able to evade its own necessary acknowledgment of human limitation and inadequacy, a confirmation of the inevitability of subjection.

This is a grim scenario, to be sure, with its roots in the Burkean/Lockean anxiety Arensberg discusses, but the sublime experience is rescued from nihilist despair by locating in the failure of the imagination a desire for fulfillment inherent in the transcendent impulse:

> The metaphorical moment of the sublime would be understood as an internalization or sublimation of the imagination's relation to the object. The "unattainability" of the object with respect to the mind would be duplicated as an inner structure, so that in the sublime moment the mind would discover or posit an undefinable (ungraspable) domain within. . . . We call an object sublime if the attempt to represent it determines the mind to regard its inability to grasp wholly the object as a symbol of the mind's relation to a transcendent order. (Weiskel 23)

David Laurence perceptively identifies this aesthetic as an "ironic gesture" that is "philosophically dubious if poetically interesting," for it is one in which "failure, defeat, and inadequacy in the world of experience indirectly and ironically vouch for the reality of a realm of supersensible ideas . . . in relation to which alone humanity discovers the spiritual vocation for which it is born" (58). The roots of this irony are those of the sublime itself: the need to convert the apparently empty Copernican universe into a signifier of divine presence.

Much of the horror of Gothic supernaturalism is a consequence of the unmasking of this irony, the rendering direct of the sublime's inverted equation. The conventional sublime demands irony in order to transmute physical emptiness and boundlessness into metaphysical plenitude; Gothic sublimity often insists on a direct correlation, and thus physical emptiness (or, perhaps more accurately, the vast unknowable complexity of the universe) signifies or at least suggests a corresponding metaphysical absence or disorder. Gothic supernaturalism is often unable to discover that sense of "rhapsodic oneness with a divine ordering power" (Price 196) upon which the positive implications of the conventional sublime depend; the supernatural sublime often is unable to endorse—or even, in some cases, identify—a numinous or transcendent ordering principle consistently operative in the universe. Nor, without the intimation of some sort of spiritual Other, does Gothic supernaturalism enable the mind to transform its own failure into some compensatory gesture of transcendence. Beginning to register the nascent anxieties of its age, Gothic fiction often finds suspect the moral and metaphysical certainties implicit in the conventional sublime. As Eugenia DeLamotte observes, "The Gothic focus on evil balances the impulse toward transcendence with suspicion. Perhaps unity with the Other is not something to seek but something to shrink from. Gothic works and Romantic works that use the Gothic tradition are filled with symbols of this ambivalent and frustrated impulse toward transcendent unity" (134). The absence of clear metaphysical landmarks is revealed, by the Gothic appropriation of the sublime, to be a source of a terror that by its very nature subverts the project of conventional sublimity.

*P*roceeding from a religious point of departure, Dennis made Christian supernatural imagery (and its attendant horror) a major element in the poetics of sublimity. Indeed, his famous list of the causes of sublimity—which Morris notes "might furnish the quasi-religious claptrap for a shelf of Gothic novels" (*Religious* 74)—privileges the Christian supernatural: "Gods, Daemons, Hell, Spirits and Souls of Men, Miracles, Prodigies, Enchantments, Witchcrafts, Thunder, Tempests, raging Seas, Inundations, Torrents, Earthquakes, Volcanoes, Monsters, Serpents, Lions, Tygers, Fire, War, Pestilence, Famine, etc." (87–88). While, as this list reveals, Dennis recognized the emotional power of nature's more violent aspects, his concern with the spiritual dimensions of poetic transport led him to valorize the extranatural. As one of the first English theorists of the sublime, Dennis helped establish the linkage between terror and supernatural beings as an integral part of sublime theory. Yet while Christianity's pantheon of immortals figured prominently even in Gothic sublimity, it is impossible to overlook the shift away from the religious foundation of sublime terror that took place in the time between Dennis and Burke.

Burke agreed with Dennis on terror's centrality in the sublime experience, but he recast his predecessor's terror-sublime on an empirical, physiological foundation, effectively clearing the way for Gothic supernaturalism and its frequent denial of the efficacy of received religious consolations. For Burke, the role of terror is simple and unequivocal: it is "in all cases whatsoever, either more openly or latently the ruling principle of the sublime" (58).

> Whatever is fitted in any sort to excite the ideas of pain, and danger, that is to say, whatever is in any sort terrible, or is conversant about terrible objects, or operates in a manner analogous to terror, is a source of the sublime; that is, it is productive of the strongest emotion which the mind is capable of feeling. (39)

In the *Enquiry* Burke is concerned almost exclusively with the natural sublime; one of the rare passages in which he directly discusses the supernatural reveals he had little interest in it per se. Yet consideration of this brief passage reveals how his theory came to be held responsible for what his detractors saw as a flood of "bad taste . . . which has been imposed on the world" in the form of "all sorts of terrific and horrific monsters and hobgoblins" (Knight 384):

> As to the association of ghosts and goblins, surely it is more natural to think, that darkness being originally an idea of terror, [it] was chosen as a fit scene for such terrible representations, than that such representations have made darkness terrible. . . . (Burke 144)

Clearly, the supernatural here is a secondary consideration, a superstitious gloss on a rational experience. Darkness is terrible for Burke because it may conceal real threat and danger (143). We are far from the supernatural sublime here, obviously; Burke, solidly empiricist, explained away the supernatural on physiological and psychological grounds while still allowing—one might say barely tolerating—the aesthetic operation of the supernatural. It is this aspect of Burkean theory that Radcliffe and her followers would later invoke. Suffering from emotional and social traumas, her protagonists could experience intimations of the supernatural without having to engage it, allowing the author to reject supernaturalism while drawing both narrative and didactic benefit from its false presence. Yet despite (or because of) this rationalism, Burke's theory and its subsequent popularity helped to establish the definitive catalogue of sublime events and agents that would supply most writers of Gothic fiction, regardless of their disposition toward the supernatural.

While his influence on aesthetic theory may have depended in large degree upon negative reaction and rebuttal, Burke's influence is nonetheless immense. Indeed, according to Samuel Holt Monk, Burke is

> responsible for much of the popularity of terror during the last half of the [eighteenth] century. No idea that became attached to the sublime failed to become popular. Terror enjoyed almost half a century of prominence, thanks to Burke, and out of the conviction that terror is sublime, came some, though not all, of the impulse that brought into existence the tale of terror. (218)

The emphasis Burke's theory placed on terror largely accounted for its popularity, particularly in that it was the first systematic application of terror to sublimity (Boulton lvi, Hipple 88) and that it conferred on terror "a major and worthwhile literary role" (Punter 45). The considerable response to this empirical, secular system and that it quickly found widespread literary application suggest quite strongly that it held particular appeal for late-eighteenth-century Western culture. The absence of moral content generated some opposition to Burke's aesthetic, as Martin Price has reported (195–96), but it seems not to have proven much of a barrier to its adoption or influence. Indeed, it may well have been precisely this lack or absence that contributed to the attraction the *Enquiry* held for writers. Burke did not create the link between terror and the sublime experience, but his achievement was to forge this link in secular fire. In consequence, Gothic supernaturalism was able to raise the tenor and intensity of the sublime so much that it became, in effect, a metasublime, participating not just in aesthetic debate but commenting on the intellectual and metaphysical contexts of that debate.

I must emphasize that I am using the term "metaphysical" throughout this study in a popular sense, for Gothic fiction may well be considered an examination of metaphysical matters in a way accessible to ordinary readers. As Marshall Brown remarks, "both the self-indulgent frivolity of the gothic and the self-sacrificing seriousness of philosophy were dedicated, at least in part, to imagining the unimaginable powers surrounding and conditioning our everyday world" (280). Such an understanding goes far to explain the prominence of Gothic fiction in the last decade of the eighteenth century, and accounts also for the confluence of sublimity and supernatural terror in Gothic literature. With the natural world no longer consistently providing sure access to the divine, Augustan rationalism and its privileging of didactic realism increasingly gave way to literary speculation willing to employ the language and tropes of the supernatural.

Both supernaturalism and sublimity were aesthetic systems (the former much less rigid than the latter, to be sure) that posited an unattainable or unknowable Other and sought, in the encounter with intimations of that Other, some trace of meaning. These aesthetics were in many regards structurally cognate, a fact that explains the ready confluence of sublimity and supernaturalism. Gothic supernaturalism seems to have been built almost according to a Burkean model.

The kinship between the two is powerfully evident in that the unapprehendable realm of the supernatural and its denizens simultaneously embody the two primary elements of Burkean terror: threat and domination. The supernatural is threatening because it is often explicitly hostile, and even when indifferent or benign it intimates a superior and indeterminate power. Here again, Burke was developing in accord with empirical principles an idea expressed in Dennis, who found the greatest terror to reside in the confluence of power and inscrutability:

> Now of things which are terrible those are the most terrible which are the most wonderful, because that seeing them both threatening and powerful, and not being able to fathom the greatness and extent of their Power, we know not how far and how soon they may hurt us.
>
> But further nothing is so terrible as the wrath of infinite Power. . . . (Dennis 88)

For Dennis, "infinite Power" resided exclusively in God, but in the age of Burke and Gothic fiction such metaphysical certitude was eroding rapidly. If we, like most Gothicists, accept the long-standing equation of the sublime with terror (and/or power), it becomes inevitable that the desire to body forth the most intense or extreme sublimity would produce a literature of supernatural horror.

*T*he experience of conventional sublimity, we have seen, is marked by loss or suspension of self in the face of an implied transcendent, a suspension that overwhelms and leaves us momentarily "wrapped in silence and inquisitive horror" (Usher 103). Such a dynamic leads to the inevitable conclusion that the Burkean sublime is effectively a prerational sublime, one that operates in the space between perception and consciousness; the sublime's intimations of overwhelming power owe their existence to the fact that this space is necessarily a space of helplessness. Here the mind retains only awareness; it can neither control perception nor exercise rationalization. Burke explicitly remarks the mind's passivity during this experience: it is "filled with its object." This passivity is not only an obvious point of entrance for supernatural terror but also the deconstructive key that enables the supernatural sublime to reveal the failure of conventional sublimity's paradigm of engagement with the transcendent.

While it is legitimate to find the conventional sublime to be "a movement into a sacred precinct. . . . sacred because it is inhabited by a power, and to be drawn into its realm is to be made one with that power" (Price 199), such conclusions do not obtain for supernatural sublimity. The latter is an experience of suspension and powerlessness, a moment of confrontation with the supernatural, in which the Gothic protagonist comes much closer to, but does not pass beyond, the state Rudolph Otto identifies as the consequence of the sublime or transcendent moment. In this moment,

> [t]he truly "mysterious" object is beyond our apprehension and comprehension, not only because our knowledge has certain irremovable

limits, but because in it we come upon something inherently "wholly other", whose kind and character are incommensurable with our own, and before which we therefore recoil in a wonder that strikes us chill and numb. (28)

It is clear by now the supernatural sublime has the same structure of emotional transport inherent in the conventional sublime[3] but achieves neither the sense of elevation and enlargement the eighteenth century found in the sublime nor the abasement of self in the veneration of object that Otto identifies as the essence of the numinous experience and that Thomas Weiskel sees, in modified form, as the basis of sublime feeling. The supernatural sublime begins with the traditional drama of the sublime experience—the "motions of the soul" are frozen in their confrontation with the suprarational or suprahuman—but the object embodying the extranatural is, if not unmasked as natural, invested with daemonic potency. In the space of helplessness sublimity opens, such objects call forth only horror and a sense of numinous dread. Thus the supernatural sublime, at least in its radical mode, questions or denies the possibility of spiritual consolation.

A result of Western culture's increasingly tenuous grip on the divine, this protonihilism is signaled by the fact that, in its most dramatic expressions—Lewis's *The Monk* (1795) and Maturin's *Melmoth the Wanderer* (1820)—metaphysical hostility is embodied in traditional signifiers of Christian evil—devils—without an accompanying intimation of divine presence. Indeed, much of Gothicism's horror is expressed through the narrative deployment of Christian icons: the Wandering Jew, the corrupt monk, the ruined abbey, the subterranean crypt. We are mistaken to assume, however, that the presence of these and other religious symbols constitutes an endorsement of Christian metaphysics.

M. H. Abrams, among others, remarks on Romanticism's participation in the "progressive secularization" of Western culture, noting that the shift was not characterized by abrupt, complete abandonment of traditional concepts and their associated imagery:

> The process . . . has not been [one of] the deletion and replacement of religious ideas but rather the assimilation and reinterpretation of religious ideas, as constitutive elements in a world view founded on secular premises. Much of what distinguishes writers I call "Romantic" derives from the fact that they undertook, whatever their religious creed or lack of creed, to save traditional concepts, schemes, and values which had been based on the relation of the Creator to his creatures and creation,

but to reformulate them within the prevailing two-term system of subject and object, ego and non-ego, the human mind or consciousness and
its transactions with nature. (13)

Gothic reassessment of religious imagery was not a wholesale rejection
of its traditional content, but rather a strict circumscription or major
recasting of its implications. Devils, we shall see in chapter 3, are still
very much associated with "evil"; the important change is that Gothic
writers are not invoking that same sense of evil once understood as
inevitably and necessarily engaged in dialectic struggle with the
"good" of God. This medieval moral topography is reconfigured in
the Romantic moment; good and evil, their boundaries increasingly
uncertain, assume a multiplicity of new meanings and nuances. One
of the consequences of this development is that the presence of devils
no longer guarantees or even implies the presence of a benevolent divinity. Like many Gothic tropes, devils became counters in Gothic fiction's preoccupation with interiority: Day suggests that in Gothic
fiction devils "function not only as images of the monstrous meaningless supernatural of the Gothic world, but also as doubles, as projec-
tions of the monstrousness of the human characters. That which seems
supernatural in these novels does not truly come from without, but
from within" (39). Supernaturalist fiction may continue to employ
biblical imagery, but the connotations of that imagery are radically
altered.

The retroping of biblical icons is revealed both in and by the supernatural sublime. In a world in which natural phenomena were no
longer understood to constitute direct evidence of the divine, sublimity
began to lose much of the function and value it had acquired during
the eighteenth century. The reassuring strategy of recovery that creates
the transcendent experience does not obtain in all Gothic fiction; confronting what it recognizes as hostility or disorder, the mind cannot
generate the consolatory belief that it failed to achieve transcendence
only because of the immensity of its desired object. Like John Melmoth or Victor Frankenstein, Gothic novelists found that beyond the
limits of the human lies that which subsumes us or marks our irrevers-
ible separation from the natural universe. Weiskel's observation that
"the sublime is cognate with the experiential structure of alienation,
whose modern form is discovered and announced in the Romantic
authors" (36) is nowhere truer than in regard to those early Romantic
authors employing the supernatural sublime. Melmoth's climactic disappearance from the cliff is the perfect literary figuration of supernatural sublimity. The mountaintop had always been a prime locus of the

sublime experience; going beyond it, as radical Gothicism did, uncovers only irrevocable loss of self unless one is quick enough to retreat, although such acts of recovery are invested with none of the metaphysical optimism that attends experience of the natural sublime. In radical Gothic fiction, the return to the world is a return from the inferno without a glimpse even of purgatory, let alone paradise.

*T*zvetan Todorov's well-known theory of the fantastic has by now some equally well-known and much-belabored limitations. Since its appearance, Todorov's schema has been questioned by scholars of the fantastic on the narrowness of its central genre, the dualistic assumptions of its structuralism, and its inability (or refusal) to account for twentieth-century fantasy. Although I agree with some of these critiques, it is not my intention to add to them. What I wish to undertake here is, rather, an application of Todorov's basic structure to Gothic supernaturalism, an application that enables important discriminations between the various modes of Gothic sublimity at the same time that it facilitates fuller acknowledgment of Gothicism's intellectual and historical value.[4]

The basis of Todorov's fantastic is the "hesitation experienced by a person who knows only the laws of nature, confronting an apparently supernatural event" (25). Todorov's study provides a useful point of departure for what follows because the Gothic supernatural experience is structurally cognate with this moment or experience of hesitation. Both involve a movement from mental equilibrium and epistemological security to a condition of profound uncertainty, an experience of emotional and intellectual trauma succeeded by either validation of the original premises of knowledge or explosion of them.

A correspondent structure informs the supernatural moment. It is immaterial whether the confronted human character believes in the independent existence of the perceived object, for even the most rationalist characters may find themselves experiencing initial doubt. The import of the encounter inheres in the fact that a signifier of the suprarational always induces, in nonparodic texts, a combined rational/emotional movement the pattern of which derives from traditional understandings of the sublime moment—with the further aspect, taken from Todorov, of epistemological uncertainty. The initial trauma freezes the "motions of the soul," a moment of arrest that impels subsequent expansion of the mind. In the conventional sublime, expansion leads to some sense of consolation and is followed by a return to the prior basis of understanding, but the same does not obtain for the supernatural sublime. Raising its investigation of transcendent possibility to the highest register, the supernatural sublime becomes, like Todorov's fantastic-uncanny or fantastic-marvelous, a movement away from certainty, a movement that cannot be endured or sustained. And like the poised moment of hesitation in Todorov's system, the supernatural sublime has two directions it may take in its escape from uncertainty.

These two directions constitute the two distinct categories or modes of supernatural sublimity. Each mode may occur in works that may either reject or endorse the supernatural; belief (of reader, character, or author) is not as important to the supernatural sublime as the metaphysical implications of the Gothic encounter. The conservative mode endorses a traditional metaphysic and therefore corresponds, albeit on another level, to Todorov's fantastic-uncanny in which the moment of hesitation is resolved in support of established laws of nature. The second mode, the radical, is akin to Todorov's fantastic-marvellous, even though some of its works contain no supernaturalism, for it constitutes an insistence on the inadequacy or even failure of received knowledge—in this case, of traditional metaphysical postulates.

CHART 1

	Todorov	Supernatural Sublime
conventional epistemology endorsed	fantastic-uncanny	conservative mode
conventional epistemology questioned	fantastic-marvelous	radical mode

Chart 1 is offered to help clarify the categories' relation to one another. It should be remembered that Todorov's system is a theory of genres and the supernatural sublime is a literary structure that may occur in any genre. The conservative mode is the literary consequence of supernatural tropes employed in the endorsement of conventional metaphysical constructs. Unlike Todorov's schema, however, the supernatural sublime requires an additional set of subcategories, the supernatural and the nonsupernatural. In the conservative mode, these subcategories or strains are best represented by the novels of Clara Reeve and Ann Radcliffe. Radcliffe's works (exclusive of the posthumously published *Glaston de Blondeville*) would be located in Todorov's "uncanny," for their supernaturalism is always finally excluded by rational explanation. Reeve, whom Todorov incorrectly identifies as an author of explained supernatural texts (41), does employ genuine supernatural elements in her best-known novel, *The Old English Baron* (1788), but hers is a work of strident didacticism. Its rigorous privileging of conventional morality and religious belief denies admission of the anxious despair widely regarded as characteristic of dark or radical Gothicism. Such validation of received tradition allies the work with Radcliffe's novels, which are equally conservative in their morality and metaphysics.

The radical mode of return from the supernatural encounter denies traditional consolations. It finds either that the supernatural does exist, and without the parental concern of Reeve's ghosts or the heavenly connections of Walpole's, or that, as in the works of Brockden Brown or Edgar Allan Poe, heightened or unusual experience of "natural" phenomena demonstrates that received intellectual and spiritual traditions are inadequate for assessing and responding to the complexities of the post-Enlightenment universe. In works of the radical mode, recovery of the mind from its moment of expansion brings limited consolation at best. The Gothic supernatural sublime, especially in its radical mode, reaches after a God who has become a *Deus absconditus*.

If this talk of modes and strains seems convoluted, it is important to keep in mind that Gothic/Romantic supernaturalism is itself a complex literary phenomenon. Similarity of imagery and atmosphere makes *The Castle of Otranto* appear to be of the same species as *Melmoth the Wanderer*, and some early works of Gothic criticism are compromised by their unequivocal assertions of such correspondences. Correspondences there are, to be sure, but there are more important differences. Approaching the Gothic from the perspective of the supernatural sublime, it is possible to retain recognition of affinities (in imagery, language, character) while discriminating among the varied, indeed at times antithetical, applications of these common properties.

A final diagram (figure 2) might help specify the relationships between the various modes and strains of Gothic supernaturalism. The point of departure for all these texts is the natural Christian world, the world of epistemological and moral surety (the horizontal line at the left of the diagram). Into this world intrudes the supernatural (the perpendicular arrow in the diagram), evidence of the inadequacy of the initial epistemology. Next comes the moment of suspension or powerlessness that follows immediately upon the confrontation (marked by the asterisk); this suspension is a constitutive element of the supernatural moment: the height or emotional climax of that moment. The two modes of recovery from this climax, each with two strains, are the final components of our schematic, which like its predecessor is chronological.

FIGURE 2   Mode of Recovery

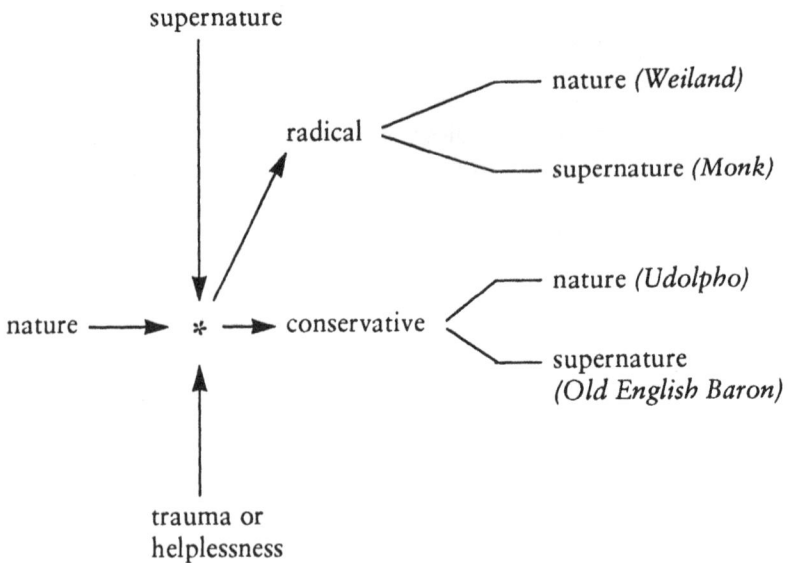

In Figure 1, recovery from the moment of trauma was a return to the horizontal level of the presublime, since natural sublimity involves no metaphysical interrogations, introduces no uncertainty as to the ordering principle(s) of the universe. Figure 2 puts the conservative mode of the supernatural sublime in a correspondent location, for it is, as its name implies, a validation of traditional epistemologies and metaphysics. The radical mode is on a different level, however, because it does not endorse conventional belief nor does it readily assimilate its supernatural to Christian dogma, even when that supernatural is Christian in its iconography. Instead, radical supernaturalism shows received wisdom to be deficient. The suprarational is found to exist, thereby challenging the established metaphysical rules.

It is readily apparent that the presence or absence of the supernatural does not by itself sufficiently discriminate between the various types of Gothic fiction. Rather, the particular *application* of the supernatural creates important differences that a full accounting of Gothic and Romantic supernaturalism must recognize. At the same time, to privilege the metaphysical implications of one element of these texts (even if it may be the dominant element) may lead to the obscuring of important and instructive similarities. By my system, *The Monk* and *The Castle of Otranto* are in opposition, yet it is obvious that both texts are concerned with themes of sexuality and that they figure these themes by using the image of the subterranean labyrinth. We can no more ignore such a correspondence than we can the metaphysical differences. Gothic fiction, one critic has noted, "has a diverse potential" (Butler 160), and this study claims not to account exhaustively for that potential but to supplement the ongoing and multivalent critical investigation of the Gothic.

It should also be noted that the supernatural sublime may structure an entire narrative as well as a particular textual moment. A work such as *The Mysteries of Udolpho* features a young heroine whose idyllic childhood is disrupted by a series of events, chief among which are sojourns in two apparently haunted structures. The supernaturalism of these episodes is eventually dispelled, and recovering from all the traumas that beset her, Emily returns to a new idyll in her childhood home. The cognitive trajectory of the conservative supernatural sublime here parallels the narrative structure of the entire text, reinforcing, in its affirmation of closure and resolvability, the consolatory gesture of the conservative supernatural sublime.

The radical supernatural sublime is the mode represented by Lewis's *The Monk;* consideration of the Bleeding Nun episode should make clear the lineaments of this aesthetic. Lewis approaches the moment carefully, preparing to elevate, by contrast with disbelief, the emotional register at the moment of the Nun's introduction. Having listened to Agnes's presentation of the Bleeding Nun's story, Raymond scoffs at her apparent belief only to be blistered by her indignant reply: "How can you ask such a question? No, no, Alphonse! I have too much reason to lament superstition's influence to be its Victim myself' " (141). The prior experience with "superstition" to which she alludes is the zealous Catholicism of her parents, who are forcing her to enter the convent unwillingly. Yet that "superstition" suddenly becomes consonant with reality as traditional, empirical formulations of knowledge, which declare ghosts to be nonexistent, are discovered to be deficient, the boundaries of epistemological certainty rendered elusive. By deploying superstition against a smug rationalism, Lewis deliberately invites us to consider the larger implications of his supernaturalism.

Raymond's emotional state, heightened in anticipation of elopement, proves vital to the episode's supernaturalism. "My bosom beat high with hope and expectation," he exclaims as it appears his desire to escape with and marry Agnes will finally be realized. When "the lovely Ghost" emerges from the castle, Raymond rushes to it, uttering the following doggerel declaration of his love:

> Agnes! Agnes! Thou art mine!
> Agnes! Agnes! I am thine!
> In my veins while blood shall roll,
> Thou art mine!
> I am thine!
> Thine my body! Thine my soul! (155–56)

His drastic language of promise and possession binds Raymond to the ghostly Nun, although he does not know the true ontological status of his "lovely Ghost"—that she really is the ghost of the Bleeding Nun, not his beloved Agnes—until the following night, due to a carriage accident and his subsequent unconsciousness.

The intensity of Raymond's near-frenzied vow invites, if indeed it does not enable, the intermingling of the natural and supernatural, and the following night at her customary hour the Nun reappears. This becomes a nightly ritual, for Raymond's misdirected devotion has opened an avenue of access for supernatural energies. The implications of this access are elucidated cogently by Peter Brooks, who identifies the episode as

> a necessary breakthrough within the novel itself, from a world which has, despite dreams and grandiose passions, up to this point been

largely natural and social. After the Bleeding Nun episode, the world
has expanded to accommodate itself to shadows from without this
world, and the consciousness of both characters and reader must ex-
pand to encompass this new dimension of experience. (256)

The new dimension Brooks speaks of is most evident in the actions of
the Nun and their effect upon Raymond. When the Nun reappears she
lifts her veil, revealing the "haggard" and "bloodless" features of "an
animated Corse" (160). At this precise moment the supernatural encounter begins; Raymond's reaction to the sight reveals very clearly
the operation of those principles central to the supernatural sublime:

> I gazed upon the Spectre with horror too great to be described. My
> blood was frozen in my veins. I would have called for aid, but the sound
> expired, ere it could pass my lips. My nerves were bound up in impo-
> tence, and I remained in the same attitude inanimate as a Statue.
>
> . . . .
>
> Her eyes were fixed earnestly upon mine: They seemed endowed
> with the property of the Rattle-snake's, for I strove in vain to look off
> her. My eyes were fascinated, and I had not the power of withdrawing
> them from the Spectre's.
>
> In this attitude She remained for a whole long hour without speaking
> or moving; nor was I able to do either. (160)

Her appointed hour having passed, the Nun departs after kissing Raymond and echoing his declaration of love. His response to her departure is a literal recovery from the suspension that marks the
supernatural moment: "Till that moment the faculties of my body had
been all suspended; Those of my mind alone had been waking. The
charm now ceased to operate: The blood which had been frozen in my
veins rushed back to my heart with violence: I uttered a deep groan,
and sank lifeless upon my pillow" (161).

Lewis has here orchestrated a near-perfect example of the supernatural sublime. The intensity of emotion with which the supernatural
is confronted (an intensity heightened by its reversal of anticipated
emotions) generates a moment of anxious uncertainty, a Burkean suspension of the motions of the soul. Raymond tells us his mind had
remained "waking," but this clearly means only that it avoided unconsciousness. No intellectual operations take place during the encounter;
there is only rudimentary sensory awareness.

Lewis has rendered, literally and with graphic precision, the sense
of helplessness that must occur if sublimity is to intimate the presence

of a transcendent object. But for the supernatural sublime in its radical mode there is no subsequent mental operation (conscious or otherwise) that offers intimations of divinity. Raymond's only response to the Nun's appearances is to become further engulfed by the terror she inspires: "Far from growing accustomed to the Ghost, every succeeding visit inspired me with greater horror. Her idea pursued me continually, and I became the prey of habitual melancholy" (163). As long as he is visited by the spectral Nun, Raymond cannot extricate himself from this space of powerlessness, yet we need not see these visits as a series of supernatural moments. They are, rather, one prolonged or aggregate moment, its duration serving to emphasize its effect. Not until the last encounter is it possible to assess the metaphysical implications of the episode's supernatural sublimity.

At first the recovery may appear to be a conservative endorsement of Christian metaphysics, for Raymond is aided by none other than the Wandering Jew. Only he can help Raymond, he claims, and he is, of course, a decidedly Christian figure. Or is he? The Wandering Jew is familiar from Christian myth, to be sure, and his narrative function involves this association, for he helps to quiet a ghost whose nocturnal terrorizing has its origins in her transgression of conventional morality. Yet this in itself is not sufficient to make him the defining factor of the episode's—let alone the novel's—metaphysical import.

While the Wandering Jew ends the supernatural moment, closing off the space of helplessness that threatens to swallow Raymond (and it is a narrative hiatus as well as one in Raymond's life), he does not determine the direction of Raymond's recovery from that moment. Conventional morality supplies some of the reference points that enable readers to understand Ambrosio's actions as "wrong," but *The Monk* is not unreservedly Christian in its metaphysics, even though Lewis himself believed that the existence of supernatural beings testified to the existence of God. If the novel were orthodox in its theology, Christian theological precepts would inform the work's supernatural moments, but we see they do not. "God's justice" may have been responsible for initiating this particular supernatural episode—a century in the past—but in the recovery from it there is no corresponding movement toward divinity. The end of supernatural suspension does not prompt any character to construe perceived absence or hostility as evidence of an ungraspable transcendent presence; supernatural sublimity uncovers only horror, a horror never transformed by the mind but only dissipated by the text. The "terror and detestation" the sight of the Wandering Jew with a cross on his forehead inspires in Raymond may vaguely be related to his status as a signifier of divine retribution—and we cannot expect a break with traditional associations to be accomplished overnight, as Abrams has explained—but the iconic aspect of this image is never developed, never relied upon in the novel's denouement.

Sight of the burning cross induces compliance from the Nun and nearly causes Raymond to faint, but the ramifications of this theological terror are pursued no further. Indeed, Lewis abruptly truncates the episode in order to dismiss the Wandering Jew as hastily as possible. After hearing the history of the Nun, Raymond, demonstrating remarkable obtuseness, inquires into that of the Wandering Jew himself. Told he will hear the story the following day, Raymond is content; the Wandering Jew takes the opportunity to vanish from both town and narrative without a trace. Responding to Lorenzo's calm assertion of the figure's true identity, Raymond remarks, with an astonishing complacence, that "for my own part I am inclined to adopt the only solution which offers itself to this riddle. I return to the narrative from which I have digressed" (177). These are not the words of a man who has undergone a profound religious experience.

The narrative to which he returns is that of his recovery from the debilitating effects of the Nun's visits and of his return to the castle where Agnes was being held. In one sentence he tells of burying the bones of the woman whose ghost was tormenting him (this being the condition of the peace) and turns then to the story of his continued pursuit of Agnes. The Bleeding Nun and any implications of her appearance or banishment are forgotten as quickly as her bones. Yet the interment of her remains, although reported briefly, may well hold the key to the readiness with which the entire episode is dismissed. The Nun's haunting of Lindenberg Castle had its origin over one hundred years prior to the time of the narrative; by burying her bones, Raymond buries the past as well, denying the vitality of any theological implications of that earlier equation of supernaturalism with divinity.

Thus the radical supernatural sublime finds in the space of suspension the key to its subversive power. The conventional sublime creates, out of the failure that occurs in this moment of arrest and expansion, a sense of transcendent achievement and metaphysical plenitude. The project of the radical supernatural sublime is to seize that moment, foreground it, and by close scrutiny reveal it to be a moment of absence, a revelation enabled by the supernatural sublime's inversion of the traditional understanding of infinity as evidence of an omnipotent divine presence. In its radical mode, Gothic fiction unmasks the dissimulation, the necessary trope of irony, inherent in previous literary figurations of transcendence, and that gesture of unmasking, that recognition of helplessness and unfulfillment *as such,* is the revelation of the decaying corpse in the place of God.

Part One

Gothic Fiction
and the Supernatural Sublime

Recent scholarship has produced a number of studies that consider, to varying degrees, the role played by the sublime in Gothic fiction. I would like to approach the novels to be examined in Part I by way of brief consideration of the most salient of these critical investigations.

The first of these studies, which ranges well beyond the Gothic, is Morse Peckham's "Toward a Theory of Romanticism" (1951). While the essay does not deal with Romantic sublimity, "negative romanticism" is based on a metaphysical consideration closely akin to that present in works of the radical mode of the supernatural sublime. For Peckham, "negative romanticism" is an intermediate stage, a low point on the mental journey from the condition of "affirming the meaning of the cosmos in terms of static mechanism to affirming it in terms of dynamic organicism . . . " (20). Between these poles of affirmation lies an inevitable sense of doubt and despair, accompanied by a feeling "of religious and social isolation, of the separation of reason and creative power." In the moment of negative Romanticism inheres the sense that there "is neither beauty nor goodness in the universe, nor any significance, nor any rationality, nor indeed any order at all, not even an evil order" (20). In the identification of Romantic despair

with a loss of confidence in the ability of the universe to be intellectu-
ally apprehended, Peckham touches the heart of Gothic pessimism and
identifies the primary points of connection between Gothic and Romantic sensibilities.

At the same time there is a danger in evaluating Gothic writers by
the implicit hierarchy of the scheme Peckham (and others) advocate.
One respondent to Peckham argues that

> The early Gothic novels can be considered the precursors of romanti-
> cism in their concern with sensibility, the sublime, and the involvement
> of the reader in a more than rational way. Gothic also prepares the way
> for and shares the romantic "confusion" of good and evil. But where
> Gothic remains darkened by the necessary ambiguities of its conclu-
> sions, romantic writing assumes the ultimate existence, if not the easy
> accessibility, of clear answers to the problems which torment man in
> this world. (Hume, "Gothic" 289)

Despite its accuracy in regard to the emotional content of Gothic fiction, such statements—and this includes Peckham's theory in general—may misrepresent the single most crucial point regarding the
achievement of the Gothic, which is that the very nature of the Gothic
project differs, subtly but importantly, from that of the mainstream or
High Romantics. Gothic writers are deliberately digging in the grave;
they are not simply failed or neotenic positive romantics, as Peckham's
definition would have it. Their very purpose in writing, whether consciously recognized or not, is to assess the legitimacy of the transcendent imagination in the face of increasing cultural uncertainty and
anxiety. The "necessary ambiguities" Hume mentions are not some
lamentable by-product of the Gothic examination, nor the result of
inherent artistic or intellectual deficiencies, but the intended result.
When we as critics privilege the Romantic over the Gothic because we
understand Romanticism to have succeeded where Gothicism failed,
we are ourselves implicitly subscribing to and endorsing a Romantic
aesthetic. It is obvious that there exist profound and distinct differences between the Gothic and the Romantic, but it is necessary to
guard against uncritically adopting Romantic criteria in our relative
assessments of Romantic and Gothic literatures. Such caution is not
easily come by, since we are very much the inheritors of a Romantic
tradition, but it is nonetheless an essential precondition for an evalua-
tive approach claiming critical objectivity.[1]

Following Peckham's essay by a few years, Devendra Varma's *The*

Gothic Flame (1957) also seeks to account for the metaphysical component of Gothic fiction. Although he mentions briefly the influence of Burkean theory on Gothic fiction, Varma finally understands Gothicism's spiritual project to be figured through the numinous:

> Primarily the Gothic novels arose out of a quest for the numinous. They are characterized by an awestruck apprehension of Divine immanence penetrating diurnal reality. . . . [Gothic novelists] were moving away from the arid glare of rationalism towards the beckoning shadows of a more intimate and mystical interpretation of life, and this they encountered in the profound sense of the numinous stamped upon the architecture, paintings, and fables of the Middle Ages. (211)

Varma's privileging of Medievalism as the major influence on Gothicism and his identifying the cathedral as the central Gothic metaphor lead him to argue that Gothic literature "lifts us from the narrow rut and enables us to join the unspaced firmament; it adds eternity to our trivial hours; and gives a sense of infinity to our finite existence" (212). Such an optimistic appraisal of Gothic fiction as a whole can only be a consequence of Varma's mistaking the field of exploration for the object itself.

Alok Bhalla offers the ruin as a more fitting paradigm for Gothic fiction, suggestive as it is of chaos and decay, and notes that "in the Gothic novel the Gothic cathedral and the ruin are not symbolic of the same mystical attitude. . . . The Gothic novel, written during a specific period of socio-political strife, is not an uncanny affirmation of the world as a sacred script . . ." (207–8). In its implications, the ruin is the antithesis of the cathedral, and more apt as a symbol, at least of the radical Gothic. Varma's laudable desire to rescue Gothic fiction from its detractors led him to an untenable position, one based on an assessment of only a small part of Gothicism's spiritual project.

Many of these same conclusions hold true for S. L. Varnado's fuller study of the role of Otto's numinous in Gothic fiction. To the extent both sublimity and the numinous lend themselves to transcendent inquiry, there is indeed value in applying the latter concept to Gothic fiction. But even Otto's recognition of a "negative numinous" (the demonic, the horrifying, the "sense of sacrilege and evil that floods the mind with fear and loathing" [Varnado 35]) does not effectively provide insight into the full range and play of the metaphysical speculations of Gothic supernaturalism.

A more trenchant recent assessment of the Gothic project is made by William Patrick Day, who counters the numinous optimism of Varma and others by arguing that Gothic supernaturalism

> portrays the disintegration of the spiritual. Just as Gothic atmosphere subverts the physical world of science, the laws of time and space, it also subverts the world of the numinous, which is transformed into the monstrous or freakish, the strange and exotic. . . . The supernatural, or the sense of the supernatural . . . is the manifestation not of transcendent order, but of chaos and disruption. (35–36)

There must be a caveat added here that, in works such as *Udolpho* and others of the conservative mode, the final suppression of "disruption and chaos" is fully intended to validate a positive metaphysics. Flirtation with the supernatural is part of the attraction of such works then and now, but *Udolpho* is not *Melmoth,* and despite the real-life religious feelings of their authors, these works offer profoundly different assessments of the human condition. It is as misleading to say that Radcliffe's Gothicism is a "rejection of the spiritual" (Day 36) as it is to find all Gothic fiction working toward "a new, tentative apprehension of the Divine" (Varma 211). Much the same can be said of Marshall Brown's examination of the links between Gothic fiction and Kantian philosophy. While I agree emphatically with Brown's thesis that Gothic novels function as "pure speculative instruments that investigate the origins of experience" (279), his conclusion is more problematic: "the essence of the gothic lies in its play with unreconciled antinomies. It is not the final triumph of good or evil, explanation or irrationality, free will or fate that makes a gothic atmosphere, but the lingering uncertainties along the way" (299). While this is certainly the case for the works I identify as "radical," I would argue that some sort of "final" determination is extremely important in conservative Gothics—and I would note that Brown's two study examples, *Melmoth* and *Frankenstein,* are works well outside the conservative range. There is an ineluctable duality to Gothic supernaturalism. Confronting intimations of a metaphysical realm, it always either retreats to some traditional understanding of the divine or advances, even if reluctantly, into a cosmos in which the divine is conspicuous only by its absence.

The metaphysical aspect of Gothic fiction is approached more closely by G. Richard Thompson in an important introduction to a collection of Gothic tales. While he mentions the sublime only in passing, Thompson's exposition of Gothic metaphysics and of its general

cultural and intellectual context is superlative and has contributed significantly to my own understanding of Gothicism, as my citations of
this and other works by Thompson should indicate. More germane at
the moment, however, is the taxonomy of Gothic fiction Thompson
develops in this introduction. There are in his system four categories,
which Thompson claims are "ontologically based": (1) historical
Gothic, (2) explained Gothic, (3) supernatural Gothic, and (4) ambiguous Gothic.

One difficulty with this schema is that the first category is not as
purely ontologically based as Thompson claims. Historical Gothicism
is determined not by ghosts but by the alleged setting of the work,
regardless of the effectiveness of the author in establishing that setting.
Thompson himself admits that "The presence of an occasional witch,
demon, or ghost implies no significant ontology shaping the themes of
the work" ("Introduction" 14). The other categories do retain their
ontological distinctions, with the last mode, the ambiguous, adding
as well a "heightened psychological and philosophical perplexity—so
much so that such works may be considered not only as uncertain
metaphysical texts, but fundamentally as epistemological texts" ("Introduction" 27). Yet these epistemological considerations enter into
other works, just as do the "perplexities," as my chapters in part I
make evident.

There is another difficulty with the category of the ambiguous, akin
in some ways to Todorov's fantastic, although the uncertainty for
Thompson is more epistemological than ontological:

> In the ambiguous mode, as distinct from the supernaturalist, the ten-
> dency is not so much toward unattainable ultimate meanings as toward
> obsessive epistemological doubt in which the very medium of the narra-
> tive is called into question by unreliable narrators or interpreters. ("In-
> troduction" 26)

The implications of such narrative self-questionings are one of the
most modern aspects of the Gothic tradition, to be sure, but in
Thompson's shift of emphasis to epistemology from ontology the
foundation of his final category is challenged as much as that of his
first. Only the middle two are determined exclusively by ontological
considerations. While Thompson's schema holds value for the scholar
of the Gothic, as a tool for analyzing the metaphysical concerns of
Gothic fiction it is not sufficiently precise.

With these various discussions as background, I turn now to the most recent full account of Gothic sublimity, David Morris's "Gothic Sublimity." Positing the inadequacy of Burke's aesthetic of terror as an explanation of the Gothic sublime, Morris argues that "In exploring the entanglements of love and terror, the Gothic novel pursues a version of the sublime without transcendence. It is a vertiginous and plunging—not a soaring—sublime, which takes us deep within rather than far beyond the human sphere . . ." (306). Morris invokes Freud's *unheimlich* as the paradigm for Gothic sublime experience, finding it to account more cogently for Gothic fiction's emotional power than traditional critical formulations, which understand the supernatural as an expression of the numinous. It is a provocative and important theory. Scholarship has long recognized the centrality of sexual drama in Gothic fiction, and Morris's invocation of the uncanny is a useful adjunct in elucidating the further implications of this dynamic. Yet Morris's approach is not without limitations.

One of these is hinted at by Morris himself: "the sublime, like the Gothic novel, embraces such a variety of historical practices and of theoretical accounts that the quest for a single, unchanging feature or essence is futile. There is no essence of the sublime" (300). In terms of particular agents or effects of the sublime Morris is correct, but Gothic writers did not know a sublime free of historical baggage. The desire to recover a sense of participation in the numinous appeared frequently and prominently in earlier theories of the sublime, as we have seen. No fully successful theory of Gothic sublimity can exclude or overlook the centrality of such desire, even if it is somewhat obscured in Burke.

It is unlikely that the debate and controversy which swirled around Burke's *Enquiry* had no impact on writers obviously interested in the sublime. Yet Morris's concentration on Burke implies that his theory was the only aesthetic contributing to literary Gothicism. The *Enquiry* was a significant manifesto for writers of Gothic fiction, undeniably, but late-eighteenth-century supernaturalism was not grounded exclusively in Burke. We have already seen that, for Gothic novelists, particular explanations of the sublime reaction are not as relevant as the effects that reaction produces; what is germane is not so much the emotional foundation of the agents of sublimity (that is, physiological or psychological causes) as their value as signifiers. Confronting previously unknown or unexpressed anxieties and lacking a psychological lexicon, Gothic and Romantic artists turned, as Morris correctly argues, to the language and tropes of both natural and rhetorical sublimity, using them in a radically new way. Yet we can no more ignore the historically determined content of this language than did the Gothicists. The metaphysical implications of both the language and structure of the sublime had been conditioned and shaped by its century-long employment as a literary quest for transcendence.

The coexistence of both new and old tropings of the sublime is evident in Morris's own example, Walpole's *The Castle of Otranto*. Morris is concerned primarily with the new, with the use of image, structure, and characterization as articulations of Freud's "family romance," of the terrifying consequences of the release of "images and desires long suppressed, deeply hidden, forced into silence" ("Gothic" 306). Because of this focus, Morris limits his analysis and observation to only part of the novel, virtually ignoring its conclusion. Yet it is here that Walpole invokes a sublime moment that owes much to the purpose of the sublime as originally determined by Dennis.

Immediately upon Manfred's learning of his daughter's death, "a clap of thunder . . . shook the castle to its foundations; the earth rocked, and the clank of more than mortal armour was heard behind" (104). The now-cliché stage effects signal the climactic supernatural moment in the text; when it comes, it is a moment of sublime emotion that is the antithesis of "vertiginous and plunging":

> the walls of the castle behind Manfred were thrown down with a mighty force, and the form of Alfonso, dilated to an immense magnitude, appeared in the centre of the ruins. "Behold in Theodore the true heir of Alfonso!" said the vision: and having pronounced these words, accompanied by a clap of thunder, it ascended solemnly towards Heaven, where, the clouds parting asunder, the form of St. Nicholas was seen, and, receiving Alfonso's shade, they were soon wrapt from mortal eyes in a blaze of glory.
>
> The beholders fell prostrate on their faces, acknowledging the divine will. (104)

Despite its innovations Walpole's novel is in many ways conventional, perhaps nowhere more so than in the implications of the passage just quoted. The work's bold supernaturalism is one of its most innovative gestures, but the movement in this passage (and the novel's remaining paragraphs) is a traditional one, expressed in traditional religious rhetoric. The ascent to heaven of the novel's tutelary spirit, Alfonso, bestows conventional religious sanction on a novel that largely validates received sociomoral codes. Indeed, Alphonso's *ascent* suggests a conservative impulse in Walpole. The verticality of medieval mysticism had given way to a horizontal movement in the seventeenth century, as Ernest Tuveson has pointed out, but whereas the vertical was limited by God's closed universe, the horizontal met no boundary. The infinite became that without—without limit, without content—and religious anxiety began to grow. The concept of the sublime, we have seen, was resurrected from Longinus in order to combat this very anxiety of the infinite. Much of Gothic fiction's medievalism—a prominent feature of Walpole's Gothic aesthetics—can be understood as an attempt to return to the vertical mode of transcendent inquiry. While such a conservative gesture worked, if clumsily, for Walpole in the mid–1760s, by the time of *The Monk*'s publication in 1795 the verticality of popular metaphysics had been subverted by turning the direction of inquiry downward, into the sepulchers and catacombs, into the hollow or undermined institutions of received wisdom. There was discovered the horror characteristic of the radical Gothic.

Morris's evaluation of *Otranto*'s labyrinthine imagery and its sexual implications is astute but should not keep us from recognizing the simultaneous operation of other modes of sublimity. Gothic sublimity also demands recognition as a mainline descendant of the eighteenth-century sublime, of its history as a literary means of metaphysical speculation. Again, I do not wish to suggest that the supernatural sublime is a substitute for other accounts of Gothic and Romantic sublimity, but it does contribute, in this case, a historical perspective that a strictly psychoanalytic approach may lead us to overlook. Morris's approach excludes historical considerations except as it refutes Burkean physiology—an element of Burke's theory, it should be mentioned, disputed by some of Burke's contemporaries and tactfully minimized even by aestheticians, such as Uvedale Price, who supported him. Morris, who establishes as his Gothic paradigm *The Castle of Otranto* (the earliest and crudest Gothic expression), writes that "Walpole shows us how the intensest terror is located at the very origin of desire" (306). True, but in the history of the sublime the very origin of desire is the quest to recover intimations of divinity in and from the natural universe.

Invoking Weiskel, Morris writes that

> The Romantic sublime is . . . invariably—although not exclusively—hermeneutic. That is, it involves an experience in which words and images grow radically unstable, where meaning is continually in question, approaching or receding or fixed on a distant horizon, promising new dimensions of insight or (in its abrupt absences) unexpectedly blocking the mind. (299)

Such a post-Romantic understanding of the sublime contrasts with the preceding eighteenth-century sense of a stable sublime but should not obscure the fact that, historically speaking, sublimity itself partakes of a profound instability. The sublime is in flux at the very moment of Gothic literary activity, and it is so for precisely the same reason Gothic fiction arises when it does: cultural unease and revolutionary change. The nonrhetorical sublime first entered Western cultural consciousness in the later decades of the seventeenth century. At the end of the eighteenth, the sublime remained a major aesthetic concern but the Western world had undergone profound changes. Robert Hume accurately notes that "The key characteristics of Gothic and romantic writers are concern with ultimate questions and lack of faith in the adequacy of reason or religious faith to make comprehensible the paradoxes of human existence" ("Gothic" 289). One of the means of expressing that concern was the hopeful employment of an intense, heightened version of the sublime quest. The anxieties and uncertainties uncovered in this effort generated the characteristic horror of Gothic fiction. The rejection or revision of the Gothic supernatural sublime was one of the primary signs of the Romantic desire to create new paradigms of engagement with the transcendent. The Romantics, writing in Gothic fiction's maturity and aftermath, would discard the supernatural sublime in favor of the transforming imagination, which "recasts the objects of the exterior world into a new and more profoundly 'true' reality, giving the materials with which it chooses to work a unity and meaning which they do not possess in their original form." From this they would elicit "the emotional certainty of revealed religion directly from nature rather than from God" (Hume, "Gothic" 289). Here, in general contour, is the basis of Romantic achievement.

The Gothicists, however, had their own task: not the perception of unity, at which some scholars see them failing, but what Thompson has called the "perception of paradox":

> the Gothic begins with irreconcilable dualities and, as a form, acknowledges the triumph of paradox and ambiguity—the impossibility of ultimate synthesis. The Gothic is the dark counterforce to optimistic Romanticism. . . . As a mode of Romantic literature, the Gothic also shares many Romantic impulses toward transcendent vision; but the vision is incomplete, fragmented, blurred. . . . the high Gothic romance rarely affirms an ordered universe or man's place within it. ("Introduction" 43)

Such an assessment is true, it must quickly be added, only for those Gothic fictions that operate in the radical mode. The fact such works do not endorse a paradigm of engagement with the transcendent is not evidence of any intellectual or artistic deficiency but is the legitimate end of their inquiry and one that may well have been a necessary pre-condition for the more optimistic poetic visions of Wordsworth and Coleridge. Romantic supernaturalism, and Romantic literature in general, is engaged in a different and, by and large, later project, one predicated upon Gothic fiction being what it is, and to assess Romantic literature as somehow "higher" is to substitute aesthetic criteria for chronological advantage.

*A*n exhaustive accounting of Gothic fiction is beyond the scope of this work. My intention is to discuss in detail only four works, one representative of each category. Discussion of these works and their categorical designation will also serve to suggest a typology of Anglo-American Gothic fiction as it is configured by the operation of the supernatural sublime. Chart 2 maps the relationship of the works to be treated.

CHART 2

	Conservative Mode	Radical Mode
supernatural	*Old English Baron*	*The Monk*
natural	*Mysteries of Udolpho*	*Wieland*

Other works will be mentioned as context permits, but these four titles will be the touchstone texts of part I.

As a supplementary note, it is hardly surprising that these categories break down along gender lines, although such a division is by no means necessary or absolute. As Eugenia DeLamotte points out in her landmark study of Gothic fiction, sublimity was, for women, an oppressive or restrictive aesthetic,[2] a psychological mechanism helping the beleaguered heroine accommodate herself to her almost obligatory passivity and captivity (181–84). Denied the possibility of effective action in the physical world, Gothic heroines take flight in their interior worlds. Transcendence achieves its sublunary expression in the rescuing arms of the male, who generally takes the woman from the enclosure in which she had been confined against her will and ensconces her in another enclosure, now a "voluntary" prisoner of patriarchal power. Such narrative movements, characteristic of female-authored Gothic fiction, "reveal women's Gothic to be deeply conservative" (186). The eighteenth century's denial of autonomy to women meant that comforting enclosures, both physical and social, would be the preferred objects of desire, the goal of most female Gothic journeys. One of the compelling insights of DeLamotte's study is that such novels subvert their own insights that the place of patriarchal enclosure is in effect a prison.[3] Anne Mellor's brief chapter on the appropriation of sublimity by female writers goes further, discerning in the works of female authors two strains of sublimity, one of which functions much as DeLamotte claims, while the other is, in a gesture that anticipates the Coleridgean and Wordsworthian sublimes, a sublime that "mediates a renewed connection" between self and Other (*Romanticism* 96).

Chapter Two

Didacticism
and Romantic Error

Reeve, Radcliffe, and the
Conservative Supernatural

The popularity of Walpole's *Otranto* and Clara Reeve's *The Old English Baron* (1778) suggests that late-eighteenth-century British culture was far from surrendering its Enlightenment faith in moral and epistemological certitude. Indeed, as Marilyn Butler has shown, the history of the Gothic is shaped significantly by reaction against the genre's "subliminal frame of reference," widely perceived to be the "breakdown of control, both in the psyche and the state" (157). Reeve's novel, for example, went through thirteen editions by the late nineteenth century, clearly indicating a continuing taste for works of reassurance rather than challenge. It is not remarkable that such fame attended this novel, now read only by students of the Gothic, for *The Old English Baron* was much more—and less—than an intermediate stage between Walpole and the Gothic apogee of *The Monk*. It is more because it stakes a claim to its own moral territory; it is less because it is a deliberately reactionary modulation and restriction of the supernatural excesses of *The Castle of Otranto*.

Yet Reeve's concern is not limited to the prominence of supernatural machinery—or, at least, her concern with the propriety of ghosts could not be divorced from her firm belief that fiction must serve morality. In the Preface to the second edition of her novel (originally and more appropriately entitled *The Champion of Virtue*), Reeve writes that "The business of Romance is, first, to excite the attention; and, secondly, to direct it to some useful, or at least innocent, end" (4). She registers no direct complaint against her predecessor on either of these points, although one senses that she must have found *Otranto* morally deficient, given the obtrusiveness of the moral in her own tale. Reeve contented herself with nothing less than an explicit drawing-out and repetition of her moral point, sacrificing character complexity and narrative momentum to this end: all her characters are compressed into one dimension, and the narrative proceeds dutifully, generating little suspense or excitement. The kindly Father Oswald makes the most succinct statement of the novel's thesis: "Let this awful spectacle be a lesson to all present, that though wickedness may triumph for a season, a day of retribution will come! . . . Behold the day of retribution! of triumph to the innocent, of shame and confusion to the wicked" (131–32). Another expression of moral concern is inscribed not only into the text but onto the monument erected to the memory of Edmund's murdered parents, an inscription that serves as recapitulation both of plot and moral. It is, despite the novel's allegedly medieval setting, Reeve's only attempt at approximating the language (or culture) of the fifteenth century:

> Praye for the soules of Arthur Lord Lovele and Marie his wife, who were cut off in the flowere of theire youthe, by the trecherye and crueltie of theire neare kinnesmanne. Edmunde theire onlie sonne, one and twentie yeares after theire deathe, by the direction of Heavene, made the discoverye of the mannere of theire deathe, and at the same time proved his owne birthe. He collected theire bones together, and interred them in this place:—A warning and proofe to late posteritie, of the justice of Providence, and the certaintie of Retribution. (145)

Indeed, the events of the tale are so "proofe" of divine providence that even the wicked Lord Lovel readily acknowledges the role of the divine in his own fall and Edmund's rise to power: "The judgments of Heaven are fallen upon me!" he laments from his sick-bed (104); "I am overtaken by justice. I am brought to a severe reckoning here, and I dread to meet one more severe hereafter" (105).

These metaphysical considerations, rudimentary as they are, return us to the supernatural sublime. Reeve, having set out explicitly to correct Walpole, analyzes the earlier novel in her Preface, pointing out that

> the opening excites the attention very strongly; the conduct of the story is artful and judicious; the characters are admirably drawn and supported; the diction polished and elegant; yet, with all these brilliant advantages, it palls upon the mind (though it does not upon the ear); and the reason is obvious, the machinery is so violent, that it destroys the effect it is intended to excite. Had the story been kept within the utmost *verge* of probability, the effect had been preserved, without losing the least circumstance that excites or detains the attention. (4)

Interest in "probability" is the key to Reeve's supernaturalism and is reminiscent of Hugh Blair's concern with the same issue at the same time that it looks forward to the aesthetics of Wordsworth and Walter Scott. Indeed, Reeve seems to have taken to heart Blair's warning that without probability a work can make no lasting impression. In her own study of literary theory and practice, *The Progress of Romance* (1785), Reeve claims (in terms that prefigure Hawthorne's deliberations over the same question) that

> The Romance is an heroic fable, which treats of fabulous persons and things.—The Novel is a picture of real life and manners, and of the times in which it is written. The Romance in lofty and elevated language, describes what never happened nor is likely to happen.—The Novel gives a familiar relation of such things, as pass every day before our eyes, such as may happen to our friend, or to ourselves. . . . (I: 111)[1]

The Old English Baron is of course a Romance (it is subtitled "A Gothic Story," as were later editions of Walpole's novel), a generic siting that permits Reeve the latitude requisite for the supernatural. But she regarded Walpole's novel as excessively "Romantic" and, determined to show the reading public how it should be done, rewrote the Gothic Romance by moving it in the direction of the novel, a form she considered best represented by the works of Richardson and Defoe.

The primary adjustment in her reworking of the genre was to minimize the supernatural, restricting its signifying capability so that probability is enhanced at the same time that metaphysical and moral conservatism are served. Reeve's approach was to introduce much of her supernaturalism through hearsay and "report" and, on those rare occasions when genuinely supernatural experiences occur, to ensure they unfold under the aegis of divine retribution, thus reinforcing the legitimacy of the Christian doctrines and upper-class values Reeve seeks to valorize. In accord with her declared aesthetic, Reeve limits the supernatural to only the most thematically consequential moments in her text, as when Edmund volunteers to spend three nights (the traditional magic number) in the castle's haunted suite. With Father Oswald and the trusted servant Joseph, Edmund investigates mysterious noises, discovering in the process both physical and aural evidence that convinces him his (and others') suspicions of his noble birth are indeed worth investigating.

Notable in this scene is the reaction of the three men to the unexplainable noises they hear: "marks of fear were visible upon all three" (54). They fall to their knees to pray for divine guidance and for the peace of the improperly buried corpse they discover, and thereupon the incident is virtually forgotten. There is no lasting fear, no wild speculation, no terror. The three men calmly return to their plans for recovering Edmund's birthright. Despite the limited effect of the supernaturalism in this episode, Reeve does not suppose that the supernatural is without the ability to inspire fear, at least when it suits her moral purpose. When two wicked kinsmen of Baron Fitz-Owen (present owner of the castle that rightly belongs to Edmund) stay in the haunted suite, they too hear mysterious groans, whereupon "They staggered to a seat, and sunk down upon it, ready to faint; presently all the doors flew open, a pale glimmering light appeared at the door from the staircase, and a man in compleat armour entered the room: He stood with one hand extended, pointing to the outward door; they took the hint, and crawled away as fast as fear would let them . . ." (78).

This morally obtuse and metaphysically domesticated aspect of Reeve's supernaturalism is clearly evident in the novel's last supernatural episode. Edmund returns to the castle for the final validation of his claim to noble birth and the Lovel estates:

> The sound of the horn announced the arrival of the commissioners; at the same instant a sudden gust of wind arose, and the outward gates flew open. They entered the court-yard, and the great folding doors into the hall, were opened without any assistance. The moment Edmund entered the hall, every door in the house flew open; the servants all

rushed into the hall, and fear was written on their countenances: Joseph only was undaunted. These doors, said he, open of their own accord to receive their master! this is he indeed!—Edmund was soon apprized of what had happened.—I accept the omen! said he. (130–31)

As these passages make clear, the supernatural elements of *The Old English Baron* are insistently, almost defiantly conservative. The supernatural sublime, which barely achieves expression in Reeve's novel, contributes only to an emphatic validation of a conventional metaphysic and in this is akin to the supernaturalism of Radcliffe's novels. Indeed, the only explicit approach to sublimity in Reeve's story occurs when Edmund prays: "he felt an enlargement of the heart beyond what he had ever experienced before; all idle fears were dispersed, and his heart glowed with divine love and affiance: He seemed raised above the world and all its pursuits" (50). When she does introduce supernatural terror, Reeve carefully limits it to the novel's evil characters and, more importantly, makes as little as possible of this terror, using it to emphasize the weakness of character that marks the immoral and the unjust. Such metaphorical employment of the supernatural means even that epistemological considerations may safely be ignored. The fact of ghosts means only that divine providence works in mysterious ways to effect the proper outcome of all things.

One critic has noted that "The alterations Reeve makes in Walpole's story . . . can generally be characterized as simplifications or clarifications. She makes the story less bizarre in a narrative ontological sense, and in an ideological sense as well" (Astle 31–32). *The Old English Baron* is indeed considerably less bizarre and more conventional than its model, itself a work that lodges well within the mode of the conservative supernatural sublime.

*R*egarded by many as the first fully realized Gothic fiction, Radcliffe's *The Mysteries of Udolpho* has since its publication held a prominent place in the Gothic canon. Edith Birkhead goes so far as to credit Radcliffe with single-handedly rescuing the Gothic "from an early death" (38). It is certainly the case that the novel had a major impact on the world of mass literature. One of the most popular novels of its day, it attracted the notice and praise of Scott and Keats, among others, and even Matthew Lewis, the man who would soon alter forever the face of Gothic fiction, wrote (to his mother!) that he was prompted to resume writing *The Monk* by his reading of *Udolpho,* "which in my opinion is one of the most interesting books that ever have been published" (qtd. in Astle 44). While *The Italian* (1797) is usually accorded the status of Radcliffe's literary masterwork, *The Mysteries of Udolpho* serves here as the representative text for the conservative nonsupernatural mode of the supernatural sublime, not only because of its phenomenal popularity but for its thematic kinship with its companion conservative work, *The Old English Baron,* and because it more directly exhibits the influence of Burkean sublime theory.

Before proceeding to the question of the novel's supernaturalism, however, a few words need be said regarding the overall conservative disposition of this novel, an orientation signaled obviously (at least for all but the Gothically naive) by the genre to which *Udolpho* belongs: in traditional critical parlance, the "explained supernatural." Works of this type, which feature a supernatural always revealed to be the result of deception or error, generally serve to validate traditional understandings of the phenomenal and spiritual universe. These texts, according to most critics, endorse worldviews "informed by conventional, unambiguous natural law and morality. Human motivation to evil, aggression, and malevolence is explainable in daylight terms—in rational formulas as simple as revenge or lust—rather than as uncaused human depravity possibly paralleling cosmic malevolence from the depths" (Thompson, "Introduction" 16).

While such is certainly the case with the *surnaturel expliqué* as it is employed by Radcliffe and others, the issue of subgenre is one of the chief difficulties inherent in traditional systems of Gothic classification. If the deciding factor in a work's classification is the presence or absence of a true supernatural element, it becomes possible to place in the same category works that have profoundly contrary implications. One scholar of the Gothic, Donald Ringe, writes of the explained Gothic that "What all of these books suggest . . . is the danger inherent in the uncontrolled imagination, especially in those who have, for whatever reason, a predilection for perceiving the marvelous" (*Gothic* 26). Whereas such an assessment is sometimes valid, as it is for Radcliffe's major works, without further distinctions a phrase such as "all of these books" will group texts that in no way agree on the validity of received knowledge and may exclude texts that coincide in their worldviews. *The Old English Baron* is a conservative text, yet it features a genuine ghost. Brown's *Wieland,* to cross the Atlantic for a moment, has events that seem supernatural but are explained as natural occurrences and deceptions, yet, as the next chapter will show, on no ground except this superficial one are *Wieland* and *Udolpho* alike.

The conservative Gothic, on the other hand, asserts the validity of received intellectual traditions, a perspective it articulates through explicit concern with the social status quo. Matters of ethics and metaphysics are assumed simply to follow along in the wake of one's social class. Such assumptions are patently operative in *Udolpho,* just as they are in Reeve's novel, where "God and property" might well serve as the rallying cry of the protagonist and his allies in their struggle against the greed of Lord Lovel. Both Emily and Edmund are paragons of conventional upper-class virtue (recall Reeve's original title) pitted against the perfectly "rational" lusts of Lovel and Montoni. None of the complicating *Weltschmerz* of the Byrónic hero for these villains, nor the demonic overreaching of Melmoth; their desires have a familiar name and object, residing as they do in the realm of economics rather than spirit. As we shall see in *The Monk* and *Wieland,* concern with property and propriety, while not absent in the radical modes, has been subordinated to concerns of greater intellectual import. Neither *Udolpho* nor *The Old English Baron* question the role or efficacy, to say nothing of the existence, of divine providence. In these works, the problem is not one of apprehending the universal order or discovering the lack thereof but simply of aligning oneself with the prevailing system of order. Edmund had to assert his true identity in order to recover his "place" (read "title and wealth") in the scheme of things; Emily will have to prove her virtue so that she, too, may assume the role and assets proper to a woman of her station. Edmund, as a male, must contest and overcome a usurping male in order to validate his claim; Emily, as suits late-eighteenth-century formulations of gender, must endure exploitation and threat in order to prove the integrity of her moral and sexual virtue. Both Reeve and Radcliffe wrote what amount to fictive handbooks on becoming members of the dominant socioeconomic class. Their didacticism took priority over their fiction, most evidently in that both novels have frequently and justly been criticized for their failure to portray accurately the historical settings to which they lay claim. Both texts employ characters and morals suitable to the time of their composition rather than that of their setting for the simple reason that it is only with their own time that they are concerned.

The conservatism of *The Old English Baron* and *The Mysteries of Udolpho* is apparent even in the narrative conventions structuring these novels. *The Old English Baron* employs the ancient folk motif of unknown parentage, in which the peasant lad is revealed to be the son of nobility. *Udolpho* echoes this in Emily's discovery that she is the niece of the late Marchioness de Villeroi, but the work's primary structure is derived from the equally venerable trope of the journey outward from the home, the experience of adventures that educate and mature the protagonist, followed by a return to the home in some new capacity. Ann Ronald remarks on this structure of *Udolpho* in a provocative essay that argues that most female Gothics reveal the basic structure of an "adult fairy tale," a tale in which, with its need for an idyllic ending, there is "no sense of maturity, no suggestion of a heroine tempered by experience" (180). As the ensuing discussion of the story will suggest, I do not concur with the final part of Ronald's assessment, for it certainly seems to be Radcliffe's intention that we see Emily as, if not having learned from her experiences, having been "proofed" or tempered by them.

Orphaned by the sudden (and melodramatic) deaths of her parents, Emily becomes the charge of Madam Cheron, her aunt and the novel's equivalent of the wicked stepmother. Taken unwillingly from her ancestral home (it is even leased in her absence, making the severance of Emily from her heritage seem more complete), Emily is forced to accompany her dangerously foolish aunt into Italy, eighteenth-century England's exotic land of strange adventures, when Madame Cheron unwisely marries the wicked and duplicitous Montoni. Emotionally brutalized by her husband's remorseless pursuit of her property, Madame Montoni dies in the castle of Udolpho, leaving Emily to deal as best she can with the greed of Montoni and the lust of his companions. Although traumatized by the loss of her aunt and then her own property, which Montoni extorts from her, Emily escapes with the aid of an intrepid servant and eventually makes her way back home, just as the lease on her house is expiring. The novel concludes with Emily regaining not only her property and that of her aunt but the love of Valancourt, from whom she had withdrawn her affection after giving credence to slanderous reports of his activities in Paris.

As the foregoing précis makes clear, *Udolpho*, like *The Old English Baron*, extols the importance of material success—specifically, a success according to conservative moral and financial standards, as Richard Astle points out (70). Much of the novel's tension in financial matters centers on the possibility that Emily's inheritance has been lost by a bad investor. The loss of her estates to Montoni is represented as a loss of almost overwhelming magnitude, certainly devastating enough to make her planned marriage to Valancourt impossible. The neat wrapping up of these and other financial matters at the novel's conclusion makes for a resoundingly happy ending, at least as far as Emily and her author are concerned.

Desire for conventional closure achieves expression at the level of the novel's metaphysics as well. A passage cited in the first chapter of the present study showed how contemplation of nature leads Emily to lift her thoughts to the Great Creator. There is never any suggestion that conventional religion and morality are anything other than entirely sufficient, equipping one successfully to meet and overcome life's vicissitudes. The villains are such because they do not subscribe to accepted moral standards; the heroes and heroines are such precisely because they do. *Udolpho* features the usual Anglican reservations about the monastic life, of course. At one point Blanche, having only recently ended a lengthy period as a convent boarder, has a sublime experience upon seeing an oceanscape at night:

> Blanche's thoughts arose involuntarily to the Great Author of the sublime objects she contemplated, and she breathed a prayer of finer devotion, than any she had ever uttered beneath the vaulted roof of a cloister.
> "Who could first invent convents!" said she, "and who could first persuade people to go into them? and to make religion a pretence, too, where all that should inspire it, is so carefully shut out! God is best pleased with the homage of a grateful heart, and, when we view his glories, we feel most grateful. I never felt so much devotion, during the many dull years I was in the convent, as I have done in the few hours, that I have been here, where I need only look on all around me—to adore God in my inmost heart!" (475–76)

Yet Radcliffe is finally more concerned here with making a point about natural beauty rather than about the unnaturalness of the religious life (something Lewis would push to its most notorious expression). For Radcliffe, in this novel at least, religious characters are harmless if somewhat ineffectual. We see Emily spend many happy days in retreat at the convent of St. Claire, in the chapel of which her father is buried. Except for the mad nun Agnes (the names alone give evidence of Lewis's borrowing), who turns out to be the passion-crazed Lady Laurentini, all religious are portrayed favorably. Radcliffe will paint a much less flattering picture of the "Romish" clergy in *The Italian*, using the Inquisition to heighten her readers' distrust, but we must remember that *The Italian* follows both the success of Lewis's *The Monk* and the full course of the Terror in France.

Radcliffe's use of the supernatural matches her conservatism in other matters. Reeve and Walpole had already demonstrated the compatibility of ghosts and religiopolitical conservatism, but Radcliffe was to go further, championing rationalist intellectual conservatism. Emily's occasional indulgence of excessive sensibility is censured by both father and author; her rare lapses into superstitious belief are always followed, and thus effectively circumscribed, by acute embarrassment.

These and related gestures of containment are foundational for the novel's metaphysics, a point overlooked in Terry Castle's provocative essay on *Udolpho*. The phenomenon she identifies as "the spectralization of the other" serves not so much as a problematizing of the metaphysical, an unsettling blurring of the boundaries that define human experience, but a co-opting of the troubling implications of ongoing metaphysical reassessments. The doubling of characters and the "ghostliness of the Other" do not serve to open new avenues of inquiry, nor do they challenge the other aspects of the novel that insistently return the reader to the world of the known and knowable. Instead, such tropes reaffirm the basic psychodynamics of the novel. Although Emily's grief is as real as Montoni's greed, neither tugs at the cornerstones of Western empiricism, although both find manifestation in extreme forms of behavior. To the extent that a blurring of boundaries occurs—and Castle is correct in finding that such is indeed the case—by locating its source in grief, Radcliffe ultimately renders the "alien" territory of the afterlife familiar, thus defusing its threat, its Otherness. When Radcliffe has finished spectralizing the Other, there is even less to be troubled by in her universe; even the realm of the dead plays by the rules of bourgeois English morality. What Castle sees as a "mystification" of death in Radcliffe is perhaps more a sentimentalization of death, and although there is indeed, as Phillippe Ariès documents, a "romantic cult of the dead" that developed in the Romantic moment, it is more in the nature of a deliberate construct, an emotional gloss on the fact that death in Western civilization has become, as Ariès points out, increasingly rational and contained. The metaphysical implications of this are decidedly conservative, just as are the implications of Montoni's motivation by greed and Laurentini's madness through lust.

Indeed, Emily herself serves as one of the primary means of containing the subversive implications of the novel's most noteworthy elements. Servants are permitted to be superstitious—endorsement of class distinction is characteristic of Radcliffe's fiction—but when they exhibit belief they are lectured by Emily on the folly of their credulity. The comic servant is part of Radcliffe's debt to Shakespeare, of course, and Annette is indeed comical when she reproves Emily for failing to believe in ghosts when a glance out her window reveals the cannon by which a spirit has reportedly been seen. But beyond the concern with occasional moments of levity there are crucial narrative and structural consequences to lower-class credulity and superstition, consequences made evident primarily through contrast with Emily's rationalism and cultivated sensibility.

Domestics are Radcliffe's primary means of introducing the supernatural, and thus, the lessons that Emily learns from her encounters with the nonrational. Within hours of her arrival at the half-ruined castle, Emily has been apprised by Annette of the numerous ghosts and mysterious doings at Udolpho, all of which Emily promptly ridicules. Finding herself suddenly alone that first night, however, Emily realizes that in addition to her victimization by enforced removal to Udolpho, she is now partly in the thrall of "those thousand nameless terrors, *which exist only in active imaginations,* and which set reason and examination equally at defiance" (240; emphasis added). The emphasized phrase is Radcliffe's interpolation, not Emily's, but even when Emily succumbs to night fears and superstitious terrors, she need never struggle for long to regain her footing in the world of empiricism and order. She does entertain doubts and does get frightened, to be sure, but Radcliffe never suggests that Emily's rationalist beliefs are in danger of collapse. Her belief in the supremacy of reason is both sincere and ultimately triumphant; the point is instead the very tension between reason and superstition, between empiricism and sensibility—a tension Wordsworth will exploit to similar ends. Radcliffe is no cold empiricist, for Emily's artistic talents, appreciation of natural beauty, and humanitarian compassion are clearly presented as praiseworthy attributes, but nonetheless a ratio between sense and sensibility must be struck and firmly maintained. A representative instance is the deathbed speech by Emily's father:

> Above all, my dear Emily . . . do not indulge in the pride of fine feeling, the romantic error of amiable minds. Those, who really possess sensibility, ought early to be taught, that it is a dangerous quality, which is continually extracting the excess of misery, or delight, from every surrounding circumstance. . . . we become the victims of our feelings, unless we can in some degree command them. (79–80)

Emily's story is, in large part, that of the dialectic engagement between these aspects of her character and of the striking of a proper balance between them within a social context of upper-class Anglican virtue. *Udolpho* is a conservative socializing tract, an upper-class fairy tale for young adults at the end of the eighteenth century, employing a supernaturalism that always turns out to be false and empty, a "romantic error," in support of its inculcation of conservative doctrine.

Udolpho is a cautionary tale as well as a didactic one, and the supernatural plays an important role here as well. To return to the deathbed speech of Emily's father:

> I know you will say (for you are young, my Emily) I know you will say, that you are contented sometimes to suffer, rather than to give up your refined sense of happiness, at others; but, when your mind has been long harassed by vicissitude, you will be content to rest, and you will then recover from your delusion. (80)

St. Aubert proves remarkably prescient: torn from her childhood world of (unearned) security and tranquility, Emily experiences the tumult of love, separation from her lover, belief in his subsequent moral degradation, unwanted advances (some honorable, some not) of various suitors, loss of her last surviving relative, loss of her estates and wealth, and the threat of death. Emily recovers from these tribulations only by passing through them, by returning to the point from which she began.

The sense/sensibility conflict within Emily, however, is expressed not merely in her traveling and the passage of time but involves travel to two specific locations, the two "haunted" houses of Udolpho and Château-le-Blanc. The importance of place in the novel's didactic scheme in turn puts considerable emphasis on the superstitious servants, through whose gossip and storytelling the supernatural atmosphere of each house is established. As readers we occasionally see a mysterious figure, catch a shadowy glimpse of an unexplained visage, and hear not a few groans or snatches of music; but most of the mystery surrounding the houses where Emily stays is indirect, a product of servant gossip. Annette, the attendant first to Madame Cheron-Montoni and then to Emily, is the prime channel for this reportage; also important in this regard is Dorothée, the gossip-filled housekeeper at Château-le-Blanc, whose knowledge of the past materially advances the final unraveling of the novel's mysteries.

By investing each house with a supernatural tradition, servants also contribute measurably to the novel's foremost theme: the intellectual and emotional maturation of Emily. Reported supernaturalism figures prominently in this process, for it is one of the two main constituents of the "sensibility" side of the sense/sensibility dichotomy in Emily. Supernaturalism also helps mark the boundaries of intellectual threat. Prior to her Udolpho experience, Emily is not especially prone to irrational fear. She is highly sensitive, to be sure, and we are made to understand that such sensitivity has the *potential* for excess; her father's deathbed warning is not given without reason. Yet on only two minor occasions before the Udolpho section of the novel does Emily yield to "imaginary terrors."

It is only when Emily and the others reach Udolpho that the supernatural becomes a significant element in the text; prior to this point, there is very little that is Gothic about this famous Gothic novel. The arrival at Udolpho unchains the superstitious imagination, however, and we are suddenly inundated with reports of apparitions, secret passageways, unaccountable noises, mysterious music, shadowy figures, open graves, and hints of murder. The supernatural tenor of her experiences continues even after Emily escapes from Udolpho. Although the inhabitants of Château-le-Blanc are her allies, their house seems just as haunted as the castle in the Apennines.

By the novel's conclusion, of course, all mysterious events have been explained: unknown kinship links are disclosed, hidden pasts are brought to light, the unexplained music is made by a deranged nun, the noises and sightings of apparitions are the tricks of pirates. There is, at the work's close, an emphatic return to the real world of marriage, conjugal bliss, and financial independence:

> O! how joyful it is to tell of happiness, such as that of Valancourt and Emily; to relate, that, after suffering under the oppression of the vicious and the disdain of the weak, they were, at length, restored to each other—to the beloved landscapes of their native country,—to the securest felicity of this life, that of aspiring to moral and labouring for intellectual improvement—to the pleasures of enlightened society, and to the exercise of the benevolence, which had always animated their hearts; while the bowers of La Vallée became, once more, the retreat of goodness, wisdom and domestic blessedness! (672)

All of this happiness is the result of Emily's having successfully endured her experiences, of modulating her sensibility by subordinating it to reason. Radcliffe affirms rationality's victory by quietly dropping the supernatural elements from the story: as the true natures of the terrifying phenomena are revealed, the presence of the supernatural simply becomes more diaphanous until finally it vanishes altogether. There is no single stunning revelation that strikes Emily with the folly of her occasional near-belief in the supernatural; she gradually masters her emotions and her tendency toward sentimental indulgence, and so the need for the supernatural no longer remains. Even Annette, her usefulness as gossip and tale-teller ended, is more or less put out to pasture, married off to her beloved Ludovico and put in charge of one of Emily's estates—one, tellingly, Emily and Valancourt do not use as their primary residence.

What, then, of the supernatural sublime? The moments of supposed supernatural encounter in *Udolpho* are relatively unexceptional—so much so that Radcliffe tips her hand. These encounters never deflect the narrative from its obvious trajectory; the apparently supernatural phenomena have so little practical effect that it is soon obvious these events are of little consequence in the overall scheme of the novel.

In an essay extracted from the preface of her posthumously published *Glaston de Blondeville,* Radcliffe provides some insight into her theory of the supernatural and its literary uses: "Terror and horror are so far opposite, that the first expands the soul; the other contracts, freezes, and nearly annihilates [it] . . ." ("Supernatural" 149). The Burkean linkage of terror with expansion of the soul is a fundamental component of the sublime; yet Radcliffe's notion of "expansion" is much more restricted than that endorsed by Gothicism's more notorious practitioners. Metaphysical implications do not attend the "supernatural" events in *Udolpho;* Radcliffe's expansion is a highly ephemeral intensification of emotional energies that is almost immediately dissipated by the commonplace demands of living, as well as being severely restricted by the quick reassertion of rationality. There is a brief moment of titillation, but in Radcliffe it is always full of a sound and fury that ultimately signify nothing of consequence, for we always return to the point from which we began. Her terrors were not of the other world, but of this one: for Radcliffe, "the true gothic terrors were not the black veils and spooky passages for which she is famous, but the winds of change, dissolution, and chaos which they represented" (Durant 520). Richard Astle notes how terror functions for Radcliffe as something of a straw man, its dissipation valorizing the status quo:

> Terror depends upon a balance between absence and clarity of information . . . about the dreaded object. Horror, on the other hand, goes to

limits—of certainty and of death. . . . The difference between terror and horror, then, is that horror is a response to an object too clearly, if not always correctly . . . seen, while terror is an error, for once the veil of obscurity has been lifted, terror either evaporates (the object proving non-existent or harmless) or becomes horror. Thus the existence of terror in [*Udolpho*] marks a territory for rationalism to conquer, a shadow in the reader's and/or the heroine's mind to be dispelled by the cold light of reason and/or objective evidence. . . . (52–53)

In the conservative nonsupernatural Gothic, "ghosts" are always present only so they may be exposed as shadows or delusions, validating the superiority and legitimacy of Enlightenment precepts.

The larger narrative sense in which she employs the structure, at least, of the supernatural sublime confirms the limited import of Radcliffe's supernatural. *Udolpho* has, as noted earlier, structural affinities with the quest romance. Like many of these works, *Udolpho* is a *Bildungsroman;* the education of Emily involves her confrontation with and temptation by the seducing power of the passions. Indeed, Nelson Smith sees as the "major theme" of *Udolpho* the "attempt to temper Emily's excess of sensibility" (583). She is disposed just enough toward sensibility to raise the prospect that she may succumb, although before too many pages have been turned it is rather apparent that Emily is made of fairly stern stuff. Still, the dangers into which she falls become progressively greater, culminating in the Udolpho episode—at which point she is at the greatest remove from her home, La Vallée—and apparently in the greatest danger: "Udolpho is, as it were, the hell for those who have been corrupted by society; for here the masks that normally veil behaviour in polite society are removed to reveal brutal egotism, unscrupulous greed, machination, manipulation and violence" (Morse 20). Emily must survive her confrontation with the undisguised evils of human society; they, not the supernatural, pose the true threat, but her mastery of herself and her assertion of social status and power can only be achieved by the mental discipline and intellectual maturity that overcoming her fears of the supernatural represents.

Emily's escape into France (ancien régime, of course) merely begins her reintegration into society. She is not yet finished conquering the irrational, and even when the hauntings at Château-le-Blanc are explained away, Emily still must reestablish herself as a woman of property as well as one of unassailable principle and virtue. The novel ends •
when Emily's incorporation into polite society is complete: she may

finally lay claim to wealth, property, a rational mind with just enough sensibility to permit the appreciation of beauty, and finally, a husband, when it is revealed that Valancourt's fall was the product of malicious gossip. Elizabeth MacAndrew cogently identifies both the importance and the origin of the lesson Emily must learn: "Like many an eighteenth century heroine, she has to learn the prudence by which the virtuous are to live in the real world without being corrupted" (95). Another commentator has effectively shown how "the only solution to the problems of adult existence lies in returning to traditional, conservative values" (Durant 520). Emily is a remarkable success in this return, beginning her adventures as a child and ending as a woman with what is, for Radcliffe, a fully realized sense of self and social place. This process of maturation involves a type of "suspension" on a narrative scale, one structurally cognate with that of the supernatural sublime. Emily is sent out into the world dispossessed but gradually throws off her liminal status, returning to the place from which she began with an earned security, a legitimate position in the social and physical world as well as a valorization of a particular version of those worlds.

The narrative structure of suspension, common to Western literature since *The Odyssey*, obviously is independent of supernaturalism. Yet discussion of this narrative design is relevant here because the supernatural is a key part of *Udolpho*'s suspension, figuring prominently as an obstacle to and test of Emily's maturity. Because of this testing I cannot agree with those critics for whom Radcliffe's heroines remain static and unchanged. They do, as David Durant argues, "preserve their innocence through the gothic adventures until they can revert to the hierarchical, reasonable, and safe world of the family. Her heroines devise no strategies by which to appreciate a chaotic world; no method to accept or penetrate the masked character of the adult; and no acceptance of the irrational as a positive force" (525). What Durant describes here is not failure, however: it is precisely the point. For Radcliffe's heroines to devise such strategies would be to admit the necessity of coping on new terms with what are essentially radical or revolutionary elements in the conservative world Radcliffe so obviously cherishes. What her heroines *do* learn is the strength of their traditional convictions: the lessons provided by Emily's story are that perseverance in moral virtue will lead to (conservative) reward and that an excess of sensibility, an essentially "romantic" trait, must be curbed. In learning these lessons, Emily and Radcliffe's other heroines do indeed make a sort of progression in their movement from child-hood to adulthood. The very point, in other words, is that no *new* strategies need be evolved.

Emily triumphs over the forces of unreason and anarchy with the old strategies endorsed by Radcliffe. Emily's terror is always brief, without lasting effect on her mind or character. In contrast, we might look back to Walpole's Manfred, tormented by guilt and exposed as a usurper by supernatural intervention. We might also look ahead a few years to Polidori's Aubrey, who loses his sanity after discovering that his companion Lord Ruthven is a vampire. The supernatural in Rad-cliffe is not supernatural, and when it is so revealed even the tempo-rary terrors Emily suffered are seen to be empty and foolish, the "romantic errors" of a not-yet-mature mind. It is true that the skepti-cal Count de Villefort is affected by his encounter with unexplained noises in a supposedly haunted suite, but his only reaction is to main-tain a strict silence. The only true effect of the supernatural, Radcliffe implies, is the effect we permit our undisciplined beliefs to have upon us. This, in fact, is the basic message not only of Radcliffe's novels but of the "explained Gothic" as a whole. Donald Ringe remarks that

> What [the explained Gothic writers] did was to internalize what Wal-pole, Reeve, and their followers presented as objectively real. From the point of view of the rationalists, it made no difference whether the sources of terror were real or not. What a character thought he per-ceived had the same effect on his mind as what was actually there. . . . What is important in these books, then, is not so much the Gothic ef-fects themselves as the intellectual and emotional sources of the charac-ters' misapprehensions of reality. ("Gothic" 24–25)

In important ways it must have made a difference or else these writers would have been just as comfortable with genuinely supernatural events, but Ringe's emphasis on the character's perspective is instruc-tive. A major concern in *Udolpho* is Emily's need to gain sufficient control over her mind so the world may be correctly perceived. Adher-ence to the principles of reason, "sense," and decorum is the only acceptable behavior and results in the eventual correction of any weakness or misperception. Emily learns this lesson in her encounters with the supernatural, encounters that pass her from the world of childhood to the world of the rational adult, and to the particular view of that world that Radcliffe endorses: "The terms of success for her heroines are inevitably those which deny any virtue to the revolution-ary world of chaos" (Durant 525). Indeed, Radcliffe's Gothics are a reactionary cry against the world that was emerging, its birth evident in the revolution across the Channel and in the texts soon to be produced in her own land.

For other Gothic practitioners, the safety and consolation of the explained Gothic was itself a deception, a mistaking of the appearance for the reality. For these writers, uncaused human depravity and cosmic evil were as real as the pirates in the walls of Radcliffe's chateaux, as real as the guillotines in the streets of Paris, and much more threatening both in themselves and in the implications of their mere existence. These are the writers who worked in the radical mode of the supernatural sublime, to which this study now turns.

Chapter Three

The Yawning Gulf

Lewis, Brown, and
the Radical Supernatural Sublime

My discussion of *The Monk*'s Bleeding Nun episode in chapter 1 hinted at the character of the radical supernatural sublime, but full elaboration of this aesthetic requires some consideration of the novel's main narrative line. Of greatest consequence is not the moral particulars of Ambrosio's hypocrisy—his lust, incest, and murder—but the supernatural context in which these crimes are committed.

Lewis is slow to introduce the supernatural into his primary narrative. Ambrosio's first transgressions involve his sexual liaison with Matilda; not until he tires of her and begins to lust for Antonia does the supernatural enter, a point not reached until nearly the end of the second of *The Monk*'s three volumes. Matilda's true demonic nature of course means that Ambrosio has had dealings with the supernatural much earlier, but this is revealed to neither monk nor reader until the novel's conclusion.

The already guilt-stricken Ambrosio reacts predictably to Matilda's revelation that her knowledge of the occult arts can help him consummate his lust for Antonia: "If on witchcraft depends the fruition of my desires, I renounce your aid most absolutely. The consequences are too horrible: I doat upon Antonia, but am not so blinded by lust, as to sacrifice for her enjoyment my existence both in this world and the next" (268). Yet this "Faust of sex" (Frank 129) is finally persuaded by Matilda to descend with her to the sepulcher of the convent of St. Clare, where she proposes to conjure Lucifer himself—persuaded not by Matilda's sophistry and "scoffing tone" but by her gift of a magic mirror that reveals Antonia undressing. The descent is particularly significant because the sepulcher is the primary locus of the supernatural sublime in this narrative strand (it shall figure importantly in a later episode as well, discussed below), and Ambrosio's mental state at the beginning of the episode determines the nature and consequence of his experience.

Ambrosio's customary world is that of the church and abbey; despite his affair with Matilda, he has retained his mental, spiritual, and emotional links to it. Indeed, his awareness of the increasingly tenuous nexus to his nurturing environment informs his argument against Matilda's offer to assist him with magic in his pursuit of Antonia: "Though my passions have made me deviate from her laws, I still feel in my heart an innate love of virtue. . . . though my principles have yielded to the force of temperament, I still have sufficient grace to shudder at Sorcery, and avoid a crime so monstrous, so unpardonable!" (269). While his sins remain natural ones, Ambrosio is not beyond the pale of Christian salvation and forgiveness; the ethical and intellectual structures that have ordered his life remain operative for him.

The sight of Antonia nude, however, is more than Ambrosio's "temperament" can bear, and his acceptance of Matilda's offer precipitates the crucial moment of supernatural sublimity. Exploiting his lust-weakened resolve, Matilda "gave the Monk no time for reflection" and "drew him hastily along" to the sepulcher (272). Here Ambrosio has stepped into the sublime's space of helplessness: his principles no longer guiding his actions, he becomes "unclear about the premises of morality in the post-sacred universe in which he has chosen to live" (Brooks 250). Like a child, he is led by the hand into a situation over which he will have no control, an experience to which he will remain a passive but fully implicated observer.

As the two descend into the sepulcher, the light of the moon (traditional symbol of chastity and purity) is left behind, and the monk and his guide stumble through "profound obscurity" until they come upon the statue of St. Clare, before which is a lamp perpetually burning but casting so little light that it cannot "dissipate the thick gloom, in which the Vaults above were buried" (272). Such details are not accidental for Lewis, but form instead part of his running commentary on religious institutions. Religion, particularly Roman Catholicism, is associated not with revelatory illumination but with cloaking gloom and obfuscation, with hidden chambers of the mind and heart concealing terrible secrets and destructive energies. Obscurity is a standard component of the Burkean sublime, but Lewis turns it to his polemical purpose, giving this clichéd bit of stage setting considerable symbolic potency. Indeed, the entire episode is a masterpiece of the supernatural sublime, for in its psychological topography it effectively delineates and reifies the intellectual structure of the experience. The descent from the world of Madrid and the abbey into the sepulcher—a descent that, in its motivation by lust, suggests the obvious Freudian paradigm—initiates the moment of suspension, the loss of contact with the quotidian world and its mental landmarks.

Briefly left alone by Matilda, Ambrosio is beset by doubts, beginning to fear (quite presciently, it turns out) that he has cut himself off from redemption:

> In this fearful dilemma, He would have implored God's assistance, but was conscious that He had forfeited all claim to such protection. Gladly would He have returned to the Abbey; But as He had past through innumerable Caverns and winding passages, the attempt of regaining the Stairs was hopeless. His fate was determined. . . . (273)

This recognition is a turning point, the crux of Ambrosio's subterranean experience. The literal suggestion here is that everything that happens subsequently to Ambrosio is the consequence of his inability to find his way. Anagogically, there is no question of chance or accident: Ambrosio is where he is by his own volition, because of decisions for which only he is responsible. His inability to find the stairway is the signal that Ambrosio has succumbed fully to the moment of helplessness. His perseverance in the new course of action before him is forecast by his efforts at self-consolation: "He reflected, that Antonia would be the reward of his daring: He inflamed his imagination by enumerating her charms" (273). Abandoning all attempts at virtuous restraint, Ambrosio placates the remnants of his conscience by convincing himself he may evade moral and spiritual blame by assigning responsibility for his diabolic involvement to Matilda, who does the actual conjuring. The appearance of the demon, "a Figure more beautiful, than Fancy's pencil ever drew" (276) rather than the "dreadful Apparition" Ambrosio anticipated, further comforts the monk, as does the demon's gift of a silver myrtle branch granting him unhindered access to Antonia's chamber. Safely back in his cell, Ambrosio's reflections on the night's experience unambiguously announce the moral transformation he has undergone:

> He rejoiced in the fortunate issue of his adventure, and reflecting upon the virtues of the Myrtle, looked upon Antonia as already in his power. Imagination retraced to him those secret charms, betrayed to him by the Enchanted Mirror, and He waited with impatience for the approach of midnight. (279)

Ambrosio has surrendered to the darkness within, rejecting the doubts and hesitations of a few hours before in his delight at the prospect of sexual indulgence. He has emerged from the sepulcher a different man, committed to the course of action represented by the bough of myrtle.

The nadir of this course is his rape of Antonia, the heinousness of which is compounded by premeditation. Already under suspicion by Antonia's mother, Elvira, Ambrosio unhesitatingly pursues his plan to its conclusion, fully aware that Elvira "could do no more than suspect; that no proof of his guilt could be produced" (299). The principles that once informed Ambrosio's life and action have been utterly abandoned; even his earlier concern for fame has been perverted into the belief that his spotless reputation will provide protection from Elvira's public calumnies and accusations.

Ambrosio's reputation is never tested, for he murders Elvira when she discovers him in Antonia's bedroom. His guilt over the deed, while appearing to suggest conventional Christian morality, proves instead to be both short-lived and amoral: his guilt is a consequence not of any fear of eternal damnation but fear of *earthly* punishment. As Lewis explains, "Impunity reconciled [Ambrosio] to his guilt: He began to resume his spirits; and as his fears of detection died away, He paid less attention to the reproaches of remorse" (305).

So completely is Ambrosio comforted by his discovery that "crimes were not so swiftly followed by punishment" (319) that he, with Matilda's aid, resumes his pursuit of Antonia. In a dark reworking of *Romeo and Juliet,* Matilda supplies the monk with a potion that creates the appearance of death. Having surreptitiously administered the drug to Antonia, Ambrosio has her "corpse" interred in the sepulcher in which he and Matilda had conjured Lucifer. Here Antonia is entirely at the monk's mercy.

At this point the action of the novel returns underground. In fact, the two heretofore separate strands of the narrative meet in the sepulcher of St. Clare, only to part again afterward, as though Lewis sought to emphasize the catacombs as a place of intersection, the anarchic locus at which the governing conventions of daylight life are suspended and previously disparate experiences combine to reveal new complexities and dark knowledge. Peter Brooks notes this confluence of the novel's two narrative lines in the sepulcher, finding the underground chamber to symbolize "the interdicted regions of the soul, the area of the mind where our deepest and least avowable impulses lie" (258). The structural contrast of these fetid regions and the false-seeming of the religious institutions above them further confirms the idea that these impulses, when restrained or rechanneled, are antithetical to a natural and virtuous life.

The descent of the novel's second narrative strand into the underworld mirrors that of the first. Lorenzo's hesitant exploration of the "Labyrinth of passages" is similar to that of Ambrosio's, but unlike the monk, Lorenzo has no guide familiar with the sepulcher's intricacies. The domains of life and death do not mingle for the young cavalier as they do for the corrupt monk and the institution he represents.

Many readers of the novel regard Ambrosio's death as the work's climax, but the second sepulcher episode is much closer to the novel's thematic center as it is revealed by the supernatural sublime. Here Lewis literally uncovers the hollowness and hidden corruption of religion, unmasking repressed horrors with no suggestion of life-affirming or spiritually empowering compensations. Lucifer appeared in the first sepulcher episode, and there is no doubt of the power and potency in the world of the negative metaphysic he represents. The second sepulcher visit, however, reveals not the balancing potency of the positive supernatural—that is, the Christian divine in contrast to the demonic—but only the former's corruption, hypocrisy, and impotence.

Lorenzo enters the sepulcher in pursuit of nuns escaping the destruction of their convent, the wholesale pillage and ruin aboveground presaging what is about to be revealed beneath. He finds the women cowering by the statue of St. Clare, drawn there by the votive lamp but frightened by a mysterious moan. The nuns attribute the noise to St. Clare's outrage at the destruction of her convent. Hoodwinked by the Prioress, they are only too willing to indulge the superstitiousness and intellectual timidity Lorenzo (and Lewis) ridicules: " 'Excuse me,' replied Lorenzo, 'if I am surprised, that while menaced by real woes you are capable of yielding to imaginary dangers. These terrors are puerile and groundless. . . . The idea of Ghosts is ridiculous in the extreme' " (362). This is a curious statement, coming from someone who not only believed every word of Raymond's tale of the Bleeding Nun but was surprised at Raymond's failure to ascertain the identity of the Wandering Jew; the statement is undoubtedly intended, to some degree at least, as an ironic comment upon Lorenzo's self-assurance. In this circumstance, however, he is absolutely correct. He scoffs at the belief that the statue has magical properties, disproving the nuns' assertion that a graverobber who once touched the statue found his fingers frozen to it. The "dried and shrivelled fingers" still to be seen on the statue fail to convince Lorenzo that he has encountered anything other than one of the Prioresses' many attempts to manipulate her gullible nuns.

Lorenzo unmasks further hollowness in the order of St. Clare, and this of the most literal sort: the saint's statue is wooden, not stone as it appears. His discovery of a secret mechanism releases the statue from its hollow pedestal. Through an opening in the base, beneath the dissimulation of the statue—emblematic of the hypocrisy of the Prioress and, for Lewis, of religion in general—Lorenzo discovers further mystery, a third level of hidden meaning and corrupt horror carefully guarded from the world's gaze:

> A deeper abyss now presented itself before them, whose thick obscurity the eye strove in vain to pierce. The rays of the Lamp were too feeble to be of much assistance. Nothing was discernible, save a flight of rough unshapen steps, which sank into the yawning Gulph, and were soon lost in darkness. (367)

Here is the novel's central image, the yawning gulf or dark abyss that lies concealed beneath the deceptive surface of institutional religion, an ornament gilded and willfully misrepresented for the purpose of manipulation and gain. Psychoanalytic readings of the novel's multilayered subterranean imagery understand these descents and explorations as confrontations with the id, and in the case of Ambrosio—and even, to a certain extent, in the case of Lorenzo—such readings are legitimate. Yet the novel's sexual element should not eclipse other dimensions of this imagery, for the physical abysses and chambers that underlie Madrid are matched in thematic significance by the moral abyss beneath the surface piety of the Prioress and Ambrosio, as well as by the metaphysical abyss beneath the veneer of religious consolation.

In these important subterranean passages Lewis provides a dual perspective on religious institutions. The first, presented through the actions of Ambrosio, is that of one whose life embodies the failures of religion and of the human desire to order the moral universe. MacAndrew affirms the relationship of the novel's extensive subterranean imagery with Lewis's attitude toward religion's power to shape human character and action:

> The recurrent theme of imprisonment—in cloister, castle, or dungeon—in each plot, subplot, and interpolation, and the repeated transformation of idyll into nightmare say again and again that goodness is locked up inside evil, that innocence is seduced, perverted, but that somehow it might not have been. Ambrosio in the claws of Lucifer is also a victim, a human being of great potential for good betrayed by social forces into a living hell of evil. (139)

The deforming effects of repression are particularly evident in the first sepulcher episode, where lust, the consequence of an unnatural, monastic repression of libidinal energies, drives Ambrosio to and then over the moral brink. Lewis insists on the potential Ambrosio once possessed: "Had [Ambrosio's] Youth been passed in the world, He would have shown himself possessed of many brilliant and manly qualities . . ." (236). The thematics of the novel demand that the monk had to be of such promise, for Lewis seeks to infuse a sense of the tragic into his protagonist's fall. Yet despite assurances of Ambrosio's youthful character, we encounter him almost exclusively as a hypocrite and a worker of evil. There is pathos in his corruption by religion, to be sure, but he does not attract our sympathy. Although we cannot deny his victimization, the energy of his narrative and symbolic role comes from his power as victimizer, as well as from his hypocrisy as such. In the ability of institutional religion to pervert and deform so thoroughly the character of such a one as Ambrosio lies the novel's most well-developed indictment of human religious endeavor.

The second perspective on religion, complementary to the first, is provided by Lorenzo and predicated on his being a much more sympathetic figure. His is the perspective of the morally intact individual, and the lesson Lewis draws from his story is that such a person is, in the human world, almost necessarily a victim. It is no coincidence that all the novel's good characters are victimized. Lorenzo loses his beloved Antonia; Antonia loses her mother, then is raped and murdered;

Agnes, separated from her beloved, is immured first in a convent, then in a sepulcher, where her baby dies; Raymond suffers horribly, and indeed nearly dies, because of his separation from Agnes. Ambrosio becoming his own victim only adds to the depth of the gulf that Lewis explores.

Lorenzo proves more sympathetic than the monk, despite a smaller narrative presence, because of his humanity; he has never sought nor pretended to be other than what he is. Ambrosio's grandiose conception of his social position and of his own moral capabilities is largely responsible for his fall, and for this reason we cannot sympathize with his victimization, from which Lewis carefully distances us by locating it in the novel's past. Ambrosio is already corrupt when the novel begins, and the story of his youthful promise and corruption, coming as it does after we have seen the monk as hypocrite and sinner, cannot much ameliorate our contempt. Lorenzo and his fellow victims are not hypocrites, even if only because they are permitted free expression of those energies that Ambrosio must continually restrain. It is to the second sepulcher passage that we must turn in order to see the moment of their greatest victimization, the same moment that is the apex of Ambrosio's career as victimizer.

Exploring the "yawning Gulph" beneath the statue, Lorenzo comes upon "a Creature stretched upon a bed of straw, so wretched, so emaciated, so pale, that He doubted to think her Woman" (369). "Petrified with horror" he realizes that this near-dead wretch clinging to the decomposing corpse of an infant is Agnes, his sister and Raymond's lover. Immured in a convent by her parents after her failed elopement, Agnes made a second attempt to escape with Raymond only to have her plans discovered by Ambrosio. Her death too had been feigned, and although pregnant she was imprisoned in the hidden depths of the sepulcher by the Prioress, who had been outraged that Madrid's "Man of Holiness" should uncover the perfidy of one of her novitiates.

Lewis leaves nothing to the imagination in Agnes's description of the horrors of her sepulchral imprisonment or in the drawing-out of the moral implications of her torment: "And they are God's Servants, who make me suffer thus! They think themselves holy, while they torture me like Fiends! They are cruel and unfeeling; And 'tis they who bid me repent; And 'tis they, who threaten me with eternal perdition!" (370). Realizing she is about to be rescued, Agnes cries out that "There is a God then, and a just one!" (372), but lest we attribute too much significance to this lone outburst of religious affirmation, Lewis quickly has Agnes add that she must take the corpse of her child with her, for "It shall convince the world, how dreadful are the abodes so falsely termed religious" (372).

The hypocrisy of the human institution of religion is not, certainly, a complete indictment of religion's spiritual content, especially given the anti-Catholicism of much English Gothic, but it is with *human* possibility that the Gothic is ultimately concerned. For the radical Gothic, even an extant divinity is as good as absent if it cannot be reached, and certainly the institutions humans have created in their quest for the divine are understood to have failed:

> It is as if the conventional morality of *The Monk,* such as it is, together with the institutions founded upon it, were presented chiefly in order to demonstrate their own inadequacy in the face of the truly perverse. . . . it seems that the very existence of moral taboos *generates* the villain's desire to destroy them. (Lea 23)

Since Ambrosio's moral character was formed in the abbey in which he was raised, the source (or, at the very least, the agent) of the perversion on which Sydney Lea remarks is the institution of religion, a connection nowhere more evident in *The Monk* than in the sepulcher episodes, which painfully reveal the emptiness and corruption masked by the facades of institutional spirituality.

Immediately prior to his discovery by Lorenzo, Ambrosio commits his greatest act of victimization, raping the helpless Antonia. Yet even here, in the literal and figurative depths of his depravity, Ambrosio is not utterly without compassion: "As his gloomy rage abated, in proportion did his compassion augment for Antonia. He stopped, and would have spoken to her words of comfort. But He knew not from whence to draw them . . ." (386). The impulse is notable, although Ambrosio's inability to speak is telling, and it remains impossible to muster sympathy for the monk. Ambrosio can think of nothing to do either with or for Antonia: he is reluctant to leave her imprisoned, yet cannot bring himself to liberate her and thus jeopardize his own freedom. He refuses, finally, to acknowledge the consequences of and responsibility for his hypocrisy and violence:

> What was the alternative? A resolution far more terrible for Antonia, but which at least would insure the Abbot's safety. He determined to leave the world persuaded of her death, and to retain her a captive in this gloomy prison: There He proposed to visit her every night, to bring her food, to profess his penitence, and mingle his tears with hers. (387)

He proposes, in essence, to leave the status quo intact and condemn Antonia to a half-life as his perpetual victim. Some readers might think, on first reading this passage, that Ambrosio has put himself in the place of his prisoner, joining her for prayer and repentance, but his postcoital remorse is fundamentally undermined by its motive of self-interest. His concern for the appearance of propriety outweighs concern for Antonia, and repentance that refuses to accept fully the consequences of earlier action is incomplete and inadequate. Ambrosio's change of mind when Antonia swears she will remain silent and flee Madrid remains indicative more of the monk's hypocrisy than of any "sincere wish to repair his fault as much as possible" (388). The true depth of his sincerity is revealed shortly hereafter, when Ambrosio stabs Antonia in a vain attempt to silence her cries for help.

As I remarked earlier, the novel's conclusion is often regarded as its climax, but nothing transpires in those final pages that does not confirm what is already known. Given over to the Inquisition, by whom he is tried, tortured, and condemned to the *auto-da-fé,* all of Ambrosio's attempts to evade the emotional and moral consequences of his predicament collapse in failure:

> In this Labyrinth of terrors, fain would He have taken his refuge in the gloom of Atheism: Fain would He have denied the soul's immortality; have persuaded himself that when his eyes once closed, they would never more open, and the same moment would annihilate his soul and body. Even this resource was refused to him. To permit his being blind to the fallacy of this belief, his knowledge was too extensive, his understanding too solid and just. He could not help feeling the existence of a God. Those truths, once his comfort, now presented themselves before him in the clearest light; But they served only to drive him to distraction. (425)

Such a passage makes a necessary contribution to Lewis's purpose, for the agony of Ambrosio's position is dependent upon his simultaneous belief in God and his overriding conviction that there is only a vengeful God, that God's forgiveness cannot be extended to a sinner such as himself. Yet even here the implications are more practical than theological: "He sorrowed for the punishment of his crimes, not their commission. . . . [In his dream] He found himself in sulphurous realms and burning Caverns, surrounded by Fiends appointed his Tormentors, and who drove him through a variety of tortures, each of which was more dreadful than the former" (426–27). Ambrosio's concerns are far from transcendent; his belief in God has failed him, existing only as an ancillary agent of his self-torment and fear and his desire to evade punishment. For the monk, God is known only by absence and failure—or, at best, by threat. God may, in the words of one critic,

> exist still, but no longer as holy mystery and as moral principle eliciting love, worship, and respect. No longer the source and guarantee of ethics, "God" has become rather an interdiction, a primitive force within nature that strikes fear into men's hearts but does not move them to allegiance and worship. . . . "God" is simply one figure in a manichaeistic daemonology. (Brooks 251)

Perhaps the greatest hypocrisy committed by Ambrosio is his surrendering the love of God for fear of God, but in his surrender is radical Gothicism's tacit acknowledgment of the waning potency of the Christian transcendent.

In the despair born of such perception of absence and the fear of punishment, Ambrosio commits himself to the only powers whose efficacy has been demonstrated: those of the devil, of abyss and darkness. At Matilda's urging Ambrosio sells his soul to Lucifer, appearing now not as a beautiful youth but "in all that ugliness, which since his fall from heaven has been his portion" (433). Carried out of his Inquisition cell by the demon, Ambrosio achieves his precious freedom, although we learn that his "Gaoler" had been coming not with orders for his execution, as the monk had believed, but with his pardon. Since fear of a painful death was one of the primary motives for Ambrosio's pact with Lucifer, it is evident the monk had been terribly deceived, the irony of his situation an appropriate comment on the hypocrisy of his life. His damnation was unnecessary, but such is the course of things, Lewis implies, that it was unavoidable.

The futility of human endeavor is underscored further by Lewis, who explains that Ambrosio "was soon forgotten as totally, as if He never had existed" (438). The yawning gulf hidden by the statue of St. Clare has swallowed the monk, tricked into embracing the darkest horrors of his moral universe and robbed of any significance in the social: even memory of him lingers only momentarily. Once the most influential "Man of Holiness" in his city, Ambrosio has become an absence, an empty cipher signifying only its own failure, its own hell.

Even the physical world of nature renounces all involvement with the monk and man Ambrosio. Carried to a mountainous waste by Lucifer, Ambrosio is hurled onto jagged rocks where he lies broken and bleeding, tormented by heat, thirst, and insects; carrion birds pick out his eyes.

Blind, maimed, helpless, and despairing, venting his rage in blasphemy and curses, execrating his existence, yet dreading the arrival of death destined to yield him up to greater torments, six miserable days did the Villain languish. On the Seventh a violent storm arose: The winds in fury rent up rocks and forests: The sky was now black with clouds, now sheeted with fire: The rain fell in torrents; It swelled the stream; The waves overflowed their banks; They reached the spot where Ambrosio lay, and when they abated carried with them into the river the Corse of the despairing Monk. (442)

The novel concludes with this strangely biblical passage. On one hand Lewis has inverted the opening of Genesis: the seventh day is not the final achievement of creation, but of moral and physical dissolution. Here is not the perfection of Eden but of anti-Eden, a world so corrupt the innocent are victimized repeatedly and even the best of human intention and endeavor ends in despair. On the other hand is Ambrosio as Jesus, the sacrificial victim whose passing is marked with storm and chaos, portent and violence. Yet if Ambrosio is a sacrifice, he is so only in the aspect of victim, not redeemer. A dark or inverted Christ, Ambrosio dies not so that we may be saved, but that we may know the impossibility of salvation. The monk is even party to a mountaintop theophany, but it is a meeting not with God in his radiance but with Lucifer in all his duplicity, ugliness, and malevolence. The flood recedes, not to deposit the ark on Ararat so that life may begin anew but to wash away decaying flesh, to cleanse the world of its human taint.

Even the morally good characters who survive continue their lives in a theological vacuum. The nuns of St. Clare are dispersed to other convents; Lorenzo forgets Antonia and marries Virginia de Villa-Franca, the innocent novice of the convent; Raymond and Agnes marry and find themselves able to "think lightly of every succeeding woe" (420) because of their past trials. No mention of matters moral or spiritual is made in Lewis's perfunctory disposal of his characters' futures, as though these are of no consequence.

And indeed they are not, for in the metaphysical terrain mapped by Lewis,

the revival of spiritualism in reaction to the desacralization wrought by the Enlightenment cannot mean reassertion of the Sacred, which has lost its unity, its force, and its ontology as the "wholly other," the designation of a realm of being and value recognized as apart from and superior to man. Instead, there is a reassertion of magic, taboo, superstition, a recognition of the diabolical forces which inhabit our world and, indeed, our inner being. (Brooks 252)

David Punter makes a similar point: "Antonia's 'sensibility of countenance' . . . betokens an unworldly faith in other people's goodness and sensitivity, and Lewis has her abducted, poisoned, raped, and murdered as a savage indication of the inadequacy of this faith" (74). The value of goodness proves alarmingly, even violently uncertain.

Such a moral and metaphysical posture locates *The Monk* firmly in the radical mode of the supernatural sublime; it is a novel of spiritual anxiety and absence, of the need for a God who is never present and whose children inevitably descend into the sepulcher of human horrors, to emerge traumatized if they emerge at all.

The dark gulf revealed by *The Monk* is social as well as theological in its implications, an aspect of the work often seized upon in contemporaneous reviews, which attacked the novel for its failures of propriety, decorum, and utility. Such response was predictable, given the sensitized conservatism of much of English society, for Lewis's exposure of religious hypocrisy and his depictions of mob action were decidedly dangerous in the years of the French Revolution— dangerous and exciting:

> No doubt the book's popularity sprang from the same sort of revolutionary impetus which Paine's radical political pronouncements were receiving. *The Monk* made a shambles of tradition, authority, and the virtue of self-denial. What officially disturbed and secretly delighted its broad audience was the cataclysm which Lewis' Gothic inflicted upon the neoclassic *Zeitgeist*: the frozen social codes; the emphasis on self-control; the positive sense of social and spiritual identity. (Frank 115)

David Morse is even more succinct: "*The Monk* reflects the intellectual ferment and confusion in the aftermath of the French Revolution: its clearest message is the disintegration of all traditional moral values . . ." (50).[1]

Failure of the rational is likewise to be understood as one of the novel's implications: "What has in fact been left after the desacralization of the world is not its rationalization—man's capacity to understand and to manage everything in terms of a rational epistemology and a humanistic ethics—but rather a terrifying and essentially uncontrollable network of violent primitive forces and taboos which are summoned into play by the dialectics of man's desire" (Brooks 262).

As overwrought and inexpert as the novel is, its publication gave compelling voice to the nascent anxieties of the emerging modern world.

Indeed, much of Gothic fiction's assault on conventional institutions is due perhaps as much to *The Monk* as to any sociocultural phenomena. Sydney Lea notes the influence of the novel on later works:

> In the progress of Gothic romance toward high art, the erosive effect of *The Monk* upon facile moral formulae is crucial: no work which claims to push beyond Lewis's achievement may now revert to such nostrums. The Gothic context is permanently altered, so that the task of future practitioners of supernatural fiction must be to develop new strategies for rendering the approach to that explosive moment when human sensibility passes into another sphere. (32)

The enduring revision of the Gothic context will be the subject of the second part of this study.

The very success of *The Monk* and similar works of radical supernaturalism in exploring the moral and intellectual boundaries of the human realm was one of the primary factors responsible for the Romantics' rejection of the conventional Gothic as a literary formula or device. The major Romantics were certainly very much interested in "that explosive moment when human sensibility passes into another sphere," but they did not render that moment with the usual Gothic tropes, which had, in essence, burned themselves out. Frank remarks that "Lewis was convinced that he was now producing the *ne plus ultra* Gothic novel" (114); Lewis was more correct than he knew. The only major radical Gothic novel to appear after *The Monk* was *Melmoth* (1820), and Maturin's novel was Gothic fiction's swan song. The tradition of supernaturalist inquiry changed dramatically in the flowering of "high" Romanticism.

*F*or the moment, however, there remains for consideration another aspect to the radicalism of supernatural sublimity, one which, while metaphysical in its implications, is more intensely focused on the personal and conducts its examination without supernaturalism. Such an approach is the foundation of Charles Brockden Brown's *Wieland* (1798).

Clearly *Wieland* is not within the immediate tradition of the conventional (read "English") Gothic novel, but its presence in the Gothic section of this study is warranted by its seminal place in the tradition of Americanized Gothic, by the novel's genesis in Brown's desire to reconfigure Gothicism in a distinctly American mode. The assessment of *Wieland* as other than a Gothic novel began with Brown himself. In an essay written nine years after the publication of *Wieland*, Brown, whose declared preference was for realism and the aberrations of the real, commented sarcastically on the development of popular fiction. The fanciful love-escapades of popular novels having become trite and "insipid" by overindulgence, the authors of the day made

> a bold and successful attempt . . . to enliven these narratives by a certain proportion of murders, ghosts, clanking chains, dead bodies, skeletons, old castles, and damp dungeons. Happily for those who are tired with themselves and all around them, this attempt produced a number of imitations, and we now rarely see a novel that is not entirely composed of the terrific materials above enumerated. ("Popularity" 411–12)

In a comment addressed "To The Public" that prefixed his fourth novel, *Edgar Huntly* (1799), Brown was more explicit about his disdain for the Gothic:

> One merit the [present] writer may at least claim:—that of calling forth the passions and engaging the sympathy of the reader by means hitherto unemployed by preceding authors. Puerile superstitions and exploded manners, Gothic castles and chimeras, are the materials usually employed for this end. The incidents of Indian hostility, and the perils of the Western wilderness, are far more suitable; and for a native of America to overlook these would admit of no apology. (3)

Brown, as would later be true of Hawthorne, was deeply concerned with an *American* literary tradition[2] and felt that the tangible dangers of American life presented sufficiently engaging subjects for a novelist. Ghosts and other Old-World Gothic terrors were, for Brown, too easy: "if once we return to the old-fashioned belief in ghosts, it is incredible with what ease we may increase our stock of personages, for every one mentioned in the work may have a ghost, and, living or dead, we may in this way exactly double our amusement" ("Popularity" 412).

Brown never wavered in his desire to anchor his fiction in the real, even if it was a real viewed obliquely, but there is some question whether his more didactic pronouncements on the subject should be taken quite at face value. It is, after all, the author of *Wieland, Arthur Mervyn, Ormond,* and *Edgar Huntly* who declared that

> The days of youth are certainly days of curiosity, and if that is directed to proper objects around us, we shall not find that real life is so devoid of variety as we imagined, or that there is any absolute necessity for relieving our minds by fabulous narratives. The page of history, to him whose mind has not been weakened by a course of superficial reading, will contain more variety and entertainment, than the utmost stretch of fiction could have produced. ("Popularity" 412)

It is hard to reconcile completely the fact that the man who wrote a passage of such dry didacticism could also produce novels that prominently featured the spontaneous combustion of a human being, a maniac's mass murder of his own family, and ventriloquism *(Wieland)*; the horrors of the plague *(Arthur Mervyn)*; embezzlement, secret societies, and murder *(Ormond)*; a sleepwalker who is shot, attacked by Indians, and who, while lost in a cave, kills a mountain lion and eats it raw *(Edgar Huntly)*.

Brown's preferred literary territory, at least in his early novels, was indeed that "stretch of fiction" that stopped just short of the supernatural. As he wrote in the "Advertisement" to *Wieland:*

> The incidents related are extraordinary and rare. Some of them, perhaps, approach as nearly to the nature of miracles as can be done by that which is not truly miraculous. It is hoped that intelligent readers will not disapprove of the manner in which appearances are solved, but that the solution will be found to correspond with the known principles of human nature. (3)

What all these declarations add up to, finally, is the reason Brown is discussed here: although not a writer of conventional Gothic fictions, Brown (like Poe) is a writer whose arena of operations is the furthest limit of *terra cognita,* that shadowy borderland where a shake of the head or a determined peer into the shadows may dispel the ghosts but cannot dislodge the sense of strangeness and lingering disquiet generated by the events witnessed. Nor is it possible to avoid the sense of impending calamity, of terrible deeds with unknowable motives about to overtake us even as we watch for them.

It is, then, hardly inappropriate to consider some of the more-or-less Gothic elements in *Wieland,* but we must do so judiciously. Brown's early fiction has always been both claimed by the Gothicists and denied to them precisely because it works with Gothic intensity and with Gothic motifs while at the same time refusing to cross over into the realm of obvious Gothicism. Although there are recognizable

Gothic elements in Brown's fiction,[3] they are elements in a larger canvas that bears only partial resemblance to the traditional Gothic novel.

Commencing with Brown, American Gothic is a factual Gothic, rendering the dream experience as terrifyingly real or presenting actual experience in dreamlike terms. The mise-en-scène of the haunted castle gives way to the alleys, townhouses, riverbanks, and caves of the New World. The American Gothic has from the start been characterized by a pronounced realistic or material element, an indication of its roots in a troubled (and troubling) suspicion that reality itself holds the superior terror. In this, perhaps, lies the greatest accomplishment of Brown as a writer of "Gothic realism": while never relinquishing "ordinary" reality as the base of his operations, he nonetheless questions the integrity and character of that base, thereby raising doubts about the validity of our own perceptions. "Based firmly upon what is rather than what might be, Brown's Gothic is an effort to chart what Irving called a 'realm of shadows, existing in the very center of substantial realities' " (Frank 192).

The ambiguity that attends *Wieland*'s generic identity is appropriate, for it is a novel deeply concerned with ambiguities, with the uncertain and the unknowable, and in its examination of indeterminacies it strains arduously against the Scottish Common Sense philosophy so dominant in early American thought.[4] The extent to which Brown himself was influenced by Scottish Common Sense is evident in those passages quoted above. Much of his personal life as well indicates that his rebellious tendencies were strong enough to generate guilt without being able to render him as free from tradition as he apparently wished to be: Cowie accurately identifies Brown as "a nursling of the eighteenth century—but an uneasy one" (311), and Sydney Krause notes the importance of the didactic interplay in *Wieland* of Brown's rationalist and romanticist beliefs (13–24). In Brown, the neoclassic warred with the Romantic; while that tension may have produced difficult moments in Brown's personal life, it also found powerful literary expression.

The uncertainties in *Wieland,* intensified as they are by an atmosphere of murder and madness, constitute not only the most Gothic elements of the work but its supernatural sublime as well. There are times in the novel when a character believes for a moment that she has experienced a supernatural phenomenon, but this sort of Gothic posturing, employed so assiduously by Radcliffe and others, meant little to Brown. He wanted not to titillate or generate casual thrills that would soon be dispersed but to engage genuine epistemological doubts.

Although the two works are otherwise dissimilar, *Wieland* and *The Mysteries of Udolpho* are related in that each employs the supernatural sublime not primarily as the structure of individual moments—such moments do exist in both works but are of little overall importance—but as the structuring concept of the entire narrative. Yet *Udolpho*'s consoling circular structure—movement away from the house followed by return to it—is in stark opposition to *Wieland*'s linear structure, a movement from pastoral idyll to trauma, and from thence outward and away. The physical starting point of the novel is the insular Wieland estate by the Schuylkill River; it ends with the last surviving Wieland living in Montpelier, self-exiled forever from America. There is no return in *Wieland*; the novel concludes not on *Udolpho*'s note of reintegration and triumph but on one of bare survival and imperfectly recovered composure. This steady darkening of the novel's metaphysical tone makes *Wieland* a perfect representative of the radical mode of the (non)supernatural sublime.

The sense of increasing philosophical gloom is evident more in the chronological sequence of events than in their narrative order: the novel takes the form of a letter written by Clara after the events she describes, and her despair in the epistle is constant. The opening paragraphs plunge us immediately into the turbulent emotional wake of the disaster—and, just as important, into what might be called the event's metaphysical aftermath:

> The sentiment that dictates my feelings is not hope. Futurity has no power over my thoughts. To all that is to come I am perfectly indifferent. With regard to myself, I have nothing more to fear. Fate has done its worst. Henceforth, I am callous to misfortune.
> *I address no supplication to the Deity.* The power that governs the course of human affairs has chosen his path. The decree that ascertained the condition of my life, admits of no recal [*sic*]. No doubt it squares with the maxims of eternal equity. That is neither to be questioned or denied by me. (5; emphasis added)

Clara's bleak resignation is a far cry from the religious fortitude Emily repeatedly manifests, but of course the murder of his wife, children, and ward by Theodore Wieland, followed by his attempted murder of Clara and his suicide, are events a few orders of magnitude more traumatic than those Emily experienced.

Yet the difference between *Udolpho* and *Wieland* involves more than the intensity of the heroine's anguish. Radcliffe's world is watched over by a benign Providence; the wicked are duly punished and the good appropriately rewarded. Brown's universe is closer to that of Lewis. If there is a God—and little in the text leads us to suppose there is—then the faith linking humanity to the divine is a dangerous thing that may blind us to truth and plunge us into disaster. Significantly, the only surviving Wieland is the one whose faith is the least orthodox. Early in the novel Clara writes of herself and her brother that "Our education had been modelled by no religious standard. We were left to the guidance of our own understanding, and the casual impressions which society might make upon us . . ." (22). Theodore's undisciplined religious impulse led him down the same path of rigid fanaticism taken by his obsessively pious father. Clara and her friend Catherine, however, were drawn to a different sense of the holy:

> It must not be supposed that we were without religion, but with us it was the product of lively feelings, excited by reflection on our own happiness, and by the grandeur of external nature. We sought not a basis for our faith, in the weighing of proofs, and the dissection of creeds. Our devotion was a mixed and casual sentiment. . . . (22)

Frank draws an interesting parallel between the religious dispositions of the male Wielands and the sense of community that forms the backdrop to the novel's horrific central event:

> The elder Wieland's temple, like Roderick Usher's "Haunted Palace" or Richard Digby's lonely grotto in Hawthorne's "Man of Adamant," is the architectural embodiment of the madman's diseased ideal of privacy and spiritual security. The spiritual pleasure dome on the banks of the Schuylkill is the visible symbol of the artificially safe and selfish world which the elder Wieland's mind has made for itself. He has sealed himself off from the rest of the human community to seek salvation on his own. (216)

The same obtains for Wieland the younger, who himself spends considerable time in the outdoor temple.

Clara's case is different, however, and after her experiences with the religious mania of her brother, it is no surprise that she declares, "I address no supplication to the Deity." For her, that Deity is a death-god, a bringer of strange destructions who preternaturally kills her troubled father and in a mysterious voice orders her brother to strangle his wife and family. It seems the ventriloquist Carwin may have been the source of these terrible commands, but even as this possibility reaffirms a certain empiricism we cannot escape that Carwin's chief ability is dissimulation and deception. He protests that he is innocent of evil intentions, but if innocent actions lead to such results, what is to be made of guilt and evil? What is the value of innocence and empiricism?

Theodore Wieland's actions are doubly unsettling because they question the ability of reason and rationalism to restrain the darker impulses of the psyche. Indeed, Michael Davitt Bell reads the novel as being primarily concerned with "the contest between Lockean rationalism and the power of the irrational" ("Deceiver" 144). Theodore was fervently religious, it is true; but in what may be seen as an a priori hope that her brother will be spared the fate of their father, Clara notes that although the character of father and son were similar, "the mind of the son was enriched by science, and embellished with literature" (23). He is "an indefatigable student" and something of a Latin scholar, and his concern with the authenticity of voice is such that he "employed months of severe study" in collating and comparing various editions of Cicero in order to arrive at the correct text. He devotes similar effort to determining "a true scheme of pronunciation for the Latin tongue" (24). Yet the darkest irony of the novel is that "voice" is what undoes Theodore and those around him.

Theodore's rationalism, manifest in his scholarly pursuits, proves not only incapable of countering his irrational impulses but may be in the service of those impulses, an ironic subversion to be developed more fully and explicitly by Poe. In his study of Brown, Alan Axelrod captures the significance of Theodore's literary interest, noting that his "veneration is not for Cicero the archapostle of Roman reason, but for Cicero the orator, persuader of men and instigator of their actions. . . . Theodore's weakness for the Roman orator both foreshadows and reveals his susceptibility to the voices of Carwin" (79–80).

Even though he does not, apparently, instigate the novel's slaughter, Carwin and his ventriloquistic amusements do pave the way for Theodore's belief in the heavenly voice that commands him to murder. Never suspecting the voice might be the product of delusion or deception, he becomes an eighteenth-century Abraham who carries through with the deed, believing in the legitimacy of the voice only to discover later that it was the voice of madness and that everything that had given his life meaning was now lost to him forever. Full realization of his loss strikes Theodore when he learns, and despite his madness believes, that the voice which commanded him to murder was truly not from heaven:

Fallen from his lofty and heroic station; now finally restored to the perception of truth; weighed to earth by the recollection of his own deeds; consoled no longer by a consciousness of rectitude, for the loss of offspring and wife—a loss for which he was indebted to his own misguided hand; Wieland was transformed at once into the *man of sorrows*. (230)

This passage documents the primary, but certainly not the only, "transformation" of the novel's subtitle, the moment at which knowledge brings the self traumatically back to a reality that had been misperceived, misread like a corrupt text. It is also the moment at which Theodore is transformed into a creature of pathos and despair, brought down from his pinnacle of religious self-confidence and justification. At his trial he can declaim boldly,

You say that I am guilty. Impious and rash! thus to usurp the prerogatives of your Maker! to set up your bounded views and halting reason, as the measure of truth! Thou, Omnipotent and Holy! Thou knowest that my actions were conformable to thy will. I know not what is crime; what actions are evil in their ultimate and comprehensive tendency or what are good. Thy knowledge, as thy power, is unlimited. I have taken thee for my guide, and cannot err. To the arms of thy protection, I entrust my safety. In the awards of thy justice, I confide for my recompense. (176–77)

Yet err is precisely what Theodore Wieland did, and his only recompense is horror and suicide, itself the final sin against his God. In the final realization of all that has befallen him, Theodore indeed becomes "a monument of woe" (231) and, after a moment of motionless despair, plunges Clara's knife into his throat.

The moment of Theodore's death marks Clara's transformation; her world collapses with the suicide of her brother. Having grown up in a remarkably small and sheltered community, Clara was insulated from the world beyond that tight social circle of her family and her friend Henry Pleyel. Her brother's madness shatters this idyll. When the violence finally ends, all the Wielands except Clara are dead, and Pleyel, estranged from Clara by Carwin's ill-considered efforts at "amusement," has moved to Boston and married. Traumatized, only Clara remains, lingering about the otherwise-deserted grounds and house in a sort of fugue state, unwilling to leave the scene of earlier happiness:

my home is ascertained; here I have taken up my rest, and never will I go hence, till, like Wieland, I am borne to my grave.

> Importunity was tried in vain: they threatened to remove me by vio-
> lence—nay, violence was used; but my soul prizes too dearly this little
> roof to endure to be bereaved of it. Force should not prevail when the
> hoary locks and supplicating tears of my uncle were ineffectual. My
> repugnance to move gave birth to ferociousness and phrenzy when force
> was employed, and they were obliged to consent to my return. (232)

The time Clara spends at the abandoned Wieland estate is her moment
of suspension, that period following immediately the encounter with
the traumatizing phenomenon in which all intellection ceases.

After the catastrophe, Clara's suspension is almost literally figured
by Brown in the near-complete loss of her will to live: "I will eat—I
will drink—I will lie down and rise up at your bidding—all I ask is the
choice of my abode. . . . Shortly will I be at peace" (233). In a final
postscript written three years later, Clara reports how at the time of
her deepest despair she "looked forward to a speedy termination of
[her] life with the fullest confidence" and that she "had every reason
to be weary of existence, to be impatient of every tie which held [her]
from the grave" (234). When she is stricken with fever and cannot rise
from her bed, she becomes certain her death is imminent.

She is saved, however, by a fire that destroys her home: the shock
of this loss, rather than kill her, effects an improvement in her health
and spirits that initiates her recovery from the moment of suspension
and helplessness, her return to the world. Yet it is not of the same
order as the return effected by Emily or Edmund. Clara's is reluctant,
precipitated only by the violence and catastrophe of fire. She regains a
measure of enthusiasm for life and even marries Pleyel after the death
of his first wife, but her statement at *Wieland*'s conclusion is not one
of optimism or positive recovery:

> It is true that I am now changed; but I have not the consolation to
> reflect that my change was owing to my fortitude or my capacity for
> instruction. Better thoughts grew up in my mind imperceptibly. I cannot
> but congratulate myself on the change, though, perhaps, it merely ar-
> gues a fickleness of temper, and a defect of sensibility. (235)

Clara has passed through her dark night of soul only to find the ordinary light of day on the other side. Time and capricious chance have
effected her recovery; no system of philosophy or religious doctrine
has contributed to her continued survival in the world. And it is the
Old World to which Clara turns in her desire to restore her life.

Her retreat across the Atlantic does not valorize a conservative recovery, however. Clara's move to Switzerland is a response of psychological rather than philosophical implications. She needs to recover some sense of psychic balance in her life, but in this final movement back to Western Europe (the ancestral home of the Wielands, we are reminded in the first chapter), Brown does not repudiate the shadowy moral and epistemological vision conjured in the pages that precede the coda. To the end he insists on the uncertainty of knowledge and "the inherent danger of human conduct rooted in religious duty" (Rosenthal 103), an insistence that in no way prevents him from asserting the possibility of some sort of human existence. We may, like Clara, be scarred by the conditions of our world, but we need not surrender life itself.

> Clara's removal to an ancient world of ancient tranquility was doubtless an emotional and intellectual necessity for Brown. Reversing the utopian stereotype, he pictures a Europe in which forgetfulness approaches innocence, and an America made guilty by its discovery of the frontier of knowledge itself. The novelist allowed his unconscious and speculative "literary" self full expression in *Wieland,* pushing his characters through a territory of paradoxical revelation. But Charles Brockden Brown could not live wholly in the revealed gloom of this American "literary mood." Having used her to probe the New World's primeval darkness, he returns Clara to the civilized sunshine of Europe. (Axelrod 96)

In that civilized sunshine there is possibility for anxiety and uncertainty enough, as Hawthorne will reveal in *The Marble Faun,* but if we recall the strong self-therapeutic element in Brown's writing we need not wonder at the final chapter's recovery. Rather than undercutting the darker metaphysical implications of the novel, the last chapter confirms the anxiety of that vision by setting against it the possibility of contentment in this life.

The final chapter, in particular the moralizing paragraph that concludes it, also constitutes further evidence of Brown's own uncertainties regarding the value of fiction, and thus it serves as an attempt to mitigate partially the religious and intellectual despair that lie at the novel's dark heart. This desire for amelioration may also serve to explain the awkward return of the Maxwell-Stuart-Conway subplot at the novel's conclusion, which has been dismissed by critics as "irrelevant to the main theme" (Clark 169). On the contrary, the subplot

lends validity and substance to that final paragraph by providing cor-
roborating evidence and so serves Brown's desire to tip the scales
back, however slightly or symbolically, in the direction of Scottish
Common Sense restraint and morality. Ringe notes that "Brown could
not call into question the validity of the optimistic psychology of the
day without undercutting as well the whole rationalist view of man
and society that ultimately is based upon it" (*Brown* 41). It may be
going too far to fault Brown, writing in the late 1790s and himself
beset by doubt, for backing away from the brink of the yawning gulf
his fiction uncovered.

But no tentative afterthoughts on Brown's part can alter the basic
tenor of *Wieland*. An image that recurs repeatedly in the novel (as well
as in other works by Brown) is that of the abyss or gulf; here, it occurs
most significantly in Clara's two dreams. In the first, which turns out
to be premonitory, she sees her brother beckoning her toward a deep
chasm directly in her path; in the second, a tumultuous and chaotic
nightmare of "wild and phantastical incongruities" features a "dark
abyss, on the verge of which I was standing," and is characterized by
"enormous depth and hideous precipices" (236). The pit is one of the
primary images of *Wieland* because it is the place signifying the horror
and the destruction into which we may be drawn even by the actions
of a wise and benevolent sibling (let alone by the actions of our ene-
mies, as Poe will show us in "The Pit and the Pendulum"). There is no
physical abyss in *Wieland* to correspond to *The Monk*'s subterranean
sepulcher, but then Lewis's novel is thoroughly dependent on the
physical accoutrements of the Gothic. Brown's terrors are of the mind,
manifestations of the uncertainty that clouds our best efforts to ascertain the truth, the sources, or the consequences of action. Clara, for
example, is deeply affected and troubled by Carwin's presence. As
Cowie points out:

> Carwin is a danger to Clara philosophically also, for the exercise of his
> gift for ventriloquism brings to her sensory experiences that do not
> square with the empirical data on which she customarily relies; she is
> forced to reckon with unsettling ideas of an occult world which could
> imperil her stability as a disciple of "reason." (330)

Clara is, in *Wieland*, the prime embodiment of Brown's rationalist/
romanticist dichotomy (Krause 188ff), and as such is the novel's thematic center, the locus of anxiety and tension produced by the confrontation between enlightened rationalism and the irrational. Nina

Baym argues that Brown's "shift" of attention from Theodore to Clara is a flaw (93) that drags the story down from the lofty heights of tragedy to those of melodrama, but it seems more likely this shift allows us to see Clara coming to a fuller sense of herself. As author of the novel's letters, Clara shifts the focus onto herself; her increasing prominence is the evidence of her individuation and maturation, of her breaking free of the insular and repressive atmosphere of the Wieland family estate. After all, Clara too is a Wieland, and though her brother is usually referred to only by the patronymic, she is, or perhaps *becomes,* the titular character.

Given the centrality of moral and intellectual ambiguity to Brown's purpose, the Clara/Carwin narrative strand assumes primary importance, for it is where the epistemological implications of *Wieland* are most fully elaborated. Theodore, after all, exhibits only momentary doubt concerning the voices Carwin imitates; Clara is plagued by uncertainty over their origin and authenticity. It is to Clara that we must turn to register the novel's full thematic impact; she is the mediator between event and reader, the voice of a text obsessed with the authority and authenticity of voice. Consider, for example, her thoughts after the first ventriloquistic episode: "The will is the tool of the understanding, which must fashion its conclusions on the notices of sense. If the senses be depraved, it is impossible to calculate the evils that may flow from the consequent deductions of the understanding" (35). Through Clara, not her brother, do we experience the difficulty of ascertaining the truth of knowledge and experience.

Clara introduces the question of uncertainty at the beginning of the novel, warning us even before her history begins: "How will your wonder, and that of your companions, be excited by my story! Every sentiment will yield to your amazement. If my testimony were without corroborations, you would reject it as incredible. The experience of no human being can furnish a parallel" (6). Though the experiences that trouble her are not occult, their effect is no less disturbing for their "reality." Throughout the novel, her anguish is elevated by her inability to determine the true nature of the voices Wieland claims to have heard (187) and the true moral character of the "biloquist" Carwin. Yet the moment of revelation is not a resolution, but a precipitation into despair, the actualization of Clara's earlier doubts.

There are ambiguities and questions enough for the reader as well, evidence not of Brown's ineptitude but of the "purposeful" expression in characterization and structure of the ambiguity that is the novel's epistemological theme (Cleman 190–219). What was the nature or origin of the elder Wieland's death? Did Theodore really only imagine the voices and the angel on the stairway? Was Carwin indeed innocent? He claims that "my only crime was curiosity" (205–6), yet at one point deliberately deceives Pleyel into thinking Clara a woman of compromised virtue.

In the universe Brown creates, there are no sure guides; reason and religion falter, leaving the individual to survive as best she or he can, knowing very little with certainty:

> Though [Brown], like his predecessors, clearly recognizes the deceptive power of the imagination and the influence of the emotions in leading men astray, he makes it abundantly clear that the cause of error is not simple nor the cure easy. . . . [S]o thoroughgoing is Brown's treatment of the unconscious sources of human error that reason cannot be seen as ever in full control, not even at the end of the book. Throughout, the characters are lost in the maze of their own perceptions. . . . Brown permits no easy solution to the problems he raises, and unlike the Gothic novelists from whom he derived so much, he retains an aura of ambiguity and uncertainty right to the end. (Ringe, Gothic 49)

We may not, having our experience with the existentialist novel, consider Wieland an especially radical or even startling work today. Yet in 1798, before the assault on religious and intellectual convention mounted by Poe, Brown's novel was indeed an exemplar of that mode of the supernatural sublime which argues for, or at least half-suspects, the existence of madness behind the facade of reason, engulfing horror beneath the polished surface of religious belief and enlightenment. Cowie effectively sums up the source of the novel's continuing appeal:

> Clara is more than the traditional beleaguered female Gothic heroine. It is not Clara huddled in a closet of an isolated Pennsylvania farmhouse fearing specific injury to her person or her reputation that finally detains the modern reader, but Clara as representative of humanity cowering in a frightening, lonely, ambiguous universe in which man is uncertain of how to cope with the "decrees" of an apparently capricious "Fate"— this is the aspect of Clara's situation that interests readers in today's depressed existential atmosphere. (348)

This is also the aspect of the novel that attracted interest in the years shortly following Brown's death. Richard Henry Dana, reviewing a collected edition of Brown in 1827, wrote that "Brown's fatal power is unsparing, and never stops; his griefs and sufferings are not of that kind which draws tears and softens the heart; it wears out the heart and takes away the strength of our spirits, so that we lie helpless under it" (qtd. in Cowie 344). Resorting to the language of the sublime, Dana identifies the power, the spell cast by Brown's tale of a world in which the authoritative voice is uncertain and in which the guideposts of religion and reason prove deceptive.

There is a transitional point to be considered before this study moves to the Romantic supernatural sublime: the project of the supernatural sublime, like that of much Romantic literature, is made possible only by the perceived weakening of traditional religious belief to provide consolation. Robert Hume's assessment of the role of religious despair in the fiction of the time is a cogent one:

> the central impulse behind most of what we call Romantic writing stems from a profound discontent with inherited religion and world views, and the social and philosophical condition of man. A revolt against the limitations and uncertainties of the human condition combines with political-social consciousness to produce a drive to regain paradise. . . . ("Exuberant" 111)

Conservative Gothicism offered the reassuringly conventional answer of religious faith, while the radical Gothic never argued that paradise could be regained; it remained for the High Romantics to give clearer shape to the new modes of spiritual and social engagement that would come to characterize the age. Gothic writers, however, remained dominated by the transcendence models of the past regardless of the perceived efficacy of these models, a domination evident in Gothicism's simultaneous fascination with and denigration of conventional religion.

The antimonasticism and anti-Catholicism of the British Gothic is only partly accounted for by England's cultural and religious differences with France and Spain. There is also in this aspect of Gothicism a displaced desire to examine the efficacy of traditional Western systems of transcendent engagement and consolation. Avoiding explicit condemnation of Protestantism, radical English Gothic fiction finds in the failure of Catholicism a type for the failure of all received religious traditions. Brooks, writing of Gothicism's religious impulses, notes perceptively that Gothic writers "all discover that reaction against the [Enlightenment's] secularization of the world cannot take the form of a resacralization." For these writers, or at least those of the radical mode,

> the Sacred in its traditional Christian form, even in the more purely ethical version elaborated by Christian humanism, is no longer operative. . . . the Gothic re-exploration of the numinous will necessarily entail a radical redefinition of the spiritual forces at play in the universe. (250)

Indeed, the fundamental premises of traditional religious thought begin to dissolve in dark Gothic fiction, evidenced by a characteristic confusion of previously distinct moral elements. Demonic energy becomes attractive (evident also in Lord Byron and Emily Brontë, and, in a non-Gothic context, William Blake); good and evil become inextricably combined in one character or circumstance. The cause, of course, is that Gothic (and Romantic) authors "simply cannot find in religion acceptable answers to the fundamentally psychological questions of good and evil which they were posing. This failure is reflected in their satire on both religious institutions and the simplicity of a religious morality" (Hume, "Gothic" 287). Gothic fiction is replete with suggestions of the corruption, hypocrisy, and inadequacy of conventional human implementations of spiritual belief. And although Gothic novels are often populated by legions of hostile demons, only in conservative Gothicism is the idea of a benign Providence seriously invoked, and even then often in a minor key. Joel Porte argues "that much Anglo-American *genre noire* fiction from Godwin to Poe owes its gloomy 'Gothic' *ambience* to a brooding sense of religious terror which is notably Protestant in its origin and bearing" ("Hands" 45); it must be emphasized that this terror stems not, as it did for John Dennis, from the supposed immanence of an all-powerful God but rather from the absence of such a God.

These early beginnings of existentialist anxiety mark the waning of traditional sublimity. Where Dennis in 1704 could characterize the sublime as "an invincible force which commits a pleasing Rape upon the very Soul of the Reader" (79), Matthew Lewis in 1795 gives us a supernatural sublime that centers upon a violent and repulsive rape, the incestuous violation of the virgin Antonia by her matricidal brother, a violation that occurs in a crypt amid rotting corpses and overwhelming horror. In less than a century, the conventional sublime had failed, even as it struggled to evolve in order to address the increasing uncertainty and secularization of the age.

Part Two

Romanticism

and the Supernatural Sublime

The first part of this study argued for an understanding of Gothic sublimity as a considered attempt either to articulate the cosmic dread that characterizes the radical supernatural or to assert, in the face of various cultural anxieties, the legitimacy of traditional intellectual and religious systems. Directly to compare these works with the literature generally regarded as "Romantic" is problematic at best, for the projects of Romanticism and Gothicism are fundamentally distinct. Critical assessments of Gothic novels as somehow less worthy than Romantic poetry are often based, if not on some antique notion of a hierarchy of genres, on the implicit assumption that the novels fail where the poetry succeeds. The basis of such judgment is, generally speaking, the transcendent: "high" Romantic poetry customarily rejects Gothic despair in favor of the possibility of transcendence of the limited realm of human life and consciousness. The Gothic, when it suggests answers, offers tradition, reason, epistemological conservatism, and spiritual faith. The darker vision of the radical Gothic offers no answers at all, except perhaps a dogged existentialist perseverance.

Romanticism, which reaches its fullest development only after the flowering of Gothicism in the mid to late 1790s, characteristically responds to Gothic gloom with a transcendent optimism, an a priori faith in the spiritual that precludes Gothicism's metaphysical horrors: "Almost all the romantic poets begin with the sense that there is a hidden spiritual force in nature. The problem is how to reach it, for the old ways have failed, and though it is present in nature, and in the depths of man's consciousness, it is not immediately possessed by man" (Miller 14). Thus Romanticism is the quest for possession, countering through either outright denial or satire radical Gothicism's implicit claim that there is nothing to be possessed. Or that, in the conservative supernatural, possession is always and only effected through traditional intellectual and religious structures. Therefore Devendra Varma is only partially correct when he notes that

> There may well be a connection between the Romantic philosophy of composition as embodied in the *Lyrical Ballads* and the Gothic philosophy set down by Walpole thirty-four years before. In both Gothic and Romantic creeds there is a marked tendency to slip imperceptibly from the real into the other world, to demolish the barriers between the physical and the psychic or spiritual. (190)

Painting with such a broad brush leads us to overlook crucial if subtle distinctions in the manner and result of these transcendent investigations.

William Patrick Day's assessment of the Gothic/Romantic dichotomy is more useful. Arguing that Gothicism emphasizes the "escapist and transformative powers of the imagination," as opposed to the "transcendent and creative powers" celebrated by Romanticism, Day finds that "The nature of the creative capacities of the imagination, and its capacity for transcendence, are in fact called into question by the Gothic, which in effect becomes a critique of the romantic idea of imagination that dominated the nineteenth century" (69). Although I concur with Day on this point, my concern with a more historically limited Gothicism and with the Romantic response to that Gothicism means that the emphasis in part 2 of the present work will be on Romanticism as a critique of the first wave of the Gothic.

Whereas earlier scholars of the Gothic often argued that the imagery and language of Gothic fiction was a vital nexus with mainstream Romanticism, it is more the case that the Romantics were uncomfortable with Gothicism's language of the past, its iconography of ruined castles, ghosts, and crypts. Gothic supernaturalism was a language of the Middle Ages, a resurrected lexicon of superstitious belief in the intrusive power of a natural order either superior or indifferent to humankind. It is the central argument of the rest of this book that all important Romantic considerations of this literary language were marked primarily by a desire to transcend the limitations of an inherited (and vastly popular) symbolism, to refigure the heritage of the past by casting off the chains of its moribund iconography. The major Romantics asked, with Emerson, "Why should we grope among the dry bones of the past, or put the living generation into masquerade out of its faded wardrobe? . . . . Let us demand our own works and laws and worship." The work of the Romantics examined here constitutes just such a demand, and theory.

Although Samuel Taylor Coleridge is the most obviously "supernatural" of the major Romantics, his aggressive reappraisal of Gothic supernaturalism was instrumental in paving the way for Romanticism's drastic revision of Gothic tropes, including a fundamental reshaping of the supernatural sublime. For various reasons Coleridge rejected the Burkean sublime and its valorization of terror and helplessness; for him, and subsequently for William Wordsworth, the sublime was a trope of fulfillment and "intense unity." Such an understanding effectively negated the radical supernatural sublime and produced a supernatural poetry that for both Coleridge and Wordsworth insisted almost polemically on this consoling aspect of their poetics. Supernatural images and language continued not as ciphers of emptiness and despair but became instead the language of interior exploration or of a quasi-animistic transcendence.

Considerations of space necessitate an examination limited to the generally recognized "major" Romantics and to their most consequential supernaturalist achievements. William Blake is excluded because of his minimal interest in the Gothic supernatural and his rejection of, indeed hostility toward, the sublime, especially as it was expounded by Burke.

Chapter Four

Dramatic Truth

Coleridge and
the Supernatural Sublime

Sometimes taken, in popular understandings of Romanticism, as works emblematic of the age's preoccupation with the imagination and the supernatural, Coleridge's so-called mystery poems document the failure of the supernatural, denying Gothicism's horror by the disclosure of its limited capacity for transcendent speculation. Coleridge's most important commentary on the subject occurs in Chapter XIV of the *Biographia Literaria* (hereafter *BL*), in which he recounts the circumstances attending the composition of the *Lyrical Ballads*. While the extent of agreement between Wordsworth and Coleridge continues to be the subject of debate, the thematic division between the work of the two poets is distinct. Wordsworth's domain was the "things of everyday," his purpose "to excite a feeling analogous to the supernatural, by awakening the mind's attention from the lethargy of custom, and directing it to the loveliness and the wonders of the world before us . . ." (*BL* II: 7). Coleridge was to supply for the *Lyrical Ballads* pieces in which "the incidents and agents were to be, in part at least, supernatural; and the excellence aimed at was to consist in the interesting of the affections by the dramatic truth of such emotions, as would naturally accompany such situations, supposing them real" (*BL* II: 6).

Yet Coleridge had in mind not the conventional supernaturalism of English balladry nor that of Gothic fiction, for with his works the *Lyrical Ballads* were to usher in a new type of literary supernatural. Poetic supernaturalism in the eighteenth century had been mainly concerned with atmosphere, not with narrative application or significance. One critic has noted that even those supernatural poems composed by Coleridge's contemporaries "have more in common with work composed fifty years earlier than with anything in *Lyrical Ballads*" (Spacks 112). Coleridge was not concerned much with atmosphere. As J. B. Beer reports, in an overly qualified statement, "it is not unlikely that [Coleridge] intended, when he wrote his [supernatural] poems, to distinguish between literature which simply made use of supernatural 'machinery' for the sake of sensationalism, and that which was concerned with the possible significance of extra-sensory phenomena as a revelation of the metaphysical" (142–43). Such was emphatically and precisely the case, and although Coleridge's supernaturalist ventures were as much psychological as they were metaphysical in their impulse, there was considerable distance between Coleridge and even the most "interior" of the radical Gothic writers.

Assessment of this distance might best begin with a momentary return to the first of the Gothic writers, Walpole, whose work initiated, albeit in rudimentary form, the implicit and near-characteristic interiority of Gothic literature. The statement of purpose Coleridge outlined in the *Biographia* strikes an uncanny resonance with Walpole's Preface to the second edition of his *Castle of Otranto,* wherein he explains that since he was

> [d]esirous of leaving the powers of fancy at liberty to expatiate through the boundless realms of invention, and thence of creating more interesting situations, [he] wished to conduct the mortal agents in [his] drama according to the rules of probability; in short, to make them think, speak, and act, as it might be supposed mere men and women would do in extraordinary positions. (21)

The similarity of intention and terms is striking. Both men spoke of the supernatural in terms of drama; both were concerned with reconciling their "boundless realms of invention" with the empirical world. Coleridge knew Walpole's work directly and was a relentless borrower, but more importantly he was a more formidable thinker with specific aesthetic and philosophical reasons for turning his hand to supernaturalist literature:

> it was agreed, that my endeavours should be directed to persons and characters supernatural, or at least romantic; yet so *as to transfer from our inward nature a human interest and a semblance of truth* sufficient to procure for these shadows of imagination that willing suspension of disbelief for the moment, which constitutes poetic faith. (*BL* II: 6; emphasis added)

These lines are the key to Coleridge's repudiation of the supernatural sublime. As is true for both his and Wordsworth's understanding of conventional sublimity, Coleridge finds the supernatural experience to obtain its affective power and intellectual consequence only as a result of the mind's active projection or contribution, something that remained true for real-life supernatural experience as well: in a copy of *The Statesman's Manual,* Coleridge wrote that "A Ghost is *nonsense*—a contradiction in terms, if it be assumed (as in Ghost-stories it always *is* assumed) to appear to our eyes and be heard by our ears. But may not a departed Spirit act on an embodied Spirit & thus produce in the Brain a corresponding Appearance, which in proportion to the vividness of the impression will have apparent *outness?*" (*Lay Sermons* 81, n). Coleridge's interest in the "real" supernatural also finds expression in his comments on the legendary incident during which Martin Luther hurled his inkpot at the devil.

Such theorizing necessarily repudiates the Burkean sublime, which Coleridge explicitly disparaged, for therein the mind becomes passive, its operations suspended after contact with the terror-inducing object. Literary experience of the supernatural was, for Coleridge the poet, an experience predicated upon active response from the intellect. Coleridge, to be sure, also found that ". . . Images and Thoughts possess a power in and of themselves, independent of that act of the Judgement or Understanding by which we affirm or deny the existence of a reality corresponding to them" (*BL* II: 6, fn. 2),[1] but he is writing here of dreams, not literature, and the distinction is crucial. For Coleridge the mind in dreams is less powerful, less active than when awake. In sleep, "the comparing power is suspended, and without the comparing power any act of Judgement, whether affirmation or denial, is impossible," and as a result "The Forms and Thoughts act merely by their own inherent power: and the strong feelings at times apparently connected with them are in point of fact bodily sensations, which are the causes or occasions of the Images, not (as when we are awake), the effects of them" (*BL* II: 6, fn. 2). Yet the waking power of "Images" is not necessarily greater than what they possess in dreams, for the mind in sleep is unlike the mind awake. In the next sentence, Coleridge specifies the crucial distinction, one that permits (and I use the word deliberately) the operation of the supernatural: "Add to this a voluntary lending of the Will to this suspension of one of its own operations (i.e. that of comparison & consequent decision concerning the reality of any sensuous Impression) and you have the true Theory of Stage Illusion . . ." (*BL* II: 6–7, fn. 2).

The invocation of "Stage Illusion," reminiscent of Walpole's discussion of supernaturalism and belief, is particularly relevant here, linking as it does Coleridge's notions of "dramatic probability" and "the willing suspension of disbelief" to his supernaturalist poetics. Indeed, supernatural works would provide the greatest test of Coleridge's theories, for they are most likely to elicit skepticism. For these works to succeed, the Coleridgean poet must seduce his readers by careful attention to dramatic possibility, which, as one critic explains,

> implies not only truth to life, but also the propriety of imaginative setting, the exclusion of ideas which, by pointing to realities, invite comparison and expose the unreality of the supernatural. . . . What stage illusion is to the partly sensible and partly mental experience of an audience in a theatre, dramatic probability is to the purely mental experience (which, however, is possible only to a mind superior to superstitious fears) provided by a supernatural poem. (Dutt 388)

The waking mind may suspend disbelief, but unaided by the lowering of mental barriers that occurs during sleep, it must be actively encouraged to suspend judgment, an achievement that, Coleridge insists, requires some degree of intellectual sophistication:

> of all intellectual power, that of superiority to the fear of the invisible world is the most dazzling. Its influence is abundantly proved by the one circumstance, that it can bribe us into a voluntary submission of our better knowledge, into suspension of all our judgement derived from constant experience, and enable us to peruse with the liveliest interest the wildest tales of ghosts, wizards, genii, and secret talismans. On this propensity, so deeply rooted in our nature, a specific *dramatic* probability may be raised by a true poet, if the whole of his work be in harmony: a *dramatic* probability, sufficient for dramatic pleasure, even when the component characters and incidents border on impossibility.

> The poet does not require us to be awake and believe; he solicits us only to yield ourselves to a dream; and this too with our eyes open, and with our judgement *perdue* behind the curtain, ready to awaken us at the first motion of our will: and meantime, only, to *dis*believe. (*BL* II: 217–18)

The dream state is the most familiar type of such experience, but the willing suspension of disbelief—or "negative faith," to use another of Coleridge's terms—is qualitatively distinct.

These precepts move us closer to understanding Coleridge's revision of the supernatural sublime. While for Coleridge the conventional sublime was characterized by suspension of the faculty of "Comparison" (*Marginalia* 1069; Modiano 124–25)—something also true of the dream-state and the supernatural—it was not marked by limitations of either reason or, as with Kant, of the imagination. Nor, for Coleridge, was sublimity to be known by those intimations of absence detected by Knight and others and turned by Gothic authors into horror. Rather, the sublime for Coleridge—as for Wordsworth, although for different reasons—was an experience of plenitude and transcendence:[2]

> What Coleridge saw out there [in nature] was not nature's chaos but nature's luxurious richness. Hence, the threat of being engulfed by the external world was certainly less real for Coleridge than it was for Schiller, and to a lesser degree for Kant. Nowhere in his statements on the sublime did Coleridge mention Nature's formless chaos or aimless violence as a condition of attaining the triumph of man's ascent into the world of absolute freedom. (Modiano 120–21)

The supernatural sublime has a poor foothold in such a mind, for engulfment and suspension, those states that characterize the trauma of the Gothic supernatural, are not operative in Coleridge's aesthetics. Accordingly, the "dramatic truth" of Coleridge's supernatural poems derives not from the terrifying, "suspending" power of the supernatural but from the poems' deliberate engagement of the intellect. The mind, thus engaged and alerted (a function of Coleridge's prefaces, as I discuss below), works to deny the supernatural its power of absorption and to both circumscribe and focus its intentions.

Coleridge's understanding of the sublime and its characteristic suspension is predicated to a substantial degree on his understanding of—and disagreements with—Kant's theory of sublimity, articulated first in *Observations on the Feeling of the Beautiful and the Sublime* (1764) and then more fully in the *Critique of Judgement* (1790). Appropriating the idealist notion of sublimity as a subjective phenomenon, existing in the mind rather than inherent in natural objects, Coleridge established a paradigm for the revision of Gothic supernaturalism that was shared, to a large degree, by Wordsworth, and, through influence, by Byron, the Shelleys, Keats, and their American counterparts Hawthorne and Poe.

Coleridge's debt to Kant is considerable (Wellek 68–72) and is mapped in some specificity by Raimonda Modiano in part III of her book *Coleridge and the Concept of Nature.* While there is no certain evidence that Coleridge knew Kant's "Analytic of the Aesthetical Judgement" before 1810, he was acquainted with Kantian (and German idealist) thought by the time of the *Lyrical Ballads*, although its specific influence on his work will be forever difficult to trace. Perhaps of greater consequence is that the important prefaces and glosses to his supernatural poems—ancillary texts meant to guide our reading and understanding of such works—were written after Coleridge had read Kant on the sublime and considered translating the "Analytic."

On one very general point Kant's theory of sublimity is akin to Burke's, for both insist on a moment of suspension, a "momentary checking of the vital powers and a consequent stronger outflow of them" (Kant 83). Beyond this, however, Kant and Burke diverge sharply (Crowther 11–15; Modiano 101–6), perhaps nowhere more importantly than in regard to Kant's identification of the sublime as a subjective phenomenon, a condition not in or of nature but of the perceiving mind. Burke and his contemporaries debated at length the ability of various characteristics or qualities of natural objects to excite the mind; Kant, while recognizing that the stimulating object had to have some impressive power or magnitude, swept the Burke-Knight-Price controversy aside by concluding that "Sublimity . . . does not reside in anything of nature, but only in our mind, in so far as we can become conscious that we are superior to nature within, and therefore also to nature without us (so far as it influences us)" (104). It is to such a subjective, interior notion of the sublime more than to Burke's objectively founded physiological theory (which Coleridge called "a poor thing") that Coleridge is indebted.

Coleridge was particularly attracted to the implicit if indirect moral dimension of Kant's sublime. For Kant, the pleasure arising from experience of the sublime "expresses a purposiveness of the subject in respect of the object" (Bernard xix). This subjectively determined purposiveness indicates the existence of a moral common ground for humanity: while "the judgement upon the sublime in nature needs culture," it also "has its root in human nature, even in that which, alike with common understanding, we can impute to and expect of everyone, viz. in the tendency to the feeling for (practical) ideas, i.e. to what is moral" (Kant 105). Without universally recognized (and recognizable) "moral ideas," Kant claims, sublimity can never be other than mere terror, a primitive and unenlightening fear.

This moral foundation manifests itself, in Coleridge's supernatural poetry, in an endorsement of generally conservative and explicitly Christian moral principles. When Kant argued that "The *sublime* consists merely in the *relation* by which the sensible in the representation of nature is judged available for a possible supersensible use" (107), Coleridge turned this impulse toward the Christian supersensible. Clarence Thorpe, noting that as regards British aesthetic tradition Coleridge was influenced more by John Dennis and James Usher than by the empiricist Burke (206), points to Coleridge's "Hymn before Sunrise in the Vale of Chamouni" to show that for Coleridge the sublime experience, however small in its beginnings, "culminates in an intuition of the mystery and greatness of the absolute one and all of Deity" (Thorpe 216). As Modiano explains it,

> Coleridge suceeded in formulating a new and remarkably subtle version of the Romantic sublime. By denying the necessity of a crisis in the sublime, Coleridge was able to avoid an abrupt rupture from sensible objects and maintain nature in the role of a benevolent power, aiding the self towards achieving the desired experience of transcendence. Conversely, by removing the apotheosis of personal power from the structure of the sublime, Coleridge significantly narrowed the gap between the sublime and the Christian ethos. The essential and unique character of Coleridge's conception of the sublime rests on the integration of nature in an experience of transcendence tending toward a Christian "I AM." (137)

Yet it was not only the consolatory nature of the sublime that led Coleridge away from Gothicism's horror. Kantian sublimity gave a special place to the power of reason in the hierarchy of faculties, a feature that further enhanced the redemptive nature of the Romantic sublime toward which Coleridge was working.

Confronted with an object suggestive of infinity, the Kantian imagination "proceeds of itself to infinity without anything hindering it" (92), but in "mathematical" sublimity (that associated with the faculty of cognition which attempts to apprehend the magnitude of overwhelming phenomena), there is "nothing purposive and pleasing for the aesthetical judgement" (92). The "understanding," which for Kant is distinct from and subordinate to reason, is "equally served and contented" by its logical, accretive estimation of magnitude by means of readily apprehendable units, but the reason is not satisfied, and therefore the experience lacks closure:

> now the mind listens to the voice of reason which, for every given magnitude—even for those that can never be entirely apprehended, although (in sensible representation) they are judged as entirely given—requires totality. Reason consequently desires comprehension in *one* intuition. . . . It does not even exempt the infinite . . . from this requirement. (93)

The ability and need of reason alone "to think [infinity] as *a whole* indicates a faculty of mind which surpasses every standard of sense" (93), and in this "suprasensible" potency of reason lies its ability to master the sublime trauma-experience (93–94). The mathematical sublime thus exposes the inadequacy of human imagination or sensibility, but the experience is finally a positive one because the overwhelming of our sensibilities actually summons the rational faculties, which in the mathematical sublime "rescue" us by providing rationally apprehendable conceptualizations of the phenomena in their totality. As Schiller explains it,

> We are pleased with the spectacle of the sensuous infinite, because we are able to attain by thought what the senses can no longer embrace and what the understanding cannot grasp. . . . [N]ature, notwithstanding all her infinity, cannot attain to the absolute grandeur which is in ourselves. We submit willingly to physical necessity both our well-being and our existence. This is because the very power reminds us that there are in us principles that escape its empire. (133–34)

In the dynamical sublime, in which the forces of nature threaten to overwhelm, the rational faculties again prove superior to nature by "leading us to imagine a situation which, through our courageous moral bearing, we refute [fear's] (and thereby nature's) claim to dominion over us" (Crowther 111). In the Kantian sublime, then, reason always succeeds precisely where sensibility and imagination fail, "and thus in our mind we find a superiority to nature even in its immensity" (Kant 101). Coleridge differed most notably by insisting that this superiority be accompanied by the mind's recognition of the Christian supersensible, as we have seen.

Emerging from such considerations is the incompatibility of the Gothic sublime and Coleridgean thought. Supernatural sublimity as practiced in radical Gothicism discovered infinity to suggest void and absence, and therein lay horror. Kant's sublime, especially as Coleridge supplemented it with a vigorous sense of religious transcendence, denies this. With reason rescuing the mathematical sublime, and with a firm moral resolve rescuing the dynamical sublime (to say nothing of the teleological foundation of that morality), the dark universe of radical Gothicism, with its abdications of reason and the inadequacy and hypocrisy of moral systems, is never the province of the Coleridgean sublime.

Coleridge's use of the supernatural, in consequence of the aesthetics sketched here, was nothing less than a renunciation of the Gothic supernatural the poet knew well and distrusted. His supernaturalism began as an imaginative form of self-scrutiny, and since for Coleridge "Imagination" was the "prime Agent" of human perception, the literary supernatural was an incisive embodiment of "man's capacity to view the world whole, to view the world as the organic creation of the living Power, God" (Brisman 126). Coleridge himself explained it in one of the famous autobiographical letters to Thomas Poole (16 October 1797):

> From my early reading of Faery Tales, & Genii etc. etc.—my mind had been habituated *to the Vast*— & I never regarded *my senses* in any way as the criteria of my belief. I regulated all my creeds by my conceptions not by my sight—even at that age. Should children be permitted to read Romances, & Relations of Giants & Magicians, & Genii? —I know all that has been said against it; but I have formed my faith in the affirmative. —I know no other way of giving the mind a love of "the Great", & "the Whole". —Those who have been led to the same truths step by step thro' the constant testimony of their senses, seem to me to want a sense which I possess—they contemplate nothing but *parts*—and all *parts* are necessarily little—and the Universe to them is but a mass of *little things*. (*Letters* 354)

Gothic fiction occasionally approached such metaphysical desire, although rarely so consciously, but the essential distinction is that Coleridge employed similar investigative techniques to discover something sharply different from that found by practitioners of the Gothic. The universal organicism of Coleridge's metaphysic precluded the dark vision of the radical Gothic, yet by the same token Coleridge cannot comfortably be aligned with the Gothic's conservative camp. His religious orthodoxy was, especially during the years that saw the composition of the mystery poems, more subtle and oblique. Coleridge began with the same materials, the same images and tropes, as Gothic writers already were wearing out, but in his hands they served far different ends.

*C*oleridge's most famous mystery poem, "The Rime of the Ancient Mariner" (1797–98), begins as do the others with an introductory prose passage. Acutely conscious of the excesses of Gothic fiction, Coleridge used these ancillary texts to indicate to his readers something of the way in which the poems should be read, which most assuredly was not as typical Gothic narratives or supernatural ballads. This particular pre-text, a modified passage from Thomas Burnet, is as important a reading guide as "The Rime" 's marginal gloss. If it is true, as Lawrence Lipking claims, that the gloss repeatedly fractures narrative complacency by insisting that the poem be read as a parable (615), then the epigraph maps the thematic terrain of that parable, preparing the reader to undergo precisely the experience that the poem—or, more exactly, the poem-and-gloss—is "about."

"*Facile credo*," it begins, immediately invoking the Coleridgean willing suspension of disbelief: we know already that invisible spirits will be part of this narrative universe. The passage then asks a series of unanswerable questions as though to emphasize the limits of our knowledge, but there is another, more telling point Coleridge seeks to underscore: "I do not disavow that it delights, meanwhile, to contemplate sometime in the mind, as in a painting, the image of a greater and better world. . . ."

The epigraph ends by announcing lofty goals: "But meanwhile we must watch over the truth, and keep a method so that we might distinguish certainties from uncertainties and day from night" (p. 186). "*Interea*" ("meanwhile") appears twice in as many sentences in this important text, becoming almost a leit motif: the poem begins by invoking the meanwhile, the between, the unresolved, thereby locating itself in the shadowed interstices of the rational framework ordering the human universe. While awaiting answers we may indulge in the delights of intellectual speculations, but while (or perhaps even as) we indulge we continue to search for truth and certainty. We simultaneously experience both and neither, presence and absence, perpetually between two states as distinct as day and night. There is in such a dialectic an implicit suspension, which Coleridge draws to our attention, engaging us in just such a suspension because suspension is one of the tropes with which the poem is centrally concerned.

To underscore this point the epigraph effects its suspension of us, the poem's readers, by positioning us in a relationship to the text that is both privileged and subordinate. The marginal gloss, that other ancillary text of the poem, abets and continues the epigraph's suspension, for the contrast or distance between the naive blunderings of the Mariner and the hermetic wisdom of the gloss is another, ongoing *"interea,"* a displacement that accompanies the text not only in the typographic fact of the gloss but in expectation of it. This renders even the white space of the margin—those moments during which the gloss, the interpretive presence of the commentator, is itself suspended—accomplice to the ongoing suspension or dislocation of the reader. The ostensibly hermeneutic presence of the gloss distances us from the Mariner's narrative at the same time it makes us dependent upon an unknown authorial presence.

The poem's first explicit suspension is that of the Wedding Guest, who is kept from the "merry din" of the wedding feast, that joyous ritual of the human community, by the "spellbound" abdication of his will: "He holds him with his glittering eye— / The Wedding-Guest stood still, / And listens like a three year's child: / The Mariner hath his will" (13–16). To "have his will" is of course a colloquial expression for rape, but the phrase works primarily in the possessive sense, for the Mariner *commands* the will of the Wedding Guest. Or suspends it. The Mariner, the "grey-beard loon" of "glittering eye," is from the start a quasifantastic being. The Wedding Guest, after all, is us, the reader of the supernatural tale, the audience present at the "Stage Illusion," and his fascination, his loss of will, is the type and model of our own suspension of disbelief. We are perhaps more willing than the Wedding Guest, but *"facile credo"* is the watchword for that transition from the realm of certainty to uncertainty, nature to supernature, and the Wedding Guest, like Christabel, resists very little. He twice "beats his breast" as the merry din recalls to him the missed wedding feast, but these tokens of resistance are easily overborne. "Yet he cannot chose but hear" may suggest the Wedding Guest's desire to withdraw to the feast, or it may as readily suggest his own inner compulsion, his fascination *with*, rather than *by*, the "bright-eyed Mariner." The Wedding Guest capitulates fully to his suspension, emerging twice more before the end only to reaffirm his rapture.

In a layering of complexities, the Mariner's tale is also one of suspension, its fantastic elements suggestive of the supernatural sublime.

But "The Rime" is not an employment of this trope as much as it is a critique of it, a critique that, in fact, helps inaugurate a new understanding of literary supernaturalism that remains vital in our own cultural moment. The ballad-tale's suspension begins with the Mariner's journey south, away from his native country to a terra incognita where "Nor shapes of men nor beast we ken" and where the appearance of an albatross is so welcome it is regarded "As if it had been a Christian soul."

The slaying of the bird marks a turn in the story, both literally and figuratively, a reversal of direction that is also the moment in which the Mariner begins, like Odysseus, his quest for self. Asserting the "I" in the face of an indifferent and icy nature, the Mariner initiates his own self-creation. In shooting the albatross, "The Mariner does something that matters to the universe of matter, in which he finds himself, materially, less than a person. He has undertaken the adventure of individuality. . . . By it he enacts himself, only to discover the implacable isolation and exposure of identity" (Cooke 32–33). In a further parallel to Odysseus, the Mariner's establishment of self-identity is figured in large part by encounter and conflict with various supernatural agents, forces of nature, and the loss of his crew. "We were the first that ever burst / Into that silent sea"—like Odysseus and his men after the sack of the Kykones' city, the Mariner and his crew enter a universe in which the real and the familiar are lost, in which the natural gives way to the supernatural. Becalmed under a bloody Sun, the Mariner and his companions slip into the meanwhile, into the world between fact and hallucination, unreal and possible:

> The very deep did rot: O Christ!
> That ever this should be!
> Yea, slimy things did crawl with legs
> Upon the slimy sea.
>
> About, about, in reel and rout
> The death-fires danced at night;
> The water, like a witch's oils,
> Burnt green, and blue and white. (123–30)

Here is not the comforting nature of "This Lime-Tree Bower My Prison" or the "Hymn before Sunrise," but the decaying world of *The Monk*'s sepulcher. Strange fires, the ocean a volatile witch's brew—the natural order has been suspended in a disjunction so complete the sailors themselves experience failure of language, token of an experience beyond relation or understanding. Only the Mariner is able to speak, and only after vampirizing himself, drawing upon the very substance of his life.

This natural and linguistic dysfunction is attributed to a Spirit following the ship from the Antarctic ice. The Spirit's dwelling in the place of the Mariner's act of separation and its pursuit of the ship "Nine fathom deep" suggest the interiority implicit in Coleridge's dictum that the supernatural "transfer from our inward nature a human interest"—in the case of the "Rime," an interest in the psychology of alienation that attends awareness of the self's necessary separateness. The gloss of this stanza testifies that Coleridge was (or, at any rate, later became) aware of the psychological aspect of his tale: "A Spirit had followed them; one of the invisible inhabitants of this planet, neither departed souls nor angels; concerning whom the learned Jew, Josephus, and the Platonic Constantinopolitan, Michael Psellus, may be consulted" (p. 191). As Lawrence Kramer and Charles Patterson report, Coleridge and Wordsworth discussed these Platonic daemons in the later 1790s, understanding them to be objectifications of interior mental and emotional states.[3] Kathleen Coburn further specifies the psychological value of the supernatural for Coleridge, for whom "nothing is more strange, more mysterious, than the mind itself, especially the frightened, or troubled, or guilty mind, with all the spectres that haunt the margins of its semi-conscious and unconscious operations; from its projection come all the daemons, spirits, and phantoms the most 'supernatural or at least romantic' poem requires" (125). The dysfunction in Nature, it becomes apparent, has its origins in the Mariner's mind.

The poem verges even closer to supernatural sublimity when Death and his female counterpart arrive to claim the lives of the crew. And it is, in one sense, a claiming of life for the Mariner as well, for though he remains alive, his alienation anxiety is seized upon by "the Nightmare LIFE-IN-DEATH," who reifies it in the death of the Mariner's companions: "The many men, so beautiful! / And they all dead did lie: / And a thousand thousand slimy things / Lived on; and so did I." The ugliness and perversity of Nature the Mariner had earlier observed are now equated with his own existence; his separation has become so acute that his life becomes repellant, the world of Nature now a world of uncertainty: "For the sky and the sea, and the sea and the sky / Lay like a load on my weary eye" (250–51). The inversion of the noun order suggests a perceptual confusion induced by the supernaturally figured separation guilt of the Mariner, a confusion so powerful that it cannot but be the point of maximum suspension.

At this point the poem turns, and to make the crux more evident (the poem, after all, had been criticized on its initial appearance), Coleridge in later editions here located the poem's longest and most important marginal gloss:

> In his loneliness and fixedness he yearneth towards the journeying Moon, and the stars that still sojourn, and yet still move onward; and every where the blue sky belongs to them, and is their appointed rest, and their native country and their own natural homes, which yet they enter unannounced, as lords that are certainly expected and yet there is a silent joy at their arrival. (p. 197)

The Mariner's moment of greatest despair proves also to be the poem's greatest moment of affirmation. Carl Woodring identifies this gloss as the moment of the Mariner's recovery, although his reading that the stars "At home in their fixity . . . provide a vision of return to a native place" (379) does not give sufficient emphasis to that element of universal belonging which characterizes the human perception of Coleridge's "wondrous whole." The Mariner indeed returns home, but his sense of belonging is achieved prior to his actual return, for it obtains on a much vaster and grander scale. While the Mariner's isolation finds in the "moving Moon" an obvious symbol of his own desire, it is the image suggested by the stars that is most telling. Belonging everywhere, at home and at rest throughout the heavens, they are the type of the universal human, the achievement and apotheosis of the Coleridgean sublime: " 'Tis the sublime of man, / Our noontide Majesty, to know ourselves / Parts and proportions of one wondrous whole!" ("Religious Musings" 127–29). The stars, in their simultaneous journeying and fixedness, mirror the Mariner's own desire to belong and yet retain individuality, to experience the broad sweep of the natural world (he is, after all, a mariner) and yet not isolate himself from the human community. His voyage thus far has been *only* journeying, but the astronomical reminder of the Coleridgean sublime provides the key to the mariner's self-completion. Like the stars, like the lord returning home, the Mariner must locate himself in the universe, alive as self yet recognizing that self as part of larger natural and social communities.

The first of these recognitions, the one that empowers the Mariner's reintegration with the natural world, is soon effected:

O happy living things! no tongue
Their beauty might declare:
A spring of love gushed from my heart,
And I blessed them unaware:
Sure my kind saint took pity on me,
And I blessed them unaware.

The self-same moment I could pray
And from my neck so free
The Albatross fell off, and sank
Like lead into the sea. (282–91)

What earlier were crawling "slimy things" are now creatures of
beauty cavorting through the waves; spiritual torpor and the failure
of language are replaced by a sense of divine favor and the return of
prayer, by "a capacity for aesthetic admiration, for love, and for a
sacred respect for other things *in themselves*. . . . The change [in the
Mariner] is ontological, putting the Mariner in a deeper, fuller, and
truer relation to the universe *and to himself*" (Cooke 34–35).

These reintegrations are accompanied by a second storm, a correspondent breeze propelling the Mariner and his ship homeward. But
one reintegration remains. Nature and heaven may have received the
Mariner, but society has not, indeed cannot as long as he remains
isolate. His social alienation is signaled by the silence, indeed the Otherness, of the body of his nephew: "The body of my brother's son /
Stood by me, knee to knee: / The boy and I pulled at one rope, / But
he said nought to me" (341–44). The remainder of the poem traces
this final and, in some ways, most crucial engagement with the world
beyond the self.

The Mariner is welcomed back to the verge of humanity by the
"sweet jargoning" of land birds, appropriately pleasant symbols of
return, just as that silent and solitary seabird, the Albatross, was the
apt emblem of the Mariner's state of mind and spirit on his outward
journey. Yet it is the Polar Spirit that ultimately effects the Mariner's
return, and although it labors "in obedience to the angelic troop, [it]
still requireth vengeance" (p. 201). The Spirit was invoked by the slaying of the Albatross, the Mariner's great act of self-assertion, and the
consequences of that act have yet to be realized fully. Heaven and
Nature may have forgiven him, but the Mariner has yet to return to
his own kind, and some equilibrium must be established between his
solipsistic impulse and the essentially social nature of humanity.

Like the stars, the Mariner returns to his "own countree," a return signaled by the departure of the angelic spirits that had animated the crew's corpses. Appropriately, the poem's supernaturalism ends here as well, yet it is a troubled end: the Mariner's attempt at speech sends the Pilot into a fit, the Pilot's boy into insanity, and the Hermit into prayer. So terrifying is the Mariner's presence—we of course recognize him as a visionary brother of the "Kubla Khan" poet—that the Hermit, for all his experience with mariners, regards this one with dread and uncertainty: " 'Say quick,' quoth he, 'I bid thee say— / What manner of man art thou?' " (576–77). Immediately the Mariner experiences the "woful agony" that is his compulsion to speak, his "penance of life" that is also the tale being told to the Wedding Guest.

To be sure, the Mariner's recovery and reintegration is problematic, hardly a straightforward return to the comforts and close security of domestic affection, belonging, and stability:

> I pass, like night, from land to land;
> I have strange power of speech;
> That moment that this face I see,
> I know the man that must hear me:
> To him my tale I teach. (586–90)

Yet if this is not the homecoming of Odysseus, the Mariner's penance is equally removed from that of his other great predecessor, the Wandering Jew, for the Mariner is not ontologically Other, nor is he a social outcast. Quite the contrary, he goes rather to prayer than to the wedding feast, but the Mariner is far from the solitary, alienated man who slew the Albatross and endured a supernatural journey that his companions could not survive:

> O sweeter than the marriage-feast,
> 'Tis sweeter far to me,
> To walk together to the kirk,
> With a goodly company!—
>
> To walk together to the kirk,
> And all together pray,
> While each to his great Father bends,
> Old men, and babes, and loving friends
> And youths and maidens gay! (601–9)

It is hard to find, with Robert Penn Warren, that the poem is a prothalamion, but this convocation-in-prayer of such a disparate group makes equally improbable a reading of the Ancient Mariner as an outcast. His reintegration is qualified but not denied; the message of his compelled and compelling tale "is that the return to God is a return from solitude to a goodly company in one's own country" (Woodring 377); and his compulsion to speak is itself a social act, a making public of his assertion of individuality and of its consequences both ill and good. And the latter outweighs the former: just as the group walking together to the kirk is both a group—a "goodly company"—and a collection of individuals—"*each* to his great Father bends"—the Mariner's return is a balanced celebration of both self-assertion and a recognition of communal belonging. The disturbance of his auditors, the disruption of their lives, is evidence not of the Mariner's alienation, but of his power and his success. Like the poet in "Kubla Khan," the Mariner is no demonic outcast but a poet-visionary who sees into the hearts of things, and if his vision is troubling, so much the better for his effectiveness. The Wedding Guest—who is indeed something of a "psychological double of the mariner" (Magnuson 84) as well as of the reader—after hearing the Mariner's tale and appropriating his experience, "went like one that been stunned, / And is of sense forlorn: / A sadder and a wiser man, / He rose the morrow morn" (622–25). The Mariner has survived his quest, to return and preach the Coleridgean vision of the sublime, humanity as part of a vast and wondrous whole.

The positive character of this sublime is further evident in the response of the Wedding Guest. His suspension—the Mariner's hypnotic telling—having ended, the Wedding Guest registers the effect of the Mariner's story by going home instead of to the feast. But rather than marking the rejection of social consolations, the Guest's departure is, like the ambiguity of Geraldine, an acknowledgment of the complexity of human experience, of the inextricable mingling of sadness and achievement. The Wedding Guest participates vicariously in the Mariner's experience, mirroring it in his own suspension, and like the Mariner—or like the Wordsworth of "Tintern Abbey" and *The Prelude*—learns that self is not achieved and asserted without cost.

Coleridge's employment, in a supernaturalist context, of these various nested suspensions is such a departure from Gothic interpretations of the same tropes that the poem proves, finally, a critique of the supernatural sublime rather than an employment of it. Coleridge does not repudiate the supernatural, as Wordsworth generally does, but even as the Romantic poet most identified with supernaturalism, Coleridge cannot rest content with imagery and structures whose uses and thematics had been so thoroughly determined by Gothic writers and the enthusiastic public reception of their work. Just as in Coleridge's aesthetics supernatural literature requires conscious intellection, so does his supernaturalism demand a pronounced self-awareness. The supernatural characters in "The Rime" are a Polar Spirit specifically identified in the gloss as a daemon (that is, an objectification of inner states), the allegoric presentations of Death and Life-in-Death, and angelic spirits. The uncertainty or absence Gothic supernaturalism uncovers (even that supernaturalism indebted to Christianity) is here obviated. These spirits are not the avatars of moral or epistemological chaos but refer instead to specific human concepts: alienation, guilt, the moral will. The poem is not an allegory, but it is close to one, its anagogy much nearer the surface than the Polar Spirit's nine fathoms. Coleridge, we recall, answered Anna Barbauld's complaint about the lack of morality in "The Rime" by pointing out, quite accurately, that "the poem had too much; and the only, or chief fault, if I might say so, was the obtrusion of the moral sentiment so openly on the reader as a principle or cause of action in a work of such pure imagination" (*Table Talk,* May 31, 1830). Of course it was the presence of a vigorous "moral sentiment" that made the poem something less than pure imagination and restricts the signifying reach of its supernatural elements.

If we were to extend the categories of Gothic fiction to Romantic poetry, "The Rime" would be in the supernatural sublime's conservative mode, but such an extension would be reductive and distortive, for although the supernaturalism of Coleridge's poem considerably exceeds that of *Otranto* or *The Old English Baron,* mere quantity is never important. More to the point is what permits or activates supernaturalism: Coleridge may be generous with it precisely because it is not the emotional or thematic center of his text. *Otranto* and *The Old English Baron* turn on the presence of their ghosts, which must be held subservient to and cannot overwhelm the novels' moral and spiritual dimensions, so their phantoms are minimally present in the text, introduced gradually and delicately. To admit a supernaturalism that dominates the text risks broaching epistemological issues, a risk unacceptable to and unnecessary for the writers of conservative Gothics. Indeed, we can see why Reeve thought it necessary to answer Walpole: the climax of the earlier fiction must for her have uncomfortably foregrounded the ghost of Alphonso and his metaphysical implications, although Walpole's grip on a conservative, traditional metaphysic was never at risk in his story.

Despite a greater supernaturalism, Coleridge is not finally concerned with epistemology either. The overwhelming uncertainty and *interea* introduced by the Burnet epigraph are, by the poem's conclusion, dissipated, explained, and filled by the marginal glosses and the Mariner's actions, which combine to reveal that these spirits *are* known. I take it as extremely significant that Coleridge added to Burnet's text the questions of what these spirits do and where they live.⁴ Coleridge has answered his own questions, closing off uncertainty with his demonstrations of spirits that are mind, ghosts that are Providential impulses, and quests that have definite and knowable answers: moral will, social integration, transcendent love of God's "wondrous whole." Coleridge's sublime is a response to the supernatural sublime, a rendering unnecessary of its very project, a co-opting of its potential subversion by assuring there is no need even to ask such fearful questions.

Coleridge invokes the structure of the supernatural sublime, but in the midst of it, at the moment of the Mariner's emotional and spiritual nadir, Coleridge undoes the supernatural sublime. He pulls the rug out from under its ectoplasmic feet by suggesting that Gothic horror is not the consequence of being lost in the trackless waste or the shadowed catacomb, but is instead the result of deficient vision. There has always been a guidepost in the wilderness, a well-lit stairway out of the sepulcher, Coleridge implies, but in their fascination with supernatural objects, Gothic novelists could not see to find these avenues of escape from the surrounding horror.

In "The Rime" 's deepest moment of despair, when his protagonist is as isolated as Antonia in the sepulchre or Emily in Castle Udolpho, Coleridge rejects despair and facile morality for a resolution more complex, more redemptive of both mind and spirit. The Mariner ends his supernatural suspension by stepping out into Nature, something not even Emily, for all her piety and her religious sublime, can effectively do: Emily, after all, *must* determine if those ghosts are real, or, more precisely, that they *are not* real, for an indeterminate ontology cannot be borne in the Radcliffean world. The same issue is irrelevant for Coleridge, for of course his supernatural is genuine: his spirits are those that haunt the human mind. The supernatural is not explained away, for Coleridge has established his supernatural as the objectification of mental states, and these we shall always have with us. What matters most is that the supernatural per se is not the emotional or intellectual center of this (or any other) Coleridgean text; the recognition by the Mariner of his place in Nature's (and thereby God's) wondrous whole is the poem's redemptive core. The supernatural continues: let it. The Mariner's journey is about the discovery, construction, and integration of self—this, not supernaturalism, is the "dramatic truth" the poem offers. The questions raised by the supernatural sublime are shown to be superfluous. For Coleridge, Blake was right: when the doors to our perception have been cleansed, the world does indeed appear infinite. In that boundless perspective is not chaos or indifference but a clear sense of belonging and unity, of transcendent achievement that dissipates the supernatural sublime, turning it into one of its own vanishing and harmless phantoms. It has been said that Coleridge's conversation poems are the poet's "attempt to step toward an imaginative understanding of the unity of all minds while at the same time preserving his individuality" (Magnuson 18); "The Rime" 's supernaturalism provides another perspective on this same sublime endeavor.

*T*he harmless phantoms of the supernatural are not the explicit concern of "Kubla Khan" (1798), a poem more about the poetic imagination than about the supernatural. The work merits consideration here, however, on the basis of its preface. "Kubla Khan," like Coleridge's other mystery poems in their final form, begins only after it is introduced by a prose text. Such introduction is more than a reflection of Coleridge's inveterate philosophizing; very few of his other poems are preceded by such texts. The relatively lengthy prefaces attached to the mystery poems suggest Coleridge's need to comment upon their particular character, to supply "a rule for reading before the reading process even begins" (Janowitz 31), thereby containing their oddness and supernaturalism.

The two "fragmentary" mystery poems begin with prose introductions in the poet's own voice; the complete "Ancient Mariner" perhaps needs less explaining prior to its text, but its ongoing marginal glosses are more extensive than the prefaces to "Kubla Khan" and "Christabel." These ancillary texts were added to the poems in the 1817 edition of *Sybilline Leaves,* although there is some evidence, in the Notebooks and elsewhere, that Coleridge had been thinking of these pieces as much as ten years earlier—that is, at approximately the time he was becoming acquainted with Kantian sublime theory. Add to this Coleridge's cogitations on Gothic fiction in his reviews, and we see a cluster of events and experiences that would lead Coleridge to ensure that his earlier supernaturalist works would be read in a way consistent with his intentions and understanding of literary supernaturalism.

It is doubly appropriate that "Kubla Khan"'s preface identifies the work as "a psychological curiosity." Not only is its study of the poetic imagination a psychological one, with its telling imagery of caverns, chasm, and fountain, it illustrates the Coleridgean principle of active intellection. The Khan's existence in a magical space-time permits him to erect his stately pleasure-dome simply by decree or act of will. While such potency is the type of the poet's vatic imagination, the world of the Romantic poet requires something more than decree. The poet is removed from Khan's world; the first two verse paragraphs of the poem lack the "I" of the poet, for they describe the Khan's world and the source of his "making" power. The gardens and pleasure-dome are the results or effects of this power; moving to the second verse paragraph, the poem slips further into the mind, closer to the source of creative energy. Here the imagery is of a terrible and violent power with its origins buried in mystery. The source of the Khan's power of effortless creation is the "deep romantic chasm," the libidinally charged abiding place of the creative force, its energies forever erupting into the world of the conscious mind before sinking back to "the caverns measureless to man," there to undergo their inscrutable metamorphosis or recycling and burst forth again in another moment of magical and sublime creation. It is clear from the artifact that remains behind that these powers can effect with ease their miraculous "making":

> The shadow of the dome of pleasure
> Floated midway on the waves;
> Where was heard the mingled measure
> From the fountain and the caves.
> It was a miracle of rare device,
> A sunny pleasure-dome with caves of ice! (31–36)

This "mingled measure" is the combined effort of will and imagination, conscious shaping and subconscious energy, uniting in a harmonized balancing of their potentially antagonistic powers to leave behind a rare device, an artifact embodying within itself the synthesis of sun and ice, dark energy and conscious intellection.

These two verse paragraphs parallel the preface's opium reverie, that "profound sleep . . . of the external senses" which is tantamount to the lowering of rational boundaries, the unbridling of those imaginative energies necessary if we are to permit the supernatural its intended play and effect. In Kubla's Xanadu, the fountain bursts with creative violence from its magic chasm to bestow the power of magical decree. In the preface, the opium dream effects for Coleridge a similar unbinding of the creative force, and "all the images rose up before him as *things,* with a parallel production of the correspondent expressions, without any sensation or consciousness of effort" (p. 296). In *The Friend* (both in 1809 and 1818) Coleridge discusses Martin Luther's confrontation with the devil in similar terms, suggesting the deep hold the idea had in his mind. It seems to be consistently axiomatic for Coleridge that poetic creation, like the construction-by-will of the Khan's pleasure-dome, is (or should be) an effortless, almost unwilled expression of powers latent in the mind.

"Kubla Khan" 's final verse paragraph corresponds to the state following the visit of the man from Porlock, an emotional lapse because, as Paul Magnuson explains it, "Containment and control of the inspirational force are not sustained . . . the delightful dream is lost because order cannot be maintained" (39). Yet Magnuson's last phrase is misleading, for the poet's problem is one of *too much* order, of excessive contact with those forces shaping human society. The hypnagogic state has been ruptured, dissipated by the intrusion of the everyday— "a person *on business* from Porlock" (emphasis added)—and the final lines of the poem embody the poet's "mortification" at his discovery of the loss of visionary power. The "damsel with a dulcimer / In a vision" is the poetic productivity of the opium-induced dream-state, the intuitive and unwilled command of creative power exhibited earlier in the poem by the Khan, earlier in the preface by the drugged Coleridge. Once awakened, however, the poet loses his link to the mind's poetic and creative energies:

> Could I revive within me
> Her symphony and song,
>   To such a deep delight 'twould win me,
> That with music loud and long,
> I would build that dome in air,
> That sunny dome! those caves of ice! (42–47)

The subjective "could" is the leading grammatical element here for good reason. The poet can only imagine now, only dream (in the least sense of the word) of the power he cannot feel or recapture:

> And all who heard should see them there,
> And all should cry, Beware! Beware!
> His flashing eyes, his floating hair!
> Weave a circle round him thrice,
> And close your eyes with holy dread
> For he on honey-dew hath fed,
> And drunk the milk of Paradise. (48–54)

The poet longs for the haunting presence and power that infuse and compel the Ancient Mariner, but the Mariner lived his experience, and his power to command the will of his auditors is earned by his rite of passage. The vision in "Kubla Khan" has been falsely achieved, a cheat that Coleridge doubly acknowledged by adding to later editions of the poem the subtitle "A Vision in a Dream. A Fragment." It is only, for the poet, an insubstantial dream-vision and has no conclusion because Coleridge cannot end it; to explain the recovery and command of poetic powers would have exorcised one of Coleridge's lifelong demons and undone the drama of the preceding parts of the poem. The lines from "The Picture" that Coleridge included in the preface are nothing more than the expression of a wistful hope, a longing for recovery of the vision that also finds voice in the quotation from Theocritus and the reminder that "the to-morrow is yet to come." Yet for Coleridge, tomorrow never was to come, his illnesses (both real and imagined) and his poetic malaise forever postponing the realization of that vision.

C hristabel" (1797–1800) is so emphatically supernatural that Coleridge felt obliged, in his Preface, to distance the work from that of his more popular supernaturalist contemporaries, Scott and Byron.[5] Yet such an obvious *clinamen,* to borrow Harold Bloom's term, is hardly necessary: the poem's particular use of the supernatural declares the work to be Coleridge's own. It is both an emphasis of "The Rime" 's thesis and a supernaturalist precursor of "The Pains of Sleep."

Like "The Rime," "Christabel" invokes a supernaturally figured suspension to make its point, but the poem complements "The Rime" by viewing the supernatural from another perspective: that of the Wedding Guest rather than of the Mariner. The supernatural is seen not only as it signifies the imaginative and psychic forces that contribute to the establishment of self but also and more importantly as an intrusion of imaginative power and experience into the world of everyday. The poem is as much a reception study as anything else, which helps resolve persistent critical concern over Geraldine's ambiguity and the poem's problematic ending.

Once again, the preface contributes importantly to a reading of the poetic text, a fact easily overlooked since "Christabel" is introduced by the most ordinary of the supernatural poems' pre-texts, a commonplace discussion of compositional dates and meter intended to bolster Coleridge's denial of plagiarism. Few introductions could be more prosaic, more mundane; no direct mention of the supernatural is made, no hint given of the poem's nature or concerns.

The poem then abruptly begins with one of the most patently Gothic lines in Coleridge: " 'Tis the middle of night by the castle clock." Here is a clue Coleridge's readers instantly would have recognized: the castle clock tolling midnight was, by 1798, a Gothic cliché, almost a Gothic joke. The ordinariness of the preface's world has been abruptly shattered, dissipated like the dream-reverie of "Kubla Khan." Only this time, the ontological dynamic is reversed: the everyday is interrupted by the supernatural, as though a dream about businessmen from Porlock were to be interrupted by a ghost knocking at the door.

Within the world of the poem the same violation of the everyday occurs, although it is certainly a different everyday than that known to Coleridge or his readers. Like the Wedding Guest, Christabel is going about her ordinary business—here also, a business concerned with love and betrothal—and, also like the Guest, must encounter a "vision of horror" in order to break through the insulating barrier of her complacency and innocence (Enscoe 48). The ordinary world within the poem is of course that of the castle, a place of patriarchal enclosure, containment, and guardianship. It is telling that as the poem opens in the witching hour of Gothic fiction, Christabel has left the security of Langdale Hall, moving a furlong into the "midnight wood" in order to "pray / For the weal of her lover that's far away" (29–30). The feeble Leoline guards his virgin dove in a lifeless hall, its security repressive and stifling, a world of Blakean innocence that cannot endure. Thel's Happy Valley is here a sterile castle, and Christabel's journey outside it, praying for an infusion of masculine energy, is the successful completion of the task that proved too terrifying for Thel.

This brief excursion into the wood inaugurates the poem's supernatural suspension—a suspension that, for Christabel, lasts only one night, in contrast to (and complement of) "The Rime" 's extended voyage of suspension. "Christabel" is more concerned with the aftermath of the suspension, with the fate of the Wedding Guest on "the morrow morn" as *he*, not the Mariner, learns to deal with his fellow beings in light of his new and disquieting knowledge. Coleridge's concern with the supernatural in the everyday becomes most evident in part II, which scrutinizes the castle residents' reactions to the infusion of (supernatural) energy into their world; here the poem moves outward in its focus, introducing Bard Bracy and Sir Leoline directly, mentioning Sir Roland and a number of real place names, including, for the first time, the name of Leoline's castle.

In part I, however, the focus is on Christabel, the vehicle for the supernatural and all it represents. She is first seen in an active role (a necessary Coleridgean condition for the supernatural), venturing out of the castle to pray for her lover. She does not, of course, get precisely what she prays for, although in one sense her prayers are indeed answered. Just as the Wedding Guest is on his way to witness a celebration of union and sociality and gets instead a supernatural tale that celebrates a higher form of union and community, so is Christabel rewarded. She prays for "her own betrothéd knight" and encounters in that moment Geraldine, a supernatural answer to her prayers and an experiential surrogate for her lover.

Geraldine is associated immediately with the "experience" Christabel lacks, with "the part of itself that innocence must finally encounter on the way to knowledge" (Spatz 111). Whereas Christabel has, by all indications, spent her life entirely within the bounds of the castle, Geraldine has had experience in the outer world—experience with erotic undertones:

> Five warriors seized me yestermorn,
> Me, even me, a maid forlorn:
> They choked my cries with force and fright,
> And tied me on a palfrey white.
> The palfrey was as fleet as wind,
> And they rode furiously behind. (81–86)

Geraldine, whom Enscoe correctly understands as "a fully developed personification of the erotic force" (28), has that which Christabel lacks; she is, in a sense, what Christabel needs and wishes to become, and yet also fears (Spatz 111). Christabel's assisting Geraldine, especially her carrying Geraldine into the castle, is a symbolic appropriation of the more worldly lady's energy and experience by the sheltered virgin Christabel, and an ironic signal from Coleridge that the "danger" the ladies have apparently just escaped is about to be engaged.

Coleridge quickly establishes Geraldine's supernaturalism—the growling dog, the inability to pray, the flaring lamps—and then begins what is sometimes regarded as the poem's most puzzling section. Once in Christabel's chamber, Geraldine's true character begins to manifest itself. But which true character is hers? Geraldine wonders if Christabel's mother's spirit will pity her and joins with Christabel in wishing her mother were present, but a moment later utters an incantation against the protecting presence of the mother's spirit:

> Off, wandering mother! Peak and pine!
> I have power to bid thee flee.
>
> . . . .
>
> Off, woman, off! this hour is mine—
> Though thou her guardian spirit be,
> Off, woman, off! 'tis given to me. (205–6, 211–13)

Geraldine reports that "All who live in the upper sky, / Do love you, holy Christabel!" (227–28), then disrobes, revealing herself as frighteningly Other. Climbing into bed with her rescuer, Geraldine invokes another spell, one "Which is lord of thy utterance, Christabel!" (268). After acting as heavenly messenger, Geraldine assumes her aspect of evil-working lamia, ensnaring her victim in a charm of delusion and magical silence, yet the conclusion to part I reveals that "the worker of these harms, / . . . holds the maiden in her arms, / [and] Seems to slumber still and mild, / As a mother with her child." Christabel prayed for her absent lover and found the experienced Geraldine, with whom she has what appears to be an erotic experience; Christabel laments the death of her mother, yet appears to have acquired one. Nature fell silent during Geraldine's "one hour" of magic potency (a situation reminiscent of the Bleeding Nun's visit to Raymond), yet now the "cliff and tower" echo with the calls of birds, Nature's celebration of the seduction or bringing of experience to Christabel (Enscoe 51) and "The Rime" 's emblem of social acceptance and inclusion. Clearly, Geraldine's nature, her true self, is complex, neither entirely good nor evil, angelic or satanic.

"The Rime" has shown that experience is not acquired without trauma. When Christabel "Gathers herself from out her trance," her emotional response to the night's events is fittingly ambiguous:

Her limbs relax, her countenance
Grows sad and soft; the smooth thin lids
Close o'er her eyes; and tears she sheds—
Large tears that leave the lashes bright!
And oft the while she seems to smile
As infants at a sudden light!

Yea, she doth smile, and she doth weep. . . . (313–19)

Some of Christabel's emotional vacillation might be Coleridge's rendering of postcoital confusion, but more importantly it indicates the ambiguity attending Geraldine's presence and effect: she is both intruder and mother, lamia and protector, lover and rapist. Indeed, since she is "the vehicle for Christabel to experience relationships otherwise denied her, . . . on this level Geraldine lacks specific identity either as female or male" (Delson 140).

Christabel can experience Geraldine as everything she needs and wants her to be, although given the import of her visit, it is to be expected that the relationship between the two women is not without some pain and confusion. As one critic explains, "A moral crisis arises when one begins to recognize the shadow in the self, yet as painful as it is, bringing this dark side of the personality to consciousness is psychologically healthy and an index of maturity" (Holstein 123). Maturity—acknowledgment of her own "shameful" impulses and the assertion of an autonomous self—is precisely what Christabel, for all her virtues, lacks.

Geraldine's ability to be all things to all people includes Sir Leoline. Obsessed with the "world of death" since his wife's passing, the Baron finds in Geraldine both outlet and receptacle for years of repressed emotion. She reminds him, first, of his estrangement from Roland de Vaux, and it is clear that Leoline takes Geraldine to be the means of healing this long-troubling breach. The supernatural woman becomes for Leoline a way to recover his early emotional involvement, but the poem does not present such a recovery as a desirable alternative. As Paul Edwards and Macdonald Emslie show, the Baron's view of life is reductive, and his desire to recover his lost friendship is not a movement forward but a regression, a return to "the simple either/or morality of his youth" ("Limitations" 64).

Geraldine fills other lacunae in the Baron's life. Part I presents a Leoline aged and infirm; his guard dog is toothless and old, and his shield hangs "in a murky old niche in the wall" (163), compelling evidence of lost virility and power. Yet Geraldine seems capable of

restoring these, rejuvenating the old Baron, just as she promises reconciliation with his youth's companion. Having "forgot his age," the
Baron issues a challenge to Geraldine's kidnappers:

> He swore by the wounds in Jesu's side
> He would proclaim it far and wide,
> With trump and solemn heraldry,
> That they, who thus had wronged the dame,
> Were base as spotted infamy!
> "And if they dare deny the same, My herald
> shall appoint a week,
> And let the recreant traitors seek
> My tourney court—that there and then
> I may dislodge their reptile souls
> From the bodies and forms of men!" (433–43)

The Baron's metaphor, casual on his part, is significant for the reader.
All indications in the poem are that the reptile soul is Geraldine's and
hers the dissembling form of the human. Yet in her snake aspect Geraldine is not so much demonic as she is an embodiment—not unlike the
serpent of Genesis—of sexual awareness.

It is apt, then, that Christabel begins to partake of the reptilian
characteristics of Geraldine. Seeing the fond embrace of Geraldine and
her father, Christabel "drew in her breath with a hissing sound" (459),
a noise she later repeats (591). She also "passively did imitate / That
look of dull and treacherous hate!" (605–6) she registers in Geraldine's "shrunken serpent eyes." Her initiation into the world of experience has changed her, as it should, just as the Mariner is altered by
his experience, and the Wedding Guest by his hearing the tale. The
supernatural, which for Coleridge is *never just* literary supernaturalism but "a human interest and a semblance of truth," is not encountered without lasting effect, a lesson Mary Shelley would, with direct
reference to Coleridge, inscribe into her great novel. The human heart,
which Coleridge's supernatural always addresses, cannot be examined
casually.

Such wisdom is known only to Bard Bracy, and only imperfectly.
His description of the castle bell's echo, couched in ghostly and demonic imagery (345–59), establishes his sensitivity to the supernatu-
ral/psychological, but his response to Leoline's request that he travel
to Tryermaine reveals an intuitive insight weakened by his long residence in the castle of the old Baron. He has a telling dream at the
moment of Geraldine's appearance, but his own isolation in Leoline's

domain renders his visionary experience incomplete. For the bard, Geraldine's embodiment of experience is a threat to be confronted, driven out, denied: "I had vowed with music loud / To clear yon wood from thing unblest, / Warned by a vision in my rest!" (528–30). Bracy's dream is of only one of Geraldine's aspects and is thereby reductive.

The Baron also misreads the poet's dream, substituting Geraldine for his daughter and thus effecting the latter's displacement. His deficient understanding of an incomplete visionary experience marks the Baron as immune to the truth of "our inward nature"; both he and Bracy register only one of Geraldine's moral dimensions, blind to the fact she is as complex and multivalent as life itself, both good and evil in a "mingled measure" so intimately intertwined that one element cannot be separated from the other. The world Geraldine represents is, in the words of Edwards and Emslie, not "a world of simple oppositions, as Sir Leoline supposes, in which figures can be defined unambiguously as doves or serpents. . . . [I]n the adult human world dove and serpent coexist" ("Paradoxical" 245).

Leoline proves capable of further folly. Looking at Geraldine with "eyes made up of wonder and love" (567), the Baron allows—indeed, empowers—her to usurp the roles of wife and lover as well as daughter. He has transformed her, in his imagination, into precisely what he needs her to be. But whereas such transformation is similar to what Christabel has done, there is an important difference. Christabel, unlike the two men, does not decisively "read" Geraldine, does not determine her as possessing a significance either good or evil. Christabel does not quite know what to make of her visitor, but in this suspension—in her exercise of negative capability, one might say—Christabel's response is the most fruitful and legitimate. Leoline and Bracy strictly limit Geraldine's significance, thereby denying the social and experiential complexity she embodies. Leoline even seems to benefit from her presence, but his restoration is merely a return to the past, a life-denying course as enervating as the Baron's daily reminder that ours—his, at least—is a world of death.

Critics have understood Geraldine as evil because she usurps the roles of lover, daughter, and wife, but these usurpations are made possible only by Leoline and Christabel. Nor are they entirely detrimental, for they themselves partake, necessarily, of Geraldine's own complexity. This is particularly and importantly true as regards Christabel. Geraldine is able to dominate Christabel to the extent that "the maid, devoid of guile and sin" begins to assume some of Geraldine's characteristics, yet she also dreads Christabel, as though aware that the power she has over Christabel—perhaps even her very existence—is a function of Christabel's desire. Geraldine also seems to regard the spirit of the mother as a potential equal. And rightly so, for Geraldine and the mother lay claim to much of the same psychic territory. The mother, after all, combines and reconciles both sexuality and community, and it is on the path to these that Geraldine has come to set Christabel. Geraldine is seen as a proto-mother and mother surrogate because to a considerable extent that is what she is. By encouraging Christabel's sexual awareness, Geraldine prepares the girl for the eventual establishment of her own domestic community.

The greatest threat to Christabel and to the integrity of Leoline's world thus comes not from Geraldine but from the Baron himself, for his is the greatest error, the most subversive self-delusion—and thus the supernatural intruder must be female. A male, while a more direct substitute for the distant knight, could not be a surrogate daughter/ lover to Leoline, and his misappropriation of Geraldine's energy is thematically vital. Christabel, after all, senses that something is wrong, or, perhaps more accurately, that something is *different,* which is precisely true and precisely as it should be. Bracy, the poem's only artist figure, misunderstands what Geraldine represents. Like the conservative Gothic novelists, he perceives the supernatural as evil, as threat, and in Coleridge's cautionary and directive poem, warns the reader against making the same mistake. But Bracy can do very little damage; he, after all, is only a functionary in the castle's ordinary reality. The orderer of that world—and it is clear this order is inadequate—is the autocratic Leoline.

The Baron is entirely self-deceived; his demonstrated incapacity to perceive the imaginative, the poetic, and the psychological leads him to deny the value of experience, to pervert its wild energy and shape it into something it is not—or, rather, that it only partially is. The imaginative or "daemonic" energy Geraldine represents for Christabel captivates the senescent Baron, and he appropriates Geraldine for his own—she goes along because she is never more than what others want her to be—making of her his long-dead wife, deliberately estranging his daughter so that he alone may feed on Geraldine's energy of experience. There is something of the lamia in Geraldine, to be sure, but as well there is something of the vampire in Leoline, renewing his youth with another's vital energies. He misreads Bracy's dream so that he will benefit from this experience only as he wishes to, only as it fits his predetermined needs, and therefore he will not gain from it what he could. His myopic imaginative vision strictly circumscribes the value of psychological and poetic insight.

"Christabel" reveals, with its deliberate ambiguity, that the imaginative exploration of our inner depths and resources uncovers both good and evil, lamiae and angels, day and night; and few Romantics registered these conflicts more acutely than did Coleridge. Geraldine is the poem's recognition of this duality, for her supernaturalism signifies our inner experience given "outness," the Berkeleian term Coleridge frequently employed. Geraldine can enter Langdale Hall only because she is carried in by Christabel, and there could be no more apt symbol of the relationship of the Coleridgean supernatural to the human. Geraldine works her spell on Christabel in the girl's bedroom, that "chamber carved so curiously, / Carved with figures strange and sweet, / All made out of the carver's brain" (178–80). Embodying the duality of Geraldine's character—it is both "strange and sweet"—the bedroom becomes a symbol of the human mind, the abiding place of reason and imagination, of that aspect of our Selves the supernatural affects and that aspect with which we misunderstand the nonrational. The "problem" in "Christabel" is not that Geraldine gains entrance to the castle; the presence of the supernatural is not alarming, for it is only a projection of inner truth. The problem arises when these inner truths are not properly understood or acted upon. Christabel's overprotected innocence is corrected by encounter with Geraldine's experience, and the seemingly magical power and confidence the encounter provides temporarily overwhelms the unprepared Christabel. Her chief consolation is that experience, as pleasurable as it is painful, becomes the foundation of a mature and informed life.

The ostensible completion schemes advanced by James Gillman and others are irrelevant, for the poem needs no completion. "Christabel," best understood as a companion piece to "The Rime," is a cautionary tale about the misuse of the imaginative powers and about the lessons to be gained from supernaturalism's psychological insights. In one sense, "Christabel" is a warning to those readers of "The Rime" who, like Anna Barbauld, dismissed the poem as without morals, or as a fanciful and meaningless ballad imitation. Coleridge's supernatural was a psychological lexicon—something undoubtedly learned from the Gothic novelists but pushed to greater levels of intensity and insight by Coleridge—and "Christabel" is a powerful statement of the dangers of reductive misunderstanding. Completion of the poem was unnecessary, and the poem's fragmentary nature is not the result of Coleridge's own inability to understand the ambiguity of Geraldine. Completion would have made heavy-handed a point already well developed, and we know how conscious Coleridge was of the didacticism of "The Rime." His inability or refusal to complete "Christabel" constitutes a recognition of the prominence of morals already in the poem. Norman Fruman argues that "The universe of both the Ancient Mariner and Geraldine is all the more terrifying for the confusion as to whether they are as much victims as aggressors" (358–59), but the supernatural in these poems helps us to see that the poems do not turn on a victim/aggressor duality as much as they do on innocence/ experience, on insular, protracted childhood in opposition to maturing knowledge of the self and, by extension, the place of self in the world. The Ancient Mariner must, like Odysseus, sail for his identity; Christabel must step outside the stifling walls of Langdale. The Mariner returns to tell his tale, to bring to the human community the truth of his experience; Christabel introduces her completing experience into her familiar world, and Coleridge here demonstrates the need for us to read these experiences properly.

The point is driven home in the poem's conclusion, which mirrors the preface by lifting the reader abruptly out of the supernatural, Gothic world of the poem and returning to the ordinary, the fully human. Beyond providing symmetry and closure, such a strategy also reaffirms the pertinence of the poem; it is a text that does not leave its significance in the romance world of the medieval ballad.

The conclusion to part II, originally written in a letter for Coleridge's son Hartley, is not the patchwork ending for which some critics have taken it. It may be read, in fact, as a summary of the core of "Christabel," its emotional drama expressive, "in a clear and direct manner, of the feelings animating the more obscurely complicated drama of the two preceding sections" (Shapiro 69).

The little child—"a limber elf," "A fairy thing"—embodies the magical/imaginative experience Geraldine brings within the castle. Receptive to this magic, the father, like Christabel, discovers in the experience a curious blending of joy and pain: "And pleasures flow in so thick and fast / Upon his heart, that he at last / Must needs express his love's excess / With words of unmeant bitterness" (662–65). The father, aware that "in a world of sin . . . / Such giddiness of heart and brain / Comes seldom save from rage and pain" (673–76), is not unlike Christabel in her intuitive perception of the dual aspect of experience, although the father is more conscious of this duality. The Mariner too knows the mingling of love and pain, guilt and joy, and we shall see the same question addressed by Keats in his lamia poem.

For Coleridge, however, what matters about Geraldine is not her lamia heritage but her value as a supernatural signifier, and as such she is not the avatar of horror or chaos she would have been for

Gothic writers. Instead she betokens the fullness and energy of the capable human soul engaging life in all its complexity, balancing its extremes: it is not so much that "in Geraldine Coleridge has reconciled malignancy with bliss" (Holstein 119), but that by embodying both polarities, Geraldine demonstrates the need for a recognition of evil and good, angel and devil. The poem is about Christabel's need to effect the same reconciliation, and about the "strange and sweet" consequences for our childhood world when we begin to grow into adult vision. The reductive visions of Bracy and Leoline are the warning markers between which Christabel needs to steer, object lessons on how the desire to avoid the moral and emotional complexities of life can lead to sterility and isolation. Coleridge learned much from the Gothic writers but not their easy answers or their metaphysical despair, and his refusal to inscribe the supernatural as either good or bad or nonexistent emphatically declares his distance from the Gothic project.

Noting the presence of tragedy's formalist elements in the poem, Marjorie Levinson contributes importantly to an explanation of Coleridge's Gothic revisionism in "Christabel": "By conjoining the subjectivity, fantasy, and sensationalism associated with romance with the impersonal, fatalistic severity of tragedy, Coleridge would effectively naturalize the supernatural" (84). Such naturalization, effected through the interiorization of what Levinson calls Coleridge's "gothic intensity," is the foundation of Coleridge's supernaturalist revisionism, a gesture of redemption and recovery that shifts the Gothic focus inward. Deploying the tropes of Gothic fiction against what he understood to be the intellectual and philosophical deficiencies of the Gothic, Coleridge initiated a new and distinctly modern supernatural aesthetic, one both intensely personal and compellingly social. In this powerful combination, Coleridge's influential supernaturalism became capable of carrying the burden of Romantic inquiry, sounding the murky depths of self while peering into the shadowed complexities of our necessary sociality.

Chapter Five

"Inquire Not if the Faery Race"

Wordsworthian Supernaturalism

Wordsworth could never be mistaken for a proponent of the Romantic supernatural; his task in the *Lyrical Ballads,* after all, was to write of "subjects . . . chosen from ordinary life." Yet consideration of the supernatural sublime in Romantic thought and in Wordsworth specifically reveals that he was, in some important ways, affected by the Romantic supernatural project. The efficacy of the supernatural for Gothic writers has, we have begun to see with Coleridge, been denied or superseded for the Romantic poet; Wordsworth is a willing, even eager, party to this reappraisal, not only in his youthful Gothic pieces but throughout his career.

Wordsworth's repudiation of the supernatural sublime has, like Coleridge's, a theoretical basis in his understanding of conventional sublimity. In "The Sublime and the Beautiful," written for his *Guide to the Lakes,* Wordsworth proposes a sublime moment that, in its insistence on "intense unity," is a departure from much eighteenth-century sublime theory and is of course greatly indebted to Coleridge.

What W. P. Albrecht calls Wordsworth's "sublime of vision" (to distinguish it from the "visual sublime" of most eighteenth-century thinkers) is characterized most importantly by the effect it achieves, a powerful linking of the object and subject of the sublime perception. For Wordsworth, as for Coleridge and Kant, there is in the moment of sublimity not a separation of perceiver and perceived but a conjoining of them, a necessary linking that takes place through and in the mind:

> To talk of an object being sublime or beautiful in itself, without references to some subject by whom that sublimity or beauty is perceived, is absurd; nor is it of the slightest importance to mankind whether there be any object with which their minds are conversant that Men would universally agree (after having ascertained that the words were used in the same sense) to denominate sublime or beautiful. (*Prose* I: 357)

Qualities of the sublime object are devalued in favor of what the mind experiences in that moment and in favor of the characteristics of the mind that sublimity heightens, calls into play, and demands.

In Wordsworth's sublime, "the mind creates a vision in which visual images lose their identity in a transcendent oneness" (Albrecht, "Tragedy" 86). Unlike Kant, Wordsworth

> does not make the imagination, with its reliance on natural forms, go down to defeat before another faculty superior in moral comprehension and religious insight. The imagination . . . serves the supersensible not by proving itself inadequate to vision but by embracing a consciousness of ultimate and immeasurable power, power which aggrandizes the mind. (Albrecht, "Tragedy" 85)[1]

This "Power" is one of the most consequential elements of the Wordsworthian sublime:

> Power awakens the sublime either when it rouses us to a sympathetic energy & calls upon the mind to grasp at something towards which it can make approaches but which it is incapable of attaining—yet so that it participates force which is acting upon it; or, 2dly, by producing a humiliation or prostration of the mind before some external agency which it presumes not to make an effort to participate, but is absorbed in the contemplation of the might in the external power, &, as far as it has any consciousness of itself, its grandeur subsists in the naked fact of being conscious of external Power at once awful & immeasurable; so that, in both cases, the head & the front of the sensation is intense unity. (*Prose* I: 354)

Wordsworth here employs language characteristic of earlier exposi-
tions of the sublime—"incapable of attaining," "prostration of the
mind"—but the passage simultaneously underscores the difference between the Wordsworthian sublime and that of Burke and other eighteenth-century theorists. (I take it as instructive that Albert Wlecke's
discussion of the Wordsworthian sublime relegates its discussion of
Burke to a footnote, although other eighteenth-century theorists are
discussed in Wlecke's text.) Burke's emphasis on terror was fundamentally incompatible with Wordsworth's aesthetic, since for Wordsworth the simple consciousness of "external Power" is enough to
intimate directly the "intense unity" that renders the sublime a positive experience. The mind need not, as in other formulations of sublimity, convert the failure of transcendence into a compensatory
suggestion that the numinous in nature resides behind a veil of impen-
etrable obscurity and grandeur. For Wordsworth, human perception
of natural Power is evidence enough that we are at one with the transcendent presence immanent in that Power. Wordsworth could figure
the sublime's loss of self as a suspension or abeyance, but as such it is
far from the Gothic rendition of a soul suspended in horror over a
yawning gulf.

A clear sense of the Wordsworthian sublime pervades "Tintern
Abbey," where the poet speculates that to the "beauteous forms" of
nature he is indebted for a special "gift / Of aspect . . . sublime":

> that blessed mood
> In which the burthen of the mystery,
> In which the heavy and the weary weight
> Of all this unintelligible world,
> Is lightened . . . .
> Until, the breath of this corporeal frame
> And even the motion of our human blood
> Almost suspended, we are laid asleep
> In body, and become a living soul;
> While with an eye made quiet by the power
> Of harmony, and the deep power of joy,
> We see into the life of things. (37–49)

As will later prove true for Percy Shelley, Wordsworth's sense of metaphysical plenitude and of participation that derive from the natural
sublime render the supernatural, as a means of literary spiritual inquiry, decidedly uncongenial or unnecessary. Lawrence Kramer, writing of the "daemonic" in Coleridge and Wordsworth, finds that for

the latter poet recovery from the experience of pure imagination (never figured by Wordsworth in supernatural imagery) involves "a return to ordinary consciousness, but it is also an assimilation of the daemonic into ordinary consciousness, which appears as an enrichment both in the self and the world" (300). The result is a visionary consciousness fundamental to Wordsworth's mature poetics. Kramer additionally finds the Wordsworthian daemonic, with its experience of fulfillment, to be "a dialectical rejection of the Coleridgean mode" of the daemonic (312), a claim supported by comparison of the poets' use of the supernatural. Coleridge discovers in the supernatural an expressive and cogent means of interior scrutiny, of bringing to the surface and embodying the "mingled measure" of pain and bliss that characterizes his interior world. Wordsworth's calmer meditations, free of Coleridge's terrors, rejected the need for such imagery. Neither demons nor daemons are invoked by recollection in tranquillity; dejection, melancholy, and remorse are much more suitable for providing the energy and the cause of their summoning.

The Wordsworthian imagination fills, then, the lacuna that traditionally characterized the experience of sublimity. Albrecht explains that "the visionary sublime—since, through association, it brings into play the mind's resources of thought and feeling—adds a degree of cognition missing in merely visual sublimity. Wordsworth's sublime not only presupposes moral judgment but results in moral and possibly religious insight" ("Tragedy" 93). This religious insight or "spiritual reach," to use Albrecht's term, is not the disturbing vision granted by the supernatural sublime in *The Monk* or *Melmoth* but an achievement of consolation and fulfillment. Crossing the Alps (and remembering the experience in *The Prelude*), Wordsworth records a veritable catalogue of sublime objects—"the immeasurable height / Of woods decaying," "The stationary blasts of waterfalls," "Winds thwarting winds," "Black drizzling crags"—and finds these images of "tumult and peace" to be "like workings of one mind, the features / Of the same face, blossoms upon one tree; / Characters of the great Apocalypse, / The types and symbols of Eternity, / Of first, and last, and midst, and without end" (VI: 636–40). Other passages of comparable Wordsworthian achievement could be adduced, but surely enough has been said to reveal how for Wordsworth Nature initiates the experience in which the individual mind receives intimations of transcendent plenitude.

While Wordsworth admits the possibility of fear in experiences of sublimity that grow out of control, these experiences (as was true for

Kant and Burke) lose the character of sublimity once fear becomes predominant. In Wordsworth's language, "But if that Power which is exalted above our sympathy impresses the mind with personal fear, so as the sensation becomes more lively than the impression or thought of the exciting cause, then self-consideration & all its accompanying littleness takes place of the sublime, & wholly excludes it" (*Prose* I: 354). Fear may have an instructive value for Wordsworth, as the famous boat-stealing episode in Book I of *The Prelude* illustrates, but the dark form of the "huge peak, black and huge" is not sublime nor is its troubling presence the final word on the experience, as it might be in a Gothic fiction.

For Wordsworth sublimity characteristically "avoids an emphasis, which is found in many commentaries, upon the violence and the uniqueness of the experience" (Wlecke 81). Additionally, the poet's sense of the religious significance of the sublime never forces Wordsworth, as it did some Gothic writers, to see fear as having in and of itself metaphysical implications. Writing of Wordsworth, Owen points out that the sublime "is an aesthetic based on the concept of *terror removed*" ("Aesthetics" 79); the *presence* of terror thus demands an aesthetic counter to that which interested Wordsworth. Only in his youthful works, in a poetic project soon abandoned, did Wordsworth even experiment with "natural scenes which directly convey terror, not the awe or the modified or remote terror of the Burkean or Wordsworthian sublime" ("Aesthetics" 79).

It is unremarkable that Wordsworth detects no special significance in the terror produced by the supernatural, for he refers in his essay on the sublime to

> that intermixture of the terrible & the ludicrous which dramatists who understand the constitution of the human mind have not infrequently represented when they introduce a character disturbed by an agency supernatural or horrible to a degree beyond what the mind is prepared to expect from the ordinary course of human calamities or affliction. (*Prose* I: 359)

Wordsworth's deliberate closing-off of the implications of such experiences resolutely denies the possibility of a supernatural sublime.

Seeking, in the *Ballads* at least, and as Coleridge reported the division of labor, "to excite a feeling analogous to the supernatural" (*BL* II: 7) but eschewing direct invocation of supernature, "Wordsworth preserves the self from all (including mythic) encroachments because the self is not this or that but *between*. He guarantees man his own realm without separating him fatally from nature or supernature" (Hartman, *Poetry* 198). In his delineation of the mind's visionary agility, imagistically dependent upon yet continually striving beyond material nature, Wordsworth successfully walks a fine poetic line between the natural and the supernatural, consistently finding that the supernatural is an unnecessary element in the mind's visionary apparatus.

As concerned as any writer of his moment with the transcendent, Wordsworth always found in the natural world sufficient material for the contemplation of transcendence. Indeed—and this departure from Gothic convention forms the foundation of Wordsworth's anti-supernaturalism—for Wordsworth the natural world was not "beneath" or "this side of" the supernatural world but superior to it, a hierarchy evident in the early "An Evening Walk" (1788–1789):

> 'Mid groves of clouds that crest the mountain's brow,
> And round the west's proud lodge their shadows throw,
> Like Una shining on her gloomy way,
> The half-seen form of Twilight roams astray . . . .
> With restless interchange at once the bright
> Wins on the shade, the shade upon the light.
> No favoured eye was e'er allowed to gaze
> On lovelier spectacle in faery days. . . . (289–92, 297–300)

Light and shadow interact with mountain and cloud to create an imaginative experience as fanciful and compelling as any to be found in the purely imaginative realms of literary supernaturalism. Wordsworth would privilege this natural aesthetic throughout his poetic career, as demonstrated by the following lines from *The Prelude* in which the poet, recalling his Cambridge days, describes an ash tree growing alone amid a grove of elms he would visit in winter:

> Often have I stood
> Foot-bound uplooking at this lovely tree
> Beneath a frosty moon. The hemisphere
> Of magic fiction, verse of mine perchance
> May never tread; but scarcely Spenser's self
> Could have more tranquil visions in his youth,
> Or could more bright appearances create
> Of human forms with superhuman powers,
> Than I beheld loitering on calm clear nights
> Alone, beneath this fairy work of earth. (VI: 85–94)

With the world of physical nature presenting such "bright appearances" to the aesthetic or visionary imagination, Wordsworth had little need for the supernatural. Distancing himself in the above passage from Britain's greatest practitioner of the romance fantastic, Wordsworth simultaneously declares his distance from the supernatural.

An episode in the fourth book of *The Excursion* provides valuable insight into Wordsworth's assessment of the ontological inferiority of the supernatural. Imagining "The face which rural solitude might wear / To the unenlightened swains of pagan Greece" (849–50), Wordsworth concludes that the supernatural of Greek myth is founded on misperception of the natural world:

> Sunbeams, upon distant hills
> Gliding apace, with shadows in their train,
> Might, with small help from fancy, be transformed
> Into fleet Oreads sporting visibly.
> . . . .
> Withered boughs grotesque,
> Stripped of their leaves and twigs by hoary age,
> From depth of shaggy covert peeping forth
> In the low vale, or on steep mountain-side; And, sometimes,
> intermixed with stirring horns
> Of the live deer, or goat's depending beard,—
> These were the lurking Satyrs, a wild brood
> Of gamesome Deities; or Pan himself,
> The simple shepherd's awe-inspiring God! (873–76, 879–87)

The supernatural is derived from the natural in consequence of aberrant perception; little wonder Wordsworth was reluctant to use it in his examination of the natural world, especially given his belief that Nature "oft times . . . takes / The work of Fancy from her willing hands; / And such a beautiful creation makes / As renders needless spells and magic wands" (Sonnet XVIII of "Memorials of a Tour on the Continent 1820" 1–4). Untransmuted natural experience is for him the preferred subject of study, richer as it is in the truths of nature, especially given his insistence that the first of the "powers requisite for the production of poetry" is "the ability to observe with accuracy things as they are in themselves, and with fidelity to describe them . . ." (Preface of 1815; *Poems* II: 907). As Keats would later disagree, Fancy is very much for Wordsworth a "deceiving elf," subversive of poetic perception; Fancy certainly can, for Wordsworth, cheat as well as she is famed to do. Wordsworth circumvents deception by extending the process outlined above: when Fancy is invoked, "humanity and Nature work reciprocally" under its influence, thereby limiting Fancy's implications to commentary on the concrete worlds of the human and the natural (Owen, "Charm" 9), or to "the discovery of unapprehended relations" (Jones 44).

Given such an aesthetic, Wordsworth's unsympathetic response to contemporary supernaturalism is hardly surprising. In an oft-quoted passage from the 1802 Preface, Wordsworth laments those "multitude of causes, unknown to former times [that] are now acting with a combined force to blunt the discriminating powers of the mind, and, unfitting it for all voluntary exertion, to reduce it to a state of almost savage torpor" (*Poems* I: 872). He identifies as some of these forces "frantic novels, sickly and stupid German Tragedies, and deluges of idle and extravagant stories in verse" (*Poems* I: 873). Wordsworth deprecates "this degrading thirst after outrageous stimulation," a comment that certainly points to the Gothic, among other things.

Yet Wordsworth himself was not immune, at least in his poetic apprenticeship, to the influence and attractions of Gothicism. The early fragment "Vale of Esthwaite," composed when Wordsworth was in his teens and never published during his lifetime, employs conventional Gothic images: "Now did I love the dismal gloom / Of haunted Castle's panelled room / Listening the wild wind's wailing song / Whistling the rattling doors among . . ." (246–49). A mysterious "female form" leads the young poet "to a dungeon deep" with a bloody "coffer" where, with suitable melodramatics, she abandons him. His attempt at escape fails: "I moved—a form unseen I found / Twist round my hand an icy chain / And drag me to the spot again" (271–73).

This scene is followed immediately by the somewhat embarrassed and self-conscious confession that "these were poor and puny joys / Fond sickly Fancy's idle toys" (274–75). The poet later conjures up more ghosts and a "tall thin Spectre," as well as personifications of Murder, Suicide, and Madness. But little weight should be brought to bear on a fragmentary juvenile effusion that Wordsworth seems understandably to have suppressed, especially one that features, near its conclusion, a Prospero-like dismissal of the supernatural: "Adieu, ye forms of Fear that float / Wild on the shipwreck of the thought" (557–58). While it may be that Wordsworth did not know precisely what it was to which he was bidding farewell, as Geoffrey Hartman claims, it seems likely that in this early poem Wordsworth declares "his intention to put off childish things: either all poetry, because imagination and the social principles are at odds, or fantasy in favor of a poetry dealing with social man" (Hartman, *Poetry* 77). The facts of Wordsworth's life prove the latter was the case.

Irving Buchen uses Wordsworth's Gothic poems to corroborate this increasing poetic preference for the human and the social: chronologically dividing Wordsworth's Gothic pieces into two groups, Buchen finds the second and later one characterized by a much more restrained Gothicism. The poems of Buchen's first group ("Esthwaite" and "Guilt and Sorrow" are representative) are marked by "the essential fear [of] madness," and all are "artistically blemished and didactically burdensome" (86). Those of the second set ("The Thorn," "Hart-Leap Well," "Goody Blake," the Lucy poems, et al.), while thematically consonant with the first in their concern with madness and alienation, are artistically more sophisticated, by which Buchen means "the gothic machinery is no longer dominant or dominating. It is either done away with altogether or normalized into believable superstitions" (91). Buchen concludes that

> just as later in *The Prelude* Wordsworth is to exclude from his own story those elements that were so peculiar to himself as to jeopardize typicality, so Wordsworth had to shift from characters who are exceptionally villainous to those who are ordinarily distortive. But to do so, he had to find a mode that would support the transition from the peculiar to the recurrent and that would adjust the transmutation of gothic to normal psychology. This mode was the lyrical ballad. (93)

It is worth remarking that even in his earliest Gothic pieces Wordsworth, perhaps affected more than he acknowledged by Gothic fiction's blending of sublimity and supernaturalism, relied heavily on landscapes. Undoubtedly such a dependence manifests Wordsworth's characteristic reliance on place and nature, but Clifford Siskin remarks on a telling similarity between this aspect of Wordsworth's early poetry and the work of some Gothic writers: "Wordsworth's struggle to qualify the insistent Gothicism of his early works by reconciling the mind's imaginative impulses to the solidities of landscape parallels the [early Gothic] novelists' struggle to realize Walpole's Gothic goal of blending romance and novel, Fancy and Nature" (161). Espousing a poetics in which the imaginative is foundationally dependent upon the natural, Wordsworth labored to maintain the linkage even as he experimented with the material most likely to disrupt it. His experience

with Gothic tropes in these early poems served to uncover their inadequacies, and he did not so much reconcile the fantastic with the natural as he revealed the superfluity of the former.

The rapid development of Wordsworth's thought early in his career
reinforces the caveat that the other Gothic juvenilia ("Dirge Sung by
a Minstrel" and "A Ballad ['Will you leave me thus alone']") be
treated with circumspection. As Hartman explains, Wordsworth's
early sense of a "daemonic" or supernatural nature "is a sign that
imagination is beginning to reveal itself as a power separate from or
even opposed to nature" (*Poetry* 85), and the chief consequence of the
soul's "intense effort not to know its own separateness" (86) is to
transform nature into a hostile, terrifying power. And while the "conflict . . . between the homeless and the naturalized imagination . . . [is]
never to be quieted" (89), Wordsworth comes to accept "the autonomy of his imagination" (41) enough to dispense with the Gothic
troping of nature and to see that, while "the imagination must separate from nature," the separation is "part of a process providentially
encouraged by nature itself" (135). The beneficence of nature permits
Wordsworth to abandon his Gothic landscapes; in those poems that
record the process of recovery from his separation anxiety—"Tintern
Abbey" comes readily to mind—the absence of the Gothic is virtually
complete.

Yet this recovery was not effected before Wordsworth wrote other
Gothic pieces. "Guilt and Sorrow" (composed mainly in 1793) has
been identified closely with the Gothic by Oscar Campbell and Paul
Mueschke, largely on the basis of the imagery in its opening stanzas:
the storm-ravaged wasteland, the body in gibbet irons, and tales of
murder and hidden corpses. These critics find that Wordsworth's
"paraphernalia of terror" is, like that of the young Percy Shelley,
largely derivative,[2] yet their dismissal of the poem as an "aesthetic
patchwork" and a "failure" ("Study" 302), while perhaps not without
some foundation, may lead us to overlook important features of the
work. While the poem does surrender its aesthetic of terror in favor
of one of "sentimental morality" (further evidence of the influence of
Radcliffe and others), to see these aesthetic tendencies as "distinct and
inharmonious" ("Study" 302–3) is misleading. Terror and sentimentality are frequent companions in Gothic fiction; indeed, as MacAndrew and others have established, the Gothic owes much to the
eighteenth-century novel of sentiment. In linking the two Wordsworth
did not fail in his artistry; he simply followed standard Gothic practice. His error was in keeping the two aesthetic modes so sharply

apart. The Gothic atmosphere in "Guilt and Sorrow" is dissipated too abruptly: the phrase "But soon his voice and words of kind intent / Banished that dismal thought . . ." (190–91) signals the complete disappearance of the Gothic machinery. Wordsworth himself recognized that by neither talent nor disposition was he favorably disposed to the Gothic, but while "Guilt and Sorrow" 's dismissal is certainly clumsy, it casts a valuable light on Wordsworth's aesthetics. The Gothic materials have fully served their purpose, that being—as was typical, especially in Radcliffe and the other conservative Gothicists who were Wordsworth's models—to serve as objective correlative for the mood of the guilt-haunted protagonist. Most telling is that the Gothic elements in "Guilt and Sorrow" are employed strictly to enhance a moral, rather than epistemological or metaphysical point, for while technical awkwardness in employing a literary device may be mastered, a belief in the strictly circumscribed and subordinate value of the supernatural is something much less likely to change.

The last explicitly Gothic piece Wordsworth wrote (at the age of twenty-six) was the piece now known as "Fragment of a Gothic Tale" (1796), some two-hundred-plus lines of energetic description in the finest Gothic tradition, many of which made their way into *The Borderers.* The Gothicness of the fragment (and of the drama) is again Radcliffean, for the dungeon-haunting "grim shape" turns out to be human, and the terror generated is, as with "Guilt and Sorrow," strictly subordinate to the moral theme. In another essay continuing their study of Wordsworth's aesthetics, Campbell and Mueschke find that the Gothicism of *The Borderers,* while still in tension with an aesthetics of sentimentality and pity, is much more successfully integrated because it is more clearly subordinate and limited in its use ("Development" 480–81), a finding corroborated by Buchen. In this drama, Campbell and Mueschke argue, Wordsworth achieved the first tentative grasp of his mature poetics, one that depended upon a rejection of Godwinian rationalism and the centrality of recollection to transform both horror and pity "into the peace which is the essential quality of the aesthetic experience" ("Development" 481). While such a reading remains open to dispute—Hartman argues that the drama denies the possibility that moral action can be predicated on the intellect and offers no positive morality to counteract this failing ("Murder" *passim*)—it is significant that after the "Fragment" Wordsworth experimented no further with explicitly Gothic material, a clear indication of new aesthetic interests.

These interests—in the natural, in the personal community—

quickly drew Wordsworth away from the Gothic excesses of his youth. Book V of *The Prelude,* dealing with various aspects of the poet's aesthetic and intellectual growth, makes reference to "that delightful time of growing youth, / When craving for the marvellous gives way / To strengthening love for things that we have seen" (539–41). These lines express the quintessentially Wordsworthian opposition between things seen (people and places of phenomenal nature) and the marvellous (those purely imaginative, derivative, and insubstantial creations of the "sickly" Fancy). Wordsworth comes to condemn "the sensationalism characteristic of his early poems because he believes it dulls the ability of the mind to respond to, and therefore learn from, literature and life" (Siskin 165). For Wordsworth, reliance on fancy and the supernatural became anathema to the requirements of his personal poetic quest.

His gradual rejection of the supernatural is recorded by Wordsworth in the Lucy poems, which taken as a group testify to his growth away from the aesthetics of Gothicism. I concur with David Ferry's assessment that "It is the poet's imagination which is finally the subject matter of these poems" (79), and while Ferry's reading of them as a study of the mystical versus the sacramental understanding of nature that so concerned Wordsworth is convincing, they speak also to another aspect of the imagination. The first four of the five Lucy poems were written in Germany, a country associated by the British reading public with Gothic horrors, with "sickly and stupid German Tragedies" and "frantic novels." While there is no Gothicism in these brief poems, they do form a serial meditation on the relative value of the "fantastic" imagination.

"Strange fits of passion have I known" is the poem of startling discovery, of the poet's realization that the world of fancy undermines the integrity of his moral and social universe. Fancy's intrusion into the world of ordinary emotional intercourse is registered as an aberration and disturbance; the narrator, recollecting his fit of passion, makes his poem an act of confession, one fit only for sympathetic ears: "I will dare to tell, / But in the Lover's ear alone, / What once to me befell" (3–5). The poet's need to *dare* the act of discourse alerts us to the disquieting nature of his experience.

The action of the poem transpires under the magical moon of "Peter Bell" and "The Ancient Mariner," and the narrator's having "fixed [his] eye" on the moon signals the fantastic rapture, the imaginative indulgence in the worlds of fancy and romance and a (mistaken) belief that in their fanciful exuberance they adequately address the richness and complexity of human life.

For Wordsworth such indulgence conflicts with the world of the actual and with clear perception of the thing itself. The narrator remains rapt as he travels—"And all the while my eyes I kept / On the descending moon" (19–20)—but the hypnotized gaze is both deceiving and deceived. The narrator overindulges and overreaches, fastening onto an object (the symbolic correlative for a mode of "low" poetic vision) that is not of the ordinary world. Allowing his poetic imagination to be transfixed by the impossibly distant and inconstant object, the narrator fails to determine accurately his own position among and relationships with the objects of life and nature: his failure to account for the change in perspective that attends the ascent of a hill deceives him into thinking the moon has "At once" dropped behind Lucy's cottage.

"Kind Nature's gentlest boon" becomes Wordsworth's ironic comment on the "sweet dreams" of Fancy's rapture. While sweet for their duration, these dreams are traumatically undone in the necessary return to the ordinary world, or in the unconscious recognition that they are at odds with the world of the real. The narrator never explicitly acknowledges he has erred, that the moon has not really dropped; he instead reacts only to his faulty perception, itself made possible by a combination of his "Otherworldly" obsession and his movement in the real world of physical nature. These two phenomena conflict, thereby producing the shock and illogic of the narrator's reaction: "What fond and wayward thoughts will slide / Into a Lover's head! / 'O mercy!' to myself I cried, / 'If Lucy should be dead!' " (25–28). The subsequent poems' proving the narrator correct does not justify his problematic mode of seeing.

We recall from *A Midsummer Night's Dream* that "the lunatic, the lover and the poet / Are of imagination all compact" and that one of the consequences of their shared disorder is that "Lovers and madmen have such seething brains, / Such shaping fantasies, that apprehend / More than cool reason ever comprehends." Wordsworth has provided his reading of the effect of these shaping fantasies in his portrayal of the morbid self-indulgence of his self-hoodwinked narrator. "Cool reason" would teach him that the image which leads to his "fond and wayward" speculation is a false one: the moon did not set, its apparent motion and speed merely a consequence of the narrator's uphill movement. The shaping fantasies of romance (and, by extension, Gothic supernaturalism, equally overdependent on the imaginative misperception of things as they are) are for Wordsworth a trap and an illusion. The poem ends unsatisfactorily, the narrator's irrationally arrived at conclusion and his seeming discovery of discontinuity apparently rendering suspect the adequacy of our understanding.

The remaining Lucy poems gradually unfold a resolution. "She dwelt among the untrodden ways" discovers Lucy indeed to be dead, confirming the emotional truth of "Strange fits of passion" without validating the means by which this truth was determined. The earlier discontinuity between the narrator's fancy and the earthly reality of Lucy has here been overcome: the emotional correspondence between the narrator and Lucy's condition is now direct and free of distortion. It is, however, free of comprehension as well, so this poem too must end on a note of privation. The narrator-poet's understanding of Lucy's condition needs still to be freed from his emotionally charged solipsism—"But she is in her grave, and, oh, / The difference to me!" (11–12)—so that he might accurately assess the significance of what has befallen Lucy. Only then will his understanding be accompanied by his own return to the earthly world, to nature as it is, free of the distortions imposed by imaginative indulgence. "She dwelt among the untrodden ways" is only the first step of this return.

"Three years she grew in sun and shower" finds Lucy's spirit assimilated into Nature, calm in the "happy dell" of a transcendent animistic union. The poet-narrator, however, remains affected only by the fact of his loss of Lucy, her happiness matched only by his quiet despair: "She died, and left to me / This heath, this calm, and quiet scene; / The memory of what has been, / And never more will be" (39–42). Still we are left with an unsatisfactory resolution, a sharp contrast of Lucy's union and the narrator's lingering dissatisfaction with his place in time and nature.

"A slumber did my spirit seal" opens by confirming the alienation of the poet-narrator: "I had no human fears," he reports, but this is not the condition of the "sweet dreams" in the first poem. "Kind Nature's gentlest boon" has been replaced by an ossification of spirit, an inability of the "thinking heart" to determine Lucy's true state. "She *seemed* a thing that could not feel / The touch of earthly years" (3–4; emphasis added) is what the narrator reports, but "seemed" alerts us to the centrality of perception (the narrator's) in this poem.

At the same time, the emotional correspondence of "She dwelt. . ." is in the process of being supplemented by partial comprehension; this poem of transition reveals the beginning of the narrator's intuitive grasp of the significance of Lucy's death, if not yet his own reaction to it. The tense shift between the two stanzas signals this nascent understanding. In the first stanza the narrator's spirit was sealed in slumber (the past tense is crucial) but has now begun to awaken. His earlier sense that Lucy was beyond time—"She seemed a thing that could not feel / The touch of earthly years"—is in the second stanza replaced not only by the recognition of her mortality—"No motion has she now, no force; / She neither hears nor sees" (5–6)—but also by the sense there is some consolation in her death and incorporation into physical nature. Lucy is "Rolled round in earth's diurnal course, / With rocks, and stones, and trees" (7–8); although he feels himself alienated from her, the narrator is perceptive enough, intuitively if not consciously, to equate Lucy with elements of Nature. She is subject to the same forces as the things of earth—"*With* rocks, and stones, and trees"—and the narrator's list of these objects ends with and emphasizes the only living, organic element. Indeed, J. R. Watson argues that for Wordsworth even stones are invested with animistic energies, a condition that would link Lucy even more emphatically with the natural, the "*terra genetrix*" (183).

As David Ferry observes, "[Lucy's] death was right, after all, for by dying she was [made] one with the natural processes that made her die. . . . [T]he poet's first identification of her was right after all, for she had nothing to do with humanity or mortality, and her true relation was to the world of eternity, from which he was excluded" (78). What must be added is that the narrator is in "She dwelt . . ." only in the process of realizing this metaphysical truth by perceiving Lucy in and through the lens of Nature, not the distracting and deceiving fantastic imagination.

"I travelled among unknown men" takes the final step. The only Lucy poem written in England, this work finds the poet celebrating not only a return to his "own countree" but a return to or achievement of that mode of perception Wordsworth championed, that direct apprehension of the natural world without which its informing "power and presence" are either lost or distorted by the imagination in a way that alienates us, as it did the poet-narrator of the first four Lucy poems, from the consolations of nature.

> I travelled among unknown men,
> In lands beyond the sea;
> Nor, England! did I know till then
> What love I bore to thee.
>
> 'Tis past, that melancholy dream!
> Nor will I quit thy shore

A second time; for still I seem
To love thee more and more. (1–8)

Here the poet's devotion to place and nature also serves as reassurance
of Lucy's continued presence in the narrator's emotional universe. The
opening line of the second stanza marks the poet's emergence from
both the stupefying "sweet dreams" of the first poem and the anesthe-
tized sensitivity of the second through fourth. Receptive now to the
consolations of place and of being-in-nature, the poet is able as well
to respond positively to Lucy's memory, as the final stanza, an apos-
trophe to England, reveals: "Thy mornings showed, thy nights
concealed, / The bowers where Lucy played; / And thine too is the last
green field / That Lucy's eyes surveyed" (13–16). Having returned to
his native place, relocated himself in his familiar psychosocial matrix,
the poet finally vanquishes his alienation and despair and in his recovery rescues not only Lucy's memory but his own poetic vision. In the
early poems, Lucy was discussed in fanciful images of light: she is
equated with the moon, she is "Fair as a star," she "grew in sun and
shower" and shall be dear to "the stars of midnight." In this final
poem the only explicit image of light is one not of fantastic or imaginative reach but of quotidian reality: "And she I cherished turned her
wheel / Beside an English fire." The creative vision that concerns itself
with the images and languages of the imaginative fantastic, with magical moons and stars, distorts the truth of nature, the truth of the
human world. Such a vision, the "fond and wayward thoughts" of
"Strange fits of passion," is here surrendered—as it will be in "Peter
Bell"—for the more satisfyingly practical and familiar illumination of
an English fire.

"Lucy Gray," while not always regarded as one of the Lucy poems,
may be understood as affirming the pattern traced in the first five Lucy
poems. In "Lucy Gray," the young girl is again, as in "I travelled
among unknown men," associated with a familiar and prosaic light,
here a lantern. She mysteriously disappears in a snowstorm, her body
never recovered. Yet what seems to be the poem's narrative simplicity
is complicated by the final two stanzas:

—Yet some maintain that to this day
She is a living child;
That you may see sweet Lucy Gray
Upon the lonesome wild.

> O'er rough and smooth she trips along,
> And never looks behind;
> And sings a solitary song
> That whistles in the wind.

The opening stanza, it turns out, contributes to the confusion: the narrator reports that "Oft I had heard of Lucy Gray: / And, when I crossed the wild, / I chanced to see at break of day / The solitary child." Whether this seeing occurred before or after her death is left uncertain by the poem; Lucy's ontological status has become ambiguous, undecided both in the narrative and by Wordsworth. But the indecision is deliberate, for Lucy Gray, like the Lucy of the other poems, is both present and absent, physically dead but alive in nature, in the whistling of the wind, in a strange half-existence between nature and supernature, natural and human.

*M*any of Wordsworth's longer narrative poems that come closest to the supernatural serve as valuable elaborations upon the aesthetic just outlined, particularly upon its antagonistic conception of nature and supernature. In fact, so antithetical are nature and supernature that the tension between them is not only quite evident even in the most supernatural of these texts, it is often the thematic center of these poems.

"Peter Bell" (1798–1812) is very much concerned with the relative values of the natural and supernatural, especially in its prologue. Critics have even suggested that the urgency with which the poem addresses itself to the supernatural may be explained by Wordsworth's "guilt" over providing Coleridge with some of the supernaturalism in the "Ancient Mariner," including the spectral persecution of the Mariner and the working of the ship by the dead men. The supposition that Wordsworth became uncomfortable with his role, or with what Coleridge made of his suggestions, is prompted by the fact Wordsworth began work on "Peter Bell" shortly after the completion of Coleridge's poem (Charles Smith 58–60).

Wordsworth sets out deliberately to address the matter of supernaturalism and imagination, as the dedicatory letter to Southey (dated 1819) makes explicit. In it, Wordsworth writes of his

> belief that the Imagination not only does not require for its exercise the
> intervention of supernatural agency, but that, though such agency be

excluded, the faculty may be called forth as imperiously, and for kindred results of pleasure, by incidents within the compass of poetic probability, in the humblest departments of daily life. (*Poems* I: 315)

Such an aesthetic is characteristic Wordsworth, certainly, and the prologue of the poem constitutes a narrative affirmation of the letter's theory. The journey through "many a breathless field of light" in the "little Boat" has for the poet some mild attractions, but his experience of imaginative mental territories, of "the realm of Fancy" and "magic lore," finally only reinforces and proves correct his deep devotion to "the matchless Earth." The poet's response to the exhortations of the "gay and beautiful Canoe" becomes, then, a definitive statement of Wordsworth's understanding of the literary supernatural:

> Temptation lurks among your words;
> But, while these pleasures you're pursuing
> Without impediment or let,
> No wonder if you quite forget
> What on the earth is doing.
> . . . .
> Long have I loved what I behold,
> The night that calms, the day that cheers;
> The common growth of mother-earth
> Suffices me—her tears, her mirth
> . . . .
> These given, what more need I desire
> To stir, to soothe, or elevate?
> What nobler marvels than the mind
> May in life's daily prospect find,
> May find or there create? (116–20, 131–34, 141–45)

The movement of the prologue, from the fanciful heights of "the long blue field of ether" to the stone table in the garden, is "the work's main symbol of the poet's choice of earth-bound rather than supernatural subjects" (Randel, "Homecoming" 583), its literal insistence on the superiority of concrete realities and common events over the "shades of palaces and kings" (105). The prologue thus becomes part of Wordsworth's poetic manifesto: that "the imagination can be domesticated, that nature can satisfy a mind which seeks, or used to seek, the supernatural" (Hartman, *Poetry* 18).

In tracing the poet's journey the prologue recasts the supernatural sublime in accord with those principles of the Wordsworthian sublime already adduced. Moving from the world of earth (the normal state the sublime presupposes) into the "suspension" of the heavens (the realm of the fantastic), the poet experiences no awe or terror. The journey into night uncovers no intimations of despair, hostility, or absence; unlike *The Monk*, the prologue discovers in darkness only a source of aesthetic gratification, not the objectification of spiritual vacuity. The assessment of humanity's metaphysical condition is just as readily figured in the movement of each text: *The Monk* probes the shadows of mind and spirit by descending from the world of human life to the subterranean world of the dead; "Peter Bell" 's prologue ascends from earth to the heavens, Western civilization's traditional locus of spiritual consolation and presence, and then returns eagerly to the earth in a validation of the lives and aspirations of ordinary human beings. Neither in its structure nor in particular moments does the prologue endorse or even recognize the supernatural sublime's interrogative project. Indeed, the prologue serves as a powerful poetic statement against even the need for the supernatural sublime, for the poet proves essentially indifferent to what his fantastic voyage reveals.

The poem proper reinforces this indifference, although here the work moves closer to at least a Radcliffean position. The prologue's denial of the supernatural may be a consequence of Wordsworth's close identification with the boat-travelling Poet; in the poem, the character of Peter Bell mediates between Wordsworth and the supernatural and that added distance permits at least a Radcliffean pseudo-supernatural.

"Peter Bell" is doubly important as a Wordsworthian comment on the supernatural because it constitutes a nonsupernatural response to Coleridge's "Ancient Mariner." Yet the differences are more substantive than the similarities. Peter Bell is willfully malicious, unlike the Mariner, and Peter's fundamental problem—"nature ne'er could find the way / Into the heart of Peter Bell" (244–45)—is the inverse of the Mariner's, whose heart has not yet found its way to nature. Peter's vision of nature is intensely literal, hence reductively inadequate:

> In vain, through every changeful year,
> Did Nature lead him as before;
> A primrose by a river's brim
> A yellow primrose was to him,
> And it was nothing more. (246–50)

Like the Mariner, Peter needs to develop an empathic understanding of the natural world; both men must progress from apparently wanton acts of cruelty through an acceptance of guilt to a thorough reappraisal of their engagements with the natural and human worlds. There is no need here for an extended comparison of the two poems;[3] suffice it to say that in Coleridge's hands the tale of the wanderer becomes a traumatic and traumatizing quest for self, while Wordsworth uses a comparable situation to educe a conventional moral tale (Coburn 125)—and it is the "Moral nature" of humanity, after all, that figures as the essential foundation of the Wordsworthian sublime (Albrecht, "Tragedy" 88). His desire to write a nonsupernatural "Ancient Mariner" becomes reminiscent, even imitative, of Reeve's desire to correct the excesses of Walpole, but Wordsworth brings the supernatural so far within the verge of probability that it is all but eliminated. Following the pattern established by Reeve, Wordsworth also emphasizes the moral force of his text, making of Peter Bell's ass-stealing a moral parable one critic labels "Wordsworth's most doctrinaire poem" (Jacobus 266).

Only one element of the "supernatural" remains by the poem's end: the "Spirits of the Mind" that complete Peter's conversion. Charles Patterson's study of the matter is the most cogent; he identifies these spirits with the daemons Wordsworth and Coleridge often discussed at the time ("Bell" 140). Pointing out that these daemons were known to the Romantics primarily through the work of Thomas Taylor the Platonist, Patterson reports these beings were understood to be

> a mythopoeic effort to explain workings of the human mind not easy to explain rationally or empirically, that is, an effort to construct myths that will serve as objectifications and hence explanations of inward processes of mind. The myth of the daemons seems to be centered on explaining the expansion of consciousness and intensifying of awareness that occur in human beings in unusual circumstances. ("Bell" 140)

Certainly such is the case with Peter Bell, whom Patterson identifies as the victim not merely of superstition but of the isolation that the daemons signify. They are not, and the distinction is important, genuine supernatural agents, rather "only supernatural machinery to facilitate the presentation of heightened awareness within the mind of Peter, and thus . . . a *poetic* rendering rather than a clinical report" ("Bell" 145). I agree that the daemons "are means of denoting awakening areas of consciousness" (145) but am less inclined than Patterson to find that Wordsworth was unconcerned as to whether his readers took the spirits to be literal supernatural manifestations (144–45). The prefatory letter seems fairly clear in ceding the territory of the supernatural to Robert Southey, so to admit the supernatural would run counter to Wordsworth's stated purpose and general poetic disposition. One point of "Peter Bell," after all, is that "the supernatural . . . bypasses the ordinary world in a way that adds nothing to it" (Jacobus 270). "Peter Bell" may come as close to explained Gothic as any other Wordsworth poem, but it is in the final analysis less supernatural even than *The Mysteries of Udolpho* because of its warning preface. In this poem (and elsewhere), Wordsworth elaborates an antisupernaturalism that, when seen in the context of his entire poetic project, permits him to employ the supernatural against itself.

Wordsworth's most supernatural poem, "The Danish Boy: A Fragment" (1799), is at the same time a crucial text for Wordsworth's antisupernaturalism. The basic premise is that a "smooth and open dell" is haunted by "A thing no storm can e'er destroy, / The shadow of a Danish Boy" (10–11); the titular character is further described, in the poem's final lines, as being "calm and gentle in his mien; / Like a dead boy he is serene" (54–55). He is also recognized as "A Spirit of noonday. . . / Yet seems a form of flesh and blood" (23–24). Any suggestion of ambiguity in these descriptions never becomes insistent; the character is clearly supernatural. (A stanza removed after "The Danish Boy" 's first publication in 1800 makes explicit reference to graves in the dell; a note by Wordsworth added to the poem in the 1827 edition of his *Poems* makes clear the supernatural character of the boy [*Poems* I: 857].)

Yet what does become a major theme in the poem is that the presence of the supernatural in the real world has disrupted nature, violating its customary order:

> In clouds above, the lark is heard,
> But drops not here to earth for rest;
> Within this lonesome nook the bird
> Did never build her nest.
> No beast, no bird, hath here his home;
> Bees, wafted on the breezy air,
> Pass high above those fragrant bells
> To other flowers:—to other dells
> Their burdens do they bear;
> The Danish Boy walks here alone:
> The lovely dell is all his own. (12–22)

Further descriptions of the behavior and appearance of the Boy's ghost emphasize the disjunction between supernature and nature. The music of his harp makes him "the darling and the joy" (39) of nearby flocks, but this attraction is overborne by prior explicit reference to his inability ever to be a "piping shepherd" or "herd-boy of the wood." These basic functions of the workaday rural world may be performed only by flesh-and-blood beings who participate in natural process. The Danish Boy's music is heard only by sheep and mountain ponies—animals with which he can have nothing to do—and is not heard at all by any human, facts that underscore his essential isolation from the world around him. It is no accident the stanza telling of his effect on domestic animals ends with the lines "They hear the Danish Boy, / While in the dell he sings *alone* / Beside the tree and corner-stone" (42–44; emphasis added).

Details of his appearance support these impressions of Otherness. He wears a vest that is "[i]n colour like a raven's wing," at least during pleasant weather. "But in the storm 'tis fresh and blue / As budding pines in spring; / His helmet has a vernal grace, / Fresh as the bloom upon his face" (30–33). His character and appearance are in constant conflict with natural process, an antithesis confirmed even by the songs he plays on his ghostly harp: "From bloody deeds his thoughts are far; / And yet he warbles songs of war, / That seem like songs of love" (51–53). The supernatural is incoherent, at odds with itself and with nature.

What remains, finally, is an impression of the supernatural as incapable of being integrated into or coordinated with the larger world of nature. As Ferry concludes, the Danish Boy "is outside things, in a valley from which [humans] are excluded, and though they may from afar wonder at and appreciate his music, it does not give harmony to them after all. . . . There is no real relation between [the Danish Boy's] world and the world in which the poet speaks" (104). The spirit of the Danish Boy insists on lingering in the dell, and Wordsworth focuses not, as one might expect, on the reactions of the local peasantry to the supernatural associations but exclusively on the disruption of the natural by the supernatural. Indeed, perhaps because this is Wordsworth's most supernatural poem, it is characterized by the complete exclusion of the sort of rural characters who populate "The Thorn" and "Goody Blake and Harry Gill." Having earlier determined the supernatural to be of little value to human understanding, Wordsworth invokes it here to show, despite its apparent innocuous neutrality (especially in contrast to typical Gothic ghosts), that the effect it has on nature is, if not pernicious, at least that of an interruption, an unintelligible and unassimilable quantity that blocks the ordinary processes of nature.

The poem may thus be understood as a perfect counterpart to "Peter Bell." If the earlier poem reveals the poet's indifference to the supernatural, "The Danish Boy" attributes the same indifference to nature, its refusal to interact with the supernatural akin to the poet's return to earth, both signifying the supernatural's insignificance and inutility.

*T*he same point is more fully elaborated in "Hart-Leap Well" (1800), a work uniting the two perspectives on the supernatural embodied in "Peter Bell" and "The Danish Boy." As a result, the poem is more complex than its predecessors, joining in its single vision both nature's superiority to the supernatural and supernaturalism's inability to speak significantly to human concerns.

Having recounted the death of the hart, the Poet begins the second part with a statement of poetic preference that signals both the tenor and implications of the story: "The moving accident is not my trade; / To freeze the blood I have no ready arts: / 'Tis my delight, alone in summer shade, / To pipe a simple song for thinking hearts" (97–100). "Thinking hearts" is a vital clue, for in part II the Poet provides a reading of the Hart-Leap Well landscape that reveals a careful balance of thought and emotion, sense and sensibility. Were he concerned only with "hearts," with the passions, he may well find himself telling a tale of "moving accident," a semi-Gothic story of rumored murders and hidden graves, which is precisely the story told by the local peasantry. Yet Wordsworth associated the Gothic with emotional and imaginative excess; the second part of "Hart-Leap Well" is his rescuing of a tale from the lurid, a balanced reading of the ruined pleasure house and fountain that acknowledges deep compassion and feeling while never surrendering the rational and real.

The natural decay characterizing the fountain and pleasure house is attributed, by local residents, to half-guessed quasi-Gothic events, but we as readers already know the story of Hart-Leap Well, for Wordsworth wants it clear from the start there is nothing supernatural, in the Gothic sense at least, about the spot. When the Shepherd mentions the local superstition, we already know that it is incorrect: "Some say that here a murder has been done, / And blood cries out for blood: but, for my part, / I've guessed, when I've been sitting in the sun, / That it was all for that unhappy Hart" (137–40). The truth lies not in any lurid horrors appropriate to a shilling shocker but in something much more ordinary and, at the same time, profound.

The Poet (the figure present in "Peter Bell" but missing from the exclusively natural, nonhuman universe of "The Danish Boy") agrees with the Shepherd in attributing the natural decay to a transcendent organicism inherent in the natural universe:

> This Beast not unobserved by Nature fell;
> His death was mourned by sympathy divine.
> The Being, that is in the clouds and air,
> That is in the green leaves among the groves,
> Maintains a deep and reverential care
> For the unoffending creatures whom he loves. (163–68)

Such sentiment would on its own deny the implications of radical Gothicism. But the Poet goes even further; a good Wordsworthian, he insists on the eventuality of nature's recovery and renewal:

> Nature, in due course of time, once more
> Shall here put on her beauty and her bloom.
> She leaves these objects to a slow decay,
> That what we are, and have been, may be known;
> But at the coming of the milder day,
> These monuments shall all be overgrown. (171–76)

Wordsworth has gone "The Danish Boy" one better: the introduction of a supernaturally tinged mode of being into the world of nature leads to decay and disruption, as with the earlier poem, but it is an ephemeral disturbance, a decay eventually to be repaired as natural process reasserts its sway.

The implications here are considerable: Wordsworth, by joining the perspectives of humanity and nature found in the earlier works, reveals the inadequacy of the supernatural sublime *as process,* not just as structure. Where "Peter Bell" and "The Danish Boy" reveal the normalcy/trauma/recovery *structure* of the supernatural sublime to be subversive of accurate human understanding and perception of the natural universe, "Hart-Leap Well," like the "Ancient Mariner," shows the *process* of the supernatural sublime to be marked by error. Here Wordsworth permits the structure to exist—we have the normal condition of the spot disrupted or suspended by the death of the hart, followed by the (predicted) recovery of the dell—but the means by which this structure is manifested in the poem obviates the Gothic supernatural. While the three-part structure obtains, the agent of trauma in the poem is not, as is usual with the Gothic supernatural sublime, an avatar of metaphysical absence *(The Monk)* or a mistaken belief in the ghostly *(Udolpho)*. The agent of recovery is not the revelation that the ghosts are false *(Udolpho)*, the intervention of God *(Old English Baron)*, or the healing passage of time *(Wieland)*. Rather, the agent of both trauma and recovery in "Hart-Leap Well" is nature itself, nature as an animistic force or presence underlying and unifying all elements of the phenomenal universe.

This animism co-opts the supernatural implications of the story in the same way that the Shepherd's belief denies Gothicism: since the condition of Hart-Leap Well is explained by reference to an animistic sympathy in nature, the desolation of the spot is refused negative metaphysical implications. The "Gothic" ruin of the fountain and pleasure house is a consequence not of hidden murders but of nature's powers of sympathy, of an organic empathic response to the fate of the hart that is, in its demonstration of unity, evidence of an underlying harmony and order to the cosmos. Thus the poem contravenes the radical Gothic, for what lies beyond the phenomenal world is revealed to be not the yawning epistemological and metaphysical gulf of *The Monk* and *Wieland* but a unified and unifying presence of nature and of that transcendent power of which nature is both agent and symbol.

The poem at the same time distances itself from even the conservative Gothic. Fear of the supernatural is never admitted into the poem; even the Shepherd only reports the local rumors—such reportage being a common distancing device for Wordsworth—and is joined by the Poet in rejecting them. Radcliffe operated differently, relying heavily on lower-class superstition to introduce the supernatural while maintaining, through her upper-class protagonists, a clear intellectual distance from it. Wordsworth, with his "levelling Muse," rejects even this narrative strategy, admitting the supernatural only as a report to which neither of the poem's living characters gives credence.

His rejection of the technique of explained Gothicism does not, however, imply a similar denial of such fiction's moral and religious conservatism, although Wordsworth gives a characteristic turn to the ethical implications of his narrative. As does Coleridge in the "Ancient Mariner," Wordsworth pushes his work into the realm of moral fable; the events of "Hart-Leap Well" conspire to teach humankind "never to blend our pleasure or our pride / With sorrow of the meanest thing that feels" (179–80). In what constitutes another denial of the supernatural sublime, Wordsworth cannot resist directing the poem's implications emphatically to the human realm of experience, even at risk of the poem itself.

The risk stems from the reductive appending of the moral, one that restricts to exclusively ethical and humanitarian concerns a point of potential metaphysical consequence. Wordsworth's poem had, only a few lines prior to the moral, posited an organicist understanding of the universe, yet the implications of this are dismissed in preference to the didactic. Wordsworth is far from undercutting his metaphysics of animism; yet his desire to moralize the tale, perhaps in order to make it answer what he saw as the main concern of Coleridge's "Rime," serves to mute the poem's denial of the supernatural sublime.

In this denial of superstititon "Hart-Leap Well" is allied with "Goody Blake and Harry Gill" (1798), a work in which explicit attempts to distance the "miraculous" from superstition deny the necessity of supernatural sublimity. A nimbus of superstition attends "Goody Blake," although in the subtitle ("A True Story"), in notes, and in the Preface to *Lyrical Ballads* Wordsworth insists that the story of Goody and Harry is authentic. He achieves further distance from superstition by predicating the poem's supernatural element, the curse, not on pagan magic but on Christian ethics, as well as on a belief that "the power of the human imagination is sufficient to produce such changes even in our physical nature as might almost appear miraculous" (*Poems* I: 887). Yet despite any psychological undercurrents, the poem is finally a moral fable, similar to "Hart-Leap Well" but with its focus and arena of operation shifted from the natural to the human. We are, as well, beginning to see an interest on Wordsworth's part not in superstitious or folkloric materials for their own sakes but for their value as moral vehicles. Such a troping helps explain a curious fact about Wordsworth's poetic canon: despite his much-proclaimed interest in rural life and custom, there is no important Wordsworthian celebration—akin to, say, Burns's "Halloween"—of superstition as a major component of rural imaginative life. The strict subordination of potentially "supernatural" materials denies any subversive implications of such material, and the careful distance Wordsworth maintained between himself and his superstitious sources is another expression of his rigid distrust of even the tamest narrative strategies of the Gothic.

*S*uch distrust is powerfully evident in "The Thorn" (1798), the Wordsworth poem most interested in superstition. Yet precisely because of this interest, Wordsworth labored diligently to interpose distance between himself and the story being told. His efforts are most apparent in the note affixed to the poem in later editions of *Lyrical Ballads,* in which Wordsworth writes at some length about the character of the poem's narrator:

> The character which I have here introduced speaking is sufficiently common. The Reader will perhaps have a general notion of it, if he has ever known a man, a Captain of a small trading vessel, for example, who being past the middle age of life, had retired upon an annuity or small independent income to some village or country town of which he was not a native, or in which he had not been accustomed to live. Such men, having little to do, become credulous and talkative from indolence; and from the same cause . . . they are prone to superstition. (*Poems* I: 949)

Wordsworth goes on to explain that the poem is his attempt to "exhibit some of the general laws by which superstition acts upon the mind" (I: 949). Asserting that the superstitious are characterized by "slow faculties and deep feelings," Wordsworth distinguishes between their "reasonable share of imagination, by which I mean the faculty which produces impressive effects out of simple elements" and their complete lack of "fancy, the power by which pleasure and surprise are excited by sudden varieties of situation and an accumulated imagery" (I: 949).

Despite such philosophic and theoretic posturing by Wordsworth, the poem is not, finally, an aesthetic or anthropological study of rural folkways or imagination—although Alan Bewell shows how the work reconfigures and modernizes tropes of witchcraft and hysteria (162–75)—but a much more personal work than the notes and distancing interposition of a loquacious narrator suggest. The composition of the poem was occasioned by a real walking trip and a real thorn tree (*Poems* I: 948–49), with Wordsworth's imagination and sense of guilt adding the dead infant and the "wretched Woman," whose name in the poem indicates that illicit sexual liaisons were very much on his mind. Martha Ray was the name of the mother of one of Wordsworth's companions on this walk—a woman who was the mistress of the Earl of Sandwich and was murdered by a rejected lover. That in the poem Martha Ray was abandoned by the father of her child inevitably reminds us of Annette Vallon. I mention this not to initiate a psychobiographical reading of the poem but to stress that the poem's notes are a calculated device intended to introduce distance between Wordsworth and thematic materials that meant more to him than he cared openly to admit.

Certainly Wordsworth would have thought to safeguard the autobiographical dimension of his poem more than its use of superstition,
but even the latter is a target of Wordsworth's post facto distancing.
"The Thorn" verges near the supernatural, and the mask of the narrator is invoked by Wordsworth as a means of keeping his poetic principles intact. Indeed, since the narrator is repeating local superstition
without endorsement—perhaps even without understanding—the supernatural elements in the poem are twice removed from Wordsworth
himself.

The poem might best be approached by contrasting it to "The Danish Boy."[4] Both are about natural places invested with the supernatural, and while the supernatural is less overtly present in "The Thorn"
there is still an insistence on its ability to disrupt natural process. The
appearance of the thorn itself is so eldritch and unnatural it is best
described in inorganic terms:

> No leaves it has, no prickly points;
> It is a mass of knotted joints,
> A wretched thing forlorn.
> It stands erect, and like a stone
> With lichens it is overgrown. (7–11)

The troubled spot also features "a little muddy pond" with unnatural
characteristics of its own: "never dry / Though but of compass small,
and bare / To thirsting sun and parching air" (31–33).

The spot is rendered stranger still and more vivid by the contrasting
appearance of the "fresh and lovely sight, / A beauteous heap, a hill
of moss, / Just half a foot in height" (36–38). Next to the grey thorn
and muddy pond, the brilliance of the grave suggests, like the impossible colors and patterns decorating the untransformed Lamia of Keats's
poem, a strange and unsettling potential:

> Ah me! what lovely tints are there
> Of olive green and scarlet bright,
> In spikes, in branches, and in stars,
> Green, red, and pearly white!
> This heap of earth o'ergrown with moss,
> Which close beside the Thorn you see,
> So fresh in all its beauteous dyes,
> Is like an infant's grave in size,
> As like as like can be:
> But never, never anywhere,
> An infant's grave was half so fair. (45–55)

So far the poem more or less matches "The Danish Boy" in its sense of nature disordered, but here it diverges by introducing a human element, as did "Hart-Leap Well." But "The Thorn" moves further in its study of the effects of the (supposed) supernatural upon the human. While "Hart-Leap Well" was content to show human beings who were uninvolved in the events that give significance to the natural spot extracting a moral from their study of the place, "The Thorn" finds its narrative center in the human most involved in the events, the grief-crazed mother. In keeping with Wordsworth's general estrangement from the supernatural, she is never seen in contact with the supernatural; indeed, in accord with the distancing principles established in and around this poem, the "wretched Woman" comes to serve as a supernatural surrogate, a "witch/hysteric" whose presence becomes the means by which the poem explores "the original workings of the imagination" (Bewell 150).

Human responses to her presence are indicative of her supernatural status. She is, for the local inhabitants, a sort of evil *genius loci* whose presence is anathema:

> But would you gladly view the spot,
> . . . .
> Pass by her door—'tis seldom shut—
> And, if you see her in her hut—
> Then to the spot away!
> I never heard of such as dare
> Approach the spot when she is there! (91, 96–99)

Even those who wish only to cross the mountain must time their journeys so as to pass the spot when the woman is absent (56–60). And in keeping with the best Gothic tradition, her behavior is inscrutable, the motive for her actions unknown (78–90). Yet we are never allowed by Wordsworth to forget, even to doubt, that the woman is and remains fully human, her supernaturalism primarily a consequence of the perceptions of others, as we would expect given Wordsworth's theory of the origin of the supernatural. The woman's grief or grief-induced behavior prompts the locals to associate both her and the spot she frequents with witchcraft and the supernatural; they may not realize it, but we understand that their use of the only language of the mysterious available and familiar to them has made of the woman and her situation something Other, something threatening that must be alienated.

While we may witness the alienation of Martha Ray, in our privileged status as readers we do not share in it. The interposition of narrator between events and the superstitious interpretation of those events by the villagers provides us more or less with the raw data of Martha Ray's condition and leaves us, if not quite able to judge for ourselves, at least as close as we can come to the objective reality of the situation. The narrator, after all, is often an eyewitness of the events and objects he describes, and when he is not he explicitly states that fact.

There are stories, the narrator reports, of "Cries coming from the mountain head: / Some plainly living voices were; / And others, I've heard many swear, / Were voices of the dead" (160–63). Here the narrator makes a provocative comment on these voices: "I cannot think, whate'er they say, / They had to do with Martha Ray" (164–65). For someone Wordsworth is so anxious to style superstitious, the narrator seems fairly level-headed, if ultimately unable to make much sense of the events he reports.

We see a similar gesture of rational balancing—again, paradoxically—in the most "supernatural" portions of the poem, where the narrator mentions the local superstitions without endorsing them. Reporting on the rumors of the infant's murder, the narrator is careful to distinguish between hearsay and his own belief and opinion:

> I've heard, the moss is spotted red
> With drops of that poor infant's blood;
> But kill a new-born infant thus,
> I do not think she could!
> Some say, if to the pond you go,
> And fix on it a steady view,
> The shadow of a babe you trace,
> A baby and a baby's face,
> And that it looks at you;
> Whene'er you look on it, 'tis plain
> The baby looks at you again.
>
> And some had sworn an oath that she
> Should be to public justice brought;
> And for the little infant's bones
> With spades they would have sought.
> But instantly the hill of moss
> Before their eyes began to stir!
> And, for full fifty yards around,

> The grass—it shook upon the ground!
> Yet all do still aver
> The little Babe lies buried there,
> Beneath that hill of moss so fair.
>
> I cannot tell how this may be. . . . (210–32)

These events are not presented as personally witnessed; the narrator is conclusive only about that which he has seen and heard: the appearance of the thorn, the behavior of the woman, her mournful cry. The much-remarked inability of the narrator to interpret, to "tell how this may be," marks the limit of the imaginative reach of the narrator, his position on the spectrum of imaginative development: midway between the poem's readers and the superstitious villagers, the narrator serves to remind us of our own more highly developed perspective. Witness to two interpretations of the same event—the villagers' superstition and the narrator's bemused observations—we recognize our own understanding of Martha Ray as distinct from and more sophisticated than either. From such a vantage we perceive the limitations not only of superstitious belief itself but of an uninformed observation. And it is this, rather than an excess of credulity, that is the narrator's flaw. In his note Wordsworth has exaggerated the narrator's superstitious gullibility (and hedged an intensely personal poem with distancing devices) because, as regards the supernatural and human interaction with it, the poem is one of Wordsworth's most extreme and most important.[5]

"The Thorn" finally registers less supernaturalism than "The Danish Boy" because of its successful incorporation, from "Goody Blake and Harry Gill," of the idea that the human imagination is capable of powerful and convincing transformations of the material of ordinary life (a point sought by "Peter Bell" as well). In "The Thorn" the space of the supernatural is occupied by superstition, human tragedy, and human imagination. The all-important use of the narrator permits Wordsworth to tread a very fine line, presenting the supernatural as a confirmed belief and therefore powerful imaginative force while at the same time excluding true supernaturalism. Wordsworth's note, with its assertion of the narrator's superstitious propensities, thus serves two purposes. It works as a corrective to the skepticism evident in the narrator's discourse: he must be receptive to or interested in the supernatural if he is taking the trouble to repeat local legend. The note also encourages the reader's perception of rural folk as superstitious and credulous, and "The Thorn" succeeds by balancing the belief of the peasants against the narrator's skepticism and by letting us see the balancing. The end result, for the poem's readers, is a vindication and celebration of the imagination's power to extract from natural occurrences an "extranatural" significance and intensity, a transcendent perception.

*I*n the Preface to the *Lyrical Ballads* Wordsworth, speaking of poetic practice and in particular his commitment to "the very language of men," writes that "I have wished to keep my Reader in the company of flesh and blood . . ." (I: 873). He succeeded in more ways than he knew; Sukumar Dutt was correct in observing that for Wordsworth the supernatural was valuable not for "its inherent mysterious quality" but for its "relation to human things" (203). The supernatural for Wordsworth was devoid of numinous possibility and power, and his occasional use of it proves the truth of Hartman's observation that Wordsworth, like Coleridge, was "interested in effects analogous to the supernatural, but . . . chooses to achieve them by a purely realistic method and content" because "he is shying from an 'apocalyptic' position. He does not want to find imagination in violation of man or nature" (*Poetry* 124). Wordsworth never does, for imagination as embodied in supernaturalism is consistently denied preeminence over the human or the natural.

Chapter Six

That Supernatural Summer

The Shelleys and Byron

The summer of 1816 proved a watershed moment for Western supernatural fiction, witnessing as it did the beginning not only of the first English vampire fiction but also of Mary Shelley's *Frankenstein*, a work so multivalent it is variously regarded as the first novel of science fiction, as one of the early achievements of feminist fiction, and as the major novelistic expression of a Romantic *Weltanschauung*. The history of that summer's ghost-story sessions at the Villa Diodati, involving both Shelleys, Byron, John Polidori, and, later, Matthew Lewis, is too well known to need rehearsal here,[1] but this moment in history will serve as the point of departure for an investigation of the supernatural in the works of Mary Wollstonecraft Shelley, Percy Bysshe Shelley, and Lord Byron. As a comprehensive treatment of the supernatural in the canons of these writers would be both unwieldy and unnecessary, this study will confine itself to those works most directly linked to that summer's challenge, recounted by Mary Shelley in her 1831 preface to *Frankenstein*, to write a ghost story. The supernatural in one form or another interested these writers throughout their lives, but in the summer months of 1816 they were thinking of it with uncommon focus; consequently, the works that had their beginnings (at least) in the period under scrutiny provide the most illuminating insight into these writers' attitudes toward, and revisions of, Gothic supernaturalism.

*F*rankenstein is often identified as a high point of Gothic fiction, and while it evidences strong affinities with the genre, its refusal fully to subscribe to the metaphysical parameters commonly acknowledged by the classical Gothic marks it, finally, as a post-Gothic work. It is too much the progeny of a Romantic context; its modulations of sublimity transcend the sensationalism and moralism of the conventional sublime while struggling beyond the gloom of radical Gothic horror.

There is of course no supernaturalism in *Frankenstein;* despite the seductions of alchemical hubris, Victor is a scientist, not a wizard, and he invokes cutting-edge scientific discoveries to make his creature[2]—a making that is also a revising and secularizing of previous religious myths:

> *Frankenstein* echoes the old stories of Faust and Prometheus, exploring the limits of ambition and rebelliousness and their moral implications; but it is also the tale of a *"modern Prometheus,"* and as such it is a secular myth, with no metaphysical machinery, no gods: the creation is from mortal bodies with the assistance of electricity, not spirit; and the deaths are not pursued beyond the grave. (G. Levine 4)

Yet a nimbus of Gothic supernaturalism surrounds the creature; he functions, like many supernatural beings from earlier Gothic stories, as something alien and Other, a tear in the fabric of ordinary human life. The creature is obviously analogous to Milton's Satan (*Paradise Lost* being another myth rewritten by Mary Shelley) and to Lucifer in Lewis's *The Monk*. Fittingly, Victor's monster is often called a demon because he is not of this world, and dealings with him not only interrupt and suspend ordinary human life but turn it in new and horrifying directions.

The trope of suspension becomes the means by which the (non)supernatural sublime enters the novel, a suspension most tellingly operative at the level of narrative structure. The multilayered symmetry of the novel has long been remarked: the first narrator is Robert Walton, whose tale includes Victor's, whose tale includes the creature's, whose tale includes that of the De Laceys; after hearing their story, we back out through the creature's narrative, then to Victor's, then finally back to Walton's at the novel's conclusion. Viewing this structure as a series of imbedded suspensions, we gain insight into Mary Shelley's disquietingly modern revision of Gothic supernaturalism.

Both Walton and Victor begin their explorations convinced of their ability to confer "inestimable benefit . . . on all mankind to the last generation" (16), but each soon finds his enterprise suspended: Walton by the ice and the interruption of Victor, Victor by the animation of the monster. These characters mirror each other, of course, each in some way a doppelgänger of the others, marking him in his isolation, despair, or desire. The experiences and ambitions of the three protagonists/antagonists reflect and intertwine in a complex and reciprocal pattern made all the more resonant by the various suspensions or interruptions that juxtapose and contrast the experiences of Walton, Victor, and the "wretch."

In the center of the novel, in the middle of the monster's tale, is yet another suspension and a figuring in miniature of one of the work's major themes. Hiding in the hovel attached to the De Laceys' cottage, the creature acquires what he believes to be an adequate command of human language, history, and society, and armed with this command, hazards an approach to the social world of humanity. His attempt to win over the blind father is interrupted by the premature return of Agatha, Safie, and Felix, who peremptorily drive the creature off before the De Laceys abandon their cottage. In some ways the creature's intrusion is merely interruptive rather than suspensive, for we never hear of the De Laceys again, but the point gained is crucial. The De Laceys and Safie have suffered great disruptions in their social and economic fortunes; their apparent recovery of stability and domestic bliss is suddenly, traumatically, and ironically shattered by the intrusion of Victor's alienated creature.

The monster's experiences in the hovel confirm his earlier impression of his own irrevocable Otherness: "I was not even of the same nature as man" (120). His attempt to insinuate himself into human community can elicit no response other than horror despite his fervent belief that should the members of this representative community "become acquainted with my admiration of their virtues they would compassionate me, and overlook my personal deformity" (130). This hope is literally driven out of him by Felix's cudgel, however, and the pattern for the rest of the novel is established: despite his intentions, the monster will destroy and disrupt by his intrusions, his presence. His very being will alienate humanity; alienated, he will reciprocate the rejection, just as he burns the De Laceys' cottage after they abandon it and thereby intensifies the dynamic of distrust and hatred into which his appearance, in conjunction with human prejudice, forces him. He inadvertently and helplessly converts this dynamic into a circular and self-intensifying relationship, one from which neither he nor Victor can escape. Victor rejects the monster, the monster kills William; Victor refuses the monster a mate, the monster kills Clerval and Elizabeth. In the absence of compassion and sympathetic understanding, this Godwinian novel implies, horror and discontinuity are increasingly inevitable.

I have begun with the creature's story of alienation and disruption because it, more than the suspension of Walton's story by Victor or Victor's story by the creature, expresses what I take as one of the novel's most basic concerns; without understanding this episode, we cannot understand those narratives that center upon it, that pass through it, as it were, on their way to climax. Nor can we judge the effect of supernatural suspensions until they end. While the early pages of the novel hint at what is to come, these hints cannot become certainties until the suspended stories are not only resumed but completed. What can we make, for example, of Walton's likening himself to the Ancient Mariner? Both men find themselves trapped in a "land of ice and snow," but we must hear Victor out before we know how he and his story will affect Walton and his expedition.

Victor's story, a suspension of Walton's, is itself a story about suspension, about the young scientist's "withdrawal from his family into a void of detached objects and alienated activity" (Dussinger 49). Even though Victor's esoteric researches are in the field of natural science, they lead him away from all that is "natural" to him: "my eyes were insensible to the charms of nature. And the same feelings which made me neglect the scenes around me caused me also to forget those friends who were so many miles absent, and whom I had not seen for so long a time" (55). Cut off from the consolations of environment and family, Victor pursues a course of studies that culminates, almost predictably, in the creation of a being outside of nature and community, one made of human parts yet not human, and its terrifying ugliness, emblematic of its unnatural genesis and Otherness, sets it forever beyond human belonging. The creature thus reifies Victor's failure to fulfill his obligations to the natural and human worlds: "[Victor's] striving for a more than human greatness destroys the warmth of his humanity, and gradually he becomes totally involved with the monster that objectifies all his own inadequacies. Their final, mad chase to the north reflects literally their abandonment of society and their total absorption with their mutual self" (Hume, "Gothic" 286). Victor's intense studies constitute an act of almost pathological solipsism; it is not surprising that the creature, the result of these unnatural researches, literally embodies his creator's isolation, reminding Victor by his very hideousness of the moral and psychological ugliness of hubris, and of the deformity and deficiency of Victor's own capacity for communal belonging. The creature berates Victor for not fulfilling a creator's duty to his creature, but the monster might have known better: were Victor capable of the requisite sensitivity, he would never have created a being in such helplessly desperate need of its creator's succor.

Subsequent to his making of the creature Victor seeks to recover those connections abandoned during his suspension in Ingolstadt, and the timely arrival of Clerval helps Victor feel he has again become "the same happy creature who, a few years ago, loved and beloved by all, had no sorrow or care" (70). But this tranquility is delusory, soon shattered by the news of William's murder. The implication of this sequence of events is clear: a separation from natural and human communities cannot simply be resumed at whim or at will, and certainly not without an acceptance of and coming to terms with the consequences of that separation. Victor fled from his creature within moments of its animation and made no attempt to contact, control, educate, or restrain it; until it began to murder, he never even sought to ascertain its whereabouts. Clearly Victor has yet to demonstrate communal responsibility, and so his suspension from community not only remains in effect but intensifies as Victor's familial community grows smaller with the creature-induced deaths of William and Justine.

In its concentric narrowing of scope the novel lays increasing responsibility and guilt on Victor, dramatically underscoring the radical hubris of his project. Victor's researches become an attempt to appropriate the divine spark, a shifting of "the responsibilities of God . . . to mankind" (G. Levine 10), and they have the expected consequence, the murder of the beloved, of the family, by a creature who is Victor's personal proxy, his surrogate. In a vitally important sense Victor is correct when, in his frenzies, he names himself as the murderer of his friends and family; George Levine is correct when he notes that "The devil and the angel of the morality play are replaced by a modern pre-Freudian psychology that removes the moral issue from the metaphysical context—the traditional concepts of good and evil—and places it entirely within the self" (15). The catalogue of crimes in *Frankenstein*, like that in *Dr. Jekyll and Mr. Hyde*, records the split within the self, the continual struggle between internal light and darkness.

The murders of William and Justine plunge Victor into a despair beyond consolation: "not the tenderness of friendship, nor the beauty of earth, nor of heaven, could redeem my soul from woe: the very accents of love were ineffectual" (93–94). The psychological insight here is trenchant: friendship and natural beauty are indeed powerless to assuage Victor's grief not through any innate deficiency on their part but because of Victor's insensitivity to the bonds of affection and what Wordsworth identified as "natural piety." Victor's character makes nature and family of secondary importance—the creature's very being affirms this—and for Victor to turn now to the very things he earlier denied only confirms the seriousness of his prior failures of sensibility.

There is one moment during which it seems nature might provide some consolation for Victor. Immediately following the passage just quoted, Victor undertakes a solitary journey to Chamounix. The deaths of William and Justine have revealed that family is no refuge from the avenging creature, the literal embodiment of Victor's hubris; it is therefore appropriate that Victor sets off alone in quest of restoration in nature, refusing even a guide. His choice of destination is also apt, for it is among the most (conventionally) sublime landscapes in Western Europe. Seeking the consolations of nature, Victor could have chosen no better.

Mary Shelley's powerful evocation of the sublimity of Chamounix is a veritable tribute to eighteenth-century aesthetic theory:

> The weight upon my spirit was sensibly lightened as I plunged yet deeper into the ravine of Arve. The immense mountains and precipices that overhung me on every side—the sound of the river raging among the rocks, and the dashing of the waterfalls around, spoke of a power mighty as Omnipotence—and I ceased to fear, or to bend before any being less almighty than that which had created and ruled the elements, here displayed in their most terrific guise. (94)

Yet this vaguely spiritual sublimity is more than a Radcliffean indulgence in the sublime for its own sake or for the pointing of conventional moral lessons. The sublime is evoked here in such intensity precisely so that Mary Shelley may "supernaturally" reveal its limitations.

While it appears that neither of the Shelleys knew Kant's theory of the sublime (Wellek 180–82), Mary Shelley was, like her husband, familiar with British aesthetic theory, using the language of the Burkean sublime "with precision" (Rieger 85). This precision makes her use of "horror" rather than "terror" significant, since Burke, like many other eighteenth-century aestheticians, identified terror as the center and impulse of the sublime. Beyond terror, Radcliffe and others explained, lay horror, an emotion not calculated to inspire the soul but rather to freeze it, oppress it under a stultifying fear. Against the background of this emotional gradient, Mary Shelley modulates an apparently conventional sublime experience into a critique of sublimity; Victor's sublime moment is driven beyond "pleasing terror" and religous inspiration to emotions very near to the dread of radical supernatural sublimity.

Victor's visit to the sublime landscape of the Arve ravine and the Mer de Glace at first appears to instigate nothing other than the usual effects of the sublime:

> These sublime and magnificent scenes afforded me the greatest consolation that I was capable of receiving. They elevated me from all littleness of feeling; and although they did not remove my grief, they subdued and tranquilised it. In some degree, also, they diverted my mind from the thoughts over which it had brooded for the last month. (96)

Hints accumulate, however, that Victor's Alpine excursions will produce more dire consequences. On the morning of his planned ascent of Montanvert, Victor awakens with a sense of foreboding, for a storm hides "the summits of the mountains . . . , the faces of those mighty friends" (96). He reports to Walton his desire to recapture the "sublime ecstasy" he felt upon first viewing the scene in his youth; for wary readers this should be warning enough of disappointment to come.

What ensues is much more than disappointment. Mountaintops are customarily the site of sublimity's greatest intensity and of religious theophany,[3] but Victor's experience is no longer that of the conventional sublime. Traversing the barren glacier to the "bare perpendicular rock," Victor has moved beyond conventional sublimity, away from its inspiring terror and power to a blank and sterile experience of dread and horror. This alpine experience is the physical analogue of Victor's intellectual movement beyond the ancient alchemists to modern science; the juxtaposition of the sublime with the end result of his post-alchemical inquiry, the monster, constitutes Mary Shelley's comment on the limits of the sublime's capacity to transform and ameliorate the anxieties of the modern human condition.[4]

Bounding up at the moment of Victor's sublime indulgence, the creature becomes the avatar of these anxieties, his appearance shattering the positive sublime Victor had been experiencing. Close reading of the novel reveals that Shelley almost always uses "horror" (or some variant thereof) when writing of the monster or of human reactions to him, and "terror" (or a variant) when referring to experiences of conventional sublimity. Approaching Montanvert, for example, Victor remarks that the mountain "is a scene terrifically desolate" (97); upon the appearance of the monster on the glacier, "horror" and "horrible" follow in quick succession. This pattern is sustained, with only minor exceptions, throughout *Frankenstein*. In the Alpine confrontation scene, Shelley uses her terms pointedly and with deliberation. Victor begins a conventionally "terrific" sublime experience, but even as his hubristic intellectual quest has taken him beyond nature, so does his search for the consolations of the natural sublime lead beyond the terror-based ecstasy he seeks into horror. He implores the "wandering spirits" of the mountain for joy and death but is instead visited by the wandering spirit he himself created.

Victor is entitled to neither joy nor death, for he has cut himself off from joy and denied death—denied nature in the most all-encompassing sense of the word. At the moment of Victor's plea for joy and death his sublime experience should end; he would, were he a normal seeker of the sublime, recover from his suspension with some sense of uplift or exhilaration. But Victor, like Byron's Manfred, has positioned himself outside the range of the normal and the natural— Manfred by being, Victor by creating "a being of no uncommon order"—so rather than begin a recovery here, Victor discovers that his sublime experience intensifies but now in a dark register of horror.

The implications of Victor's horrific suspension develop during the monster's story. Having already considered its message of alienation and despair, we may shift consideration to the more immediate effects of this unrecoverable sublimity on Victor and Walton. I say "unrecoverable" because although the monster's tale ends and Victor returns to his own narrative, the effects of the encounter are never dissipated; so in one important sense the structure of the novel is deceptive. Victor's story resumes, but he is both in that narrative and, as he sits in Walton's cabin, still under the shadow cast by the creature, a shadow that first fell upon him during that mountaintop confrontation, that inversion of epiphany and the sublime.

Victor himself explains the effect on his life of his mountaintop encounter with the monster:

> I returned home, and entering the house, presented myself to the family. My haggard and wild appearance awoke intense alarm; but I answered no questions, scarcely did I speak. I felt as if I were placed under a ban—as if I had no right to claim their sympathies—as if never more might I enjoy companionship with them. Yet even thus I loved them to adoration; and to save them, I resolved to dedicate myself to my most abhorred task. The prospect of such an occupation made every other circumstance of existence pass before me like a dream; and that thought only had to me the reality of life. (149)

This dream, this thought, never passes, only worsens. Victor further alienates himself from his family: agreeing to marry Elizabeth, he promptly leaves Switzerland for one of the remotest of the Orkney Islands in order to construct the monster's mate, an episode that continues the suspension of the isolating "supernatural" sublime in which Victor became involved in the Alps. He destroys the nearly complete female as his creature looks on and, in consequence, loses his remaining consolations: Clerval, and his own bride, Elizabeth, and his father. It is appropriate that Victor begins to identify himself as a "wretch"— his usual term for the monster—for he has become ever more like his creature, cut off from humanity and increasingly prone to overwhelming frustration and despair. Finally all that remains to Victor is his suspension; his hatred of the creature is all that binds him to life: "I was hurried away by fury; revenge alone endowed me with strength and composure. . . . [R]evenge kept me alive; I dared not die and leave my adversary in being" (201). Fittingly, Victor has become like his creation, suspended between life and death.

If the resumption of Victor's story after the conclusion of the monster's embedded tale does not reveal a markedly different Victor as far as the outermost narrative level is concerned, the same cannot be said of Walton, who has been touched by what he has heard. The significance of Victor's impact on Walton is discovered most readily in the novel's ice imagery, which is most prominent at the beginning, middle, and end of the novel so as to tie Walton's experience to the implications of the novel's supernatural sublime, most directly addressed at the novel's center. Victor's quest, explicitly likened to Walton's, led to horror and dread, to a confrontation with forces of violence and hatred beyond human and natural control. The benevolence of the creature's original impulses only heightens the tragedy of this development; Victor's aspirations, also altruistic, were warped by his careless alienation of nature and family, and the result was a being, a force, equally outside of nature, as warped externally as Victor's goals and desires were insidiously perverted by his lack of contact with (and assimilation of) nature, family, and what Fred Randel identifies as "the female principle" ("Intertextuality" passim).

Victor's supernatural sublimity works its influence on the hearts and minds of Walton's crew, for despite Victor's eloquent exhortation they turn back when confronted with seemingly impassable ice. Some readers may take Victor's speech as an example of hypocrisy or foolishness—Victor should know better than to urge exploration of the unknown, they seem to think—but there is no contradiction here. Victor is referring to a limited sort of exploration and inquiry: he mentions "cold," "danger," "death," and, most importantly, "terror" and the "terrific." This is the language of the natural sublime and of physical exploration; Victor clearly has in mind a different sort of investigation from the one he himself conducted, an investigation beyond nature and with implications well beyond the natural. More to the point, Victor's speech falls short of hypocrisy because Victor actually seems to have learned very little. Although urging Walton to desist from scientific inquiry, Victor reveals that he himself is not irrevocably committed to a path of tranquility and intellectual stasis: "Yet why do I say this? I have myself been blasted in these hopes, yet another may succeed" (218). Victor recognizes the hollowness in his own words and remains committed to his solipsistic obsession.

Whatever Victor's ambiguous desires, it does not fall to Walton to take up Victor's quest, for he surrenders his aspirations in the face of potential mutiny and solid ice. This recurrence of ice imagery makes the connection Walton himself refuses to see: Victor's supernatural sublime has cast its dark shadow across Walton. In the novel's opening pages, Walton likens himself to the Ancient Mariner, but unlike Coleridge's voyager, Walton truncates his journey: the ice opens *behind* him, and that is the direction in which he sails. He abandons his visionary project at the moment when he finally and fully confronts the land of ice and snow, before he may undertake to slay his own albatross. (In his second letter to his sister, Walton remarks, prophetically, that he shall "slay no albatross" [21].) He has seen Victor take this action, and has heard too of the consequences of that act, consequences much more horrifying than Coleridge ever supposed. The Mariner passed through his dark night of soul psychically intact and infused with daemonic potency, able to bring his redemptive if unsettling message to his fellow beings. Victor, chasing part of himself across the indifferent ice, is similarly compelled to speak of his dark quest—and Walton, like the Wedding Guest, must listen. But Victor has no redemptive words, no exhortation to prayer and communal belonging; he urges Walton's men to precisely the opposite, to continue their solitary quest. Victor never found beauty in the ugliest of nature's creatures; he went nature one uglier, constructing a being more hideous than any sea-snake, and in consequence discovered a horror for which nature has no consolations, against which nature has no countering grace. Victor dies amid the ice; he has, in one sense, never left it since that Alpine confrontation with his creature. The ice stops Walton but not because it blocks his ship: it has become emblematic of the soul-freezing horror and dread that lies beyond the known and the safe, of that sterile and consuming whiteness we later find at the end of Poe's *Narrative of Arthur Gordon Pym* and in the color of Ahab's demon.

There is, finally, an ambivalence in Mary Shelley's novel, an uncertainty as great as that surrounding the monster's status. Just as the creature is both *of* nature and *beyond* it, so does *Frankenstein* find its themes both in nature and outside it. On one hand it is a conservative warning against Faustian/Romantic hubris,[5] yet *Frankenstein* is also a radical vision of that despair born of confrontation with a dark and chaotic universe, an "Ancient Mariner" as it might have been written by Matthew Lewis.

The novel is rescued from the vision of horror endorsed by the radical supernatural sublime, however, in that we are given to understand Victor and his enterprise as fatally flawed, an understanding presented through subtle but important contrast. The failure of Victor to accept responsibility for and nurture his creature is juxtaposed with the positive families and fathers in the book, the De Laceys and Alphonse Frankenstein particularly. As Anne Mellor explains, *Frankenstein* co-opts the horror of the masculinist sublime by subsuming it in the female aesthetic of the beautiful and by endorsing the bourgeois family as a model human dynamic that potentially redeems the moral failure of Victor's motherless creation. Since her novel is finally more concerned with moral rather than epistemological questions (Mellor, *Shelley* 134), Shelley is able to give freer rein to those dark elements of the Gothic generally eschewed by post-Gothic contemporaries, and indeed *Frankenstein* is much closer to the Gothic than any other major work considered in the second part of this study. But the horror she envisions through Victor is moral rather than metaphysical, the consequence not of the absence of the divine but of the familial, the nurturing, the human. And as such, the "solution" to Victor's problem is at least within the realm of the human, even if it often remains out of reach.

*I*n the 1818 preface to *Frankenstein,* Percy Shelley writes that the supernatural is intended to afford "a point of view to the imagination for the delineating of human passions more comprehensive and commanding than any which the normal relations of existing events can yield" (13). In his early Gothic novels, he took these "passions" quite literally: *Zastrozzi* (1810) is an emotional panoply, with swoons, fits, and tears enough to supply a handful of sentimental novels. The novel is without supernaturalism, however, and so will not be considered here. His second effort, *St. Irvyne; or the Rosicrucian* (1810–1811), reveals more clearly how Percy, very early in his career, worked out his own position between the conservatism of Reeve and Radcliffe and the radical investigations of Lewis and Maturin.

The conservative element in *St. Irvyne* is rather simple and superficial, as though it had small purchase in Percy Shelley's mind. The mysterious bandit Ginotti, having sold his soul to the devil, laments that he has paid a horrible price to discover that there is indeed a God who orders the universe, and the novel concludes with the moral that "endless life [must] be sought from Him alone who can give an eternity of happiness" (199). Such moralizing is typical of much of the period's fiction, Radcliffe's included, and is readily explained by the fact that *St. Irvyne,* like *Zastrozzi,* was a calculated attempt by the eighteen-year-old Percy Shelley to sell books and cultivate an audience (Behrendt viii). The conservative element in *St. Irvyne* is the "calculation," the veneer intended to make the work suitable for mass consumption. Indeed, the conventionality of the novel's moral element seems to have put off Shelley himself, for it is drastically undermined by the hasty patchwork conclusion with which he ended the novel when he obviously tired of it. There is nothing, in short, to suggest that these concessions to conventional piety were in any way heartfelt, especially when we recall that only three months after the publication of *St. Irvyne,* Shelley and Thomas Hogg were sent down from Oxford for writing *The Necessity of Atheism.*

The radical element, on the other hand, is worked deeply into *St.*

Irvyne. It is most evident in the repeated use of the image of the "terrifying precipice"—the Shelleyan expression of *The Monk*'s "yawning Gulph"—which occurs, like the ice in *Frankenstein,* three times in *St. Irvyne,* each time in a dream of one of the principal characters. The image also brings *Wieland* to mind, with Clara and her dream of the chasm that lies between her and her beckoning brother, and Percy Shelley's use of dream is similar.[6]

St. Irvyne begins, like the second scene of Byron's *Manfred,* with the protagonist, Wolfstein, perched on a storm-blasted mountain peak, about to hurl himself into the precipice "which yawned widely beneath his feet" (110). His unarticulated but "excessive despair" has driven him to the verge of self-destruction; he is saved only to begin those involvements that lead to a more oppressive life and, finally, to his death.

Having joined the Alpine bandits, Wolfstein one night "dreamed that he stood on the brink of a frightful precipice" (137) with jagged rocks below and fierce lightning storms above, and he is accosted by "a figure, more frightful than the imagination of man is capable of portraying" (138). In the dream Wolfstein is rescued by the man who, in waking life, is his demonic pursuer and persecutor. This pursuer, Ginotti, is Wolfstein's surrogate in the dream, hurled over the cliff by the frightful figure. Ginotti has his own dream, presented late in the novel but occurring before the others, in which he, like Wolfstein, is on a "most terrific precipice" poised between the clouds above and a cataract below. No one saves him from his dream-demon, however; faced with "a form more hideous than the imagination of man is capable of portraying" (183–84), Ginotti sells his soul rather than face the terror of the abyss. God is not to trust in, for Ginotti—better to acknowledge the devil than chaos.

Even the dream of the innocent and naive Eloise reveals the yawning gulf that undermines the apparent security of the phenomenal world. Dreaming of the mysterious stranger who, in waking life, has befriended her, Eloise "thought that she met him on a flowery plain; that the feelings of her bosom, whether she would or not, impelled her towards him; that, before she had been enfolded in his arms, a torrent of scintillating flame, accompanied by a terrific crash of thunder, made the earth yawn beneath her feet" (159–60). The hidden precipice image, in Eloise's dream much like that chasm dreamt of by Clara Wieland, reveals the true nature of *St. Irvyne*'s moral universe. All the novel's characters totter on its brink. Wolfstein, and his wife, Megalena, and Ginotti are drawn into the yawning nothingness, the consuming abyss that underlies and subverts the sublime mountainscapes of the novel, much as Victor is lost to the horror he uncovers beyond the Alps' sublime vistas. At the novel's end, Ginotti is carried off to hell; we are expressly told that "the powers of hell [had] no influence" over Wolfstein at the moment of his death (199), apparently because he resisted the devil's offer (and allowed Ginotti, in a sense, to take his place in hell). Yet at the conclusion Shelley overlooks, perhaps intentionally, the earlier fears of Wolfstein, who is after all a murderer, that he would end up in the devil's power. He does not sell his soul but does die at that moment when the devil carries Ginotti's soul to hell.

Wolfstein thus falls victim to what might be a more horrifying fate, for although conventional piety may dictate that his soul be sent to Purgatory to expiate its sins, this conventional element is superficial in *St. Irvyne*. More integral to the novel's intellectual fabric is the repeated use of the dream, the precipice image, and sublime mountain vistas. These last are hardly the landscape set-pieces found in Radcliffe, leading neither to Burke's "pleasing terrors" nor to the consolation of religious aspiration. The novel's mountaintop scenes are associated with terrifying precipices, with yawning gulfs and suicide and death but never with God. The conventional religious sentiment of the novel's final sentence does not adequately counter the repeated use of a sublime consistently associated with void, darkness, and dread. Wolfstein may not be carried off to hell with Ginotti, but his refusal to obey the devil's command that he deny his Creator is hardly the final element in the novel's metaphysical picture. As with *The Monk*, *St. Irvyne* has a present and powerful devil but an absent God who ignores all pleas and takes no action, never intervening in human affairs or providing consolation. *St. Irvyne*, again like Lewis's novel, also features some morally good characters who manage to survive the horrors that destroy others, but Percy Shelley's are much more affected by the evil dimension of their experiences rather than by the good. Eloise and Fitzeustace do find some consolation in living in accord with "the laws of God" (although they marry only when forced to by socioeconomic pressures), but evil has left an enduring reminder of its potency: Eloise gives birth not to Fitzeustace's child but to Ginotti's, the demonic thus asserting its ability to intrude into the social and familial unit.

In a dark vision of the sublime that invokes *The Monk*'s hostile universe, *St. Irvyne* counters and subverts its own token gestures toward traditional piety. Both elements are present, to be sure, engaged in a tension resulting from Shelley's desire to write a commercially successful novel and yet still incorporate some of his personal philosophical and ideological tenets. Yet it is the latter that finally dominate this early work. Shelley was, Stephen Behrendt explains, "deliberately advocating unconventional, generally liberal causes here [in his Gothic novels], purposefully embedding subversive, 'anti-Establishment' propaganda in his tales while appearing to be writing conventional, conservative Gothic romances" (ix).

Percy Shelley abandoned the Gothic after *St. Irvyne* but never lost interest in the literary supernatural: from *Queen Mab* (1811) to the end of his life, he relied heavily on the images and tropes of mythic and Gothic supernaturalism; David Punter claims, with good reason, that "Shelley appears to have been the most immersed of the poets in contemporary Gothic writing" (106). Yet his mature work evinces an understanding of the supernatural that is markedly different even from his own youthful labors in the genre. His most sophisticated literary supernaturalism is most evident in two texts written in the ghost-haunted summer of 1816.

The major poems of that season, "Mont Blanc" and "Hymn to Intellectual Beauty," seem, at first, decidedly unconcerned with the supernatural, but careful examination discovers that these texts serve, in part, as mediations upon the sublime and its capacity to investigate terror and horror. Shelley first considers, in "Mont Blanc," the relationship of the Universal Mind (the term is Earl Wasserman's) to the individual human mind, here figured, respectively, as the ravine of Arve and the "feeble brook." The stream's origins in "the ice gulphs" of an unseen Mont Blanc become for the poet the type of the human mind "Holding an unremitting interchange / With the clear universe of things around . . ." (36–40). Through the agency of the poetic imagination, the individual achieves communion with a universal presence, a process in which the active role of the mind or imagination is stressed by the poet; as Wasserman notes, the universe as it is formulated in the poem is not "a self-existent reality" but "a fusion of perception and creation. . . . a reality provoked by (although not necessarily corresponding to) the objective, but existing in the subjective" (*Language* 200). This subjectivity profoundly influences Shelley's conception of the sublime.

The poem moves to a consideration of that Power which informs the Universal Mind, a Power of considerable consequence for human thought and activity but largely beyond direct comprehension: above the mutabilities of the world, "Power dwells apart in its tranquility / Remote, serene, and inaccessible" (96–97). The poet is quick to assert, however, the link between this Power and the things of Earth: "even

these primaeval mountains / Teach the adverting mind." Such direct
and explicit reaffirmation is necessary for the crucial point made in
the poem's fifth and final section: "Mont Blanc yet gleams on
high:—the power is there. . . ." The sense of human insignificance that
concludes the fourth part is here dispelled or at least countermanded
by the declaration of Power's unchanging presence; in its eternality
lies consolation, as the poet reveals in the final lines of the poem, addressed to the mountain:

> The secret strength of things
> Which governs thought, and to the infinite dome
> Of heaven is as a law, inhabits thee!
> And what were thou, and earth, and stars, and sea,
> If to the human mind's imaginings
> Silence and solitude were vacancy? (139–44)

In this final rhetorical question, Shelley subverts the sublime's potential for terror. "Silence" and "solitude" are *not* empty or void; Richard
Payne Knight's signifiers of sublime emptiness are filled by Shelley
with intimations of transcendent Power. The passivity of mind in the
pre-Kantian sublime led writers of radical Gothics to detect only void
beyond the empirical; Shelley, imbibing the general Romantic sense of
sublimity from his predecessors Wordsworth and Coleridge, understood the void to be a self-deceit. For Shelley, "Silence and solitude . . .
are decidedly not a vacancy either in the Power or in the 'human
mind's imaginings'. . . . What is an emptiness in the objective world is
the mind's entry into the absolute, since the absolute is silent (and
therefore the essence of sound), solitary (and therefore the essence of
fullness)" (Wasserman, *Language* 237). The mind's action, stimulated
by nature, fills the lacuna perceived by the Gothic novelists. Angela
Leighton, discussing Shelley's sense of the conventional sublime, observes that

> while he refuses to concede any epistemological evidence for the exis-
> tence of a God, he is drawn to an aesthetic which idealises the immate-
> rial and numinous properties of the landscape. The conflict between
> these two perspectives will become one of the distinguishing features of
> that poetry which is written in the manner of the sublime, and which
> has as its main theme the desire of the imagination to find a presence in
> the empty scene. (40)

The fulfillment of this desire is achieved in the closing lines of "Mont Blanc," which record the poet's understanding of the fundamental impulse of the eighteenth-century sublime reconfigured in accord with his personal beliefs. As a result "Mont Blanc" celebrates not absence but a secular version of the plenitude Coleridge discovered in the same locale and celebrated in his "Hymn before Sunrise in the Vale of Chamouni" (see Webb 140–42).

What is finally evident here, then, is the explanation for Percy Shelley's rejection of the Gothic as a vehicle of literary expression: if one did not use the Gothic to uncover the horror of *The Monk*'s universe, one had, it seems, to work the Radcliffean/sentimental vein of Gothicism, an alternative even less acceptable. It is probable that the haste with which *St. Irvyne* was concluded indicates Shelley's discovery that the possibilities of the form—of the supernatural sublime itself—were limited and uncongenial. Attempts to express a metaphysical dread one does not feel are bound to be as unconvincing as efforts to console through a religious belief one rejects: *St. Irvyne* is the ambivalent result of precisely such efforts. Five years after his second Gothic fiction, "Mont Blanc" reaches deeper into Shelley's thought than any dire demon or pious platitude.

Shelley's ability to locate in the natural sublime a secular transcendence accounts for two other aspects of his career. Having rejected the Gothic novel as a form, he still relied upon many of its tropes, as John Murphy amply shows in *The Dark Angel.* Shelley was more comfortable with literary supernaturalism than was Wordsworth precisely because he was able to work *through* supernatural sublimity to the transcendence normally found in the conventional sublime. Wordsworth never believed supernaturalism could carry a spiritual burden; in all his "Gothic" or supernatural pieces, Wordsworth opposes the supernatural to either nature or Christianity (or both) and to the spiritual consolations derived from each. The young Shelley, *St. Irvyne* reveals, did believe that Gothic supernaturalism could have spiritual implications, even if mostly negative; he had read Gothic fiction carefully. Like Wordsworth, Shelley too found nature to be an agent of transcendence and consolation, but his rejection of Christian thought meant that the supernatural never became something that had to be opposed in favor of an alternate language of the suprarational. The Gothic and mythic supernatural were compatible with his poetics and his beliefs because they were, by their very nature as well as by tradition, a language of the extra-natural; they provided the artist with an effective way to treat aspects of experience that lay beyond the empirical without invoking Christianity.

Percy Shelley's positive sublime also explains why he had the least success (and interest) in composing a supernatural work in the summer of 1816. Byron started a novel and began work on *Manfred;* Mary Shelley began *Frankenstein,* and John Polidori eventually produced *The Vampyre.* Within a week of the ghost-story episode, Percy Shelley wrote his "Hymn to Intellectual Beauty." Yet while the poem lacks a supernatural story, it constitutes his most important statement *about* supernaturalism, which should not surprise us given the circumstances of its composition. Indeed, the "Hymn" may well be taken as his poetic explanation of why he wrote no ghost story that summer.

Like "Alastor" the "Hymn" is a poem of intellectual quest, in this case a search not for knowledge but for an understanding of how best to achieve knowledge; the restless energy of "Alastor" gives way to a more considered reflection. The poem's calmer mood results from the fact that the object of the quest is at least vaguely known: that "unseen Power" which the poet addresses as "Spirit of Beauty." Yet knowing the object of one's quest is hardly the same as achieving it; the poet's questions in stanza two—"where art thou gone? / Why dost thou pass away and leave our state?"—show that it is simply in the nature of things for Intellectual Beauty to be an inconstant source of illumination.

The questions are also those of a more fundamental inquiry, and at this level the poem comments on Gothic supernaturalism. The poet asks nothing less than why human nature should be as it is; the answer he himself offers has implications for our inquiry:

> No voice from some sublimer world hath ever
> > To sage or poet these responses given—
> Therefore the name of God and ghosts and Heaven,
> Remain the records of their vain endeavour,
> Frail spells—whose uttered charm might not avail to sever,
> > From all we hear and all we see,
> > Doubt, chance, and mutability. (25–31)

Both religious and supernatural modes of inquiry, taken as ends in themselves, prove inadequate. Even Intellectual Beauty, the poem's central object, provides no clear and final answers: it may give "grace and truth to life's unquiet dream" (36) but does so "like mist o'er mountains driven, / Or music by the night wind sent / Through strings of some still instrument, / Or moonlight on a midnight stream" (32–35). Hardly the images of Apollonian clarity, these metaphors suggest an intuitive apprehension, rather than a rational comprehension, of Intellectual Beauty's enlightening power. Stanza four confirms the transitory nature of Intellectual Beauty's inspiring power and the consequences for humankind.

Stanza five returns to the "ghosts" mentioned in the third stanza, and to the possibilities of gaining knowledge through an ancient mode of inquiry:

> While yet a boy I sought for ghosts, and sped
> Through many a listening chamber, cave and ruin,
> And starlight wood, with fearful steps pursuing
> Hopes of high talk with the departed dead.
> I called on poisonous names with which our youth is fed;
> I was not heard—I saw them not. . . . (49–54)

This passage has an autobiographical aspect; Percy Shelley dabbled in necromancy as a youth, but the passage refers equally well to his early literary explorations of the supernatural. Just as he raised no ghosts with his youthful incantations, the Gothic fictions supplied no answers, provided no high talk with the departed dead.

The "answer," if such it is, lies ultimately not in the realm of the supernatural but the natural:

> When musing deeply on the lot
> Of life, at that sweet time when winds are wooing
> All vital things that wake to bring
> News of buds and blossoming,—
> Sudden, thy shadow fell on me;
> I shrieked, and clasped my hands in extacy! (55–60)

Intellectual Beauty's basis in nature, not supernature, is the source of consolation; it is part of the organic natural world, of "buds and blossomings" rather than of caves and the starlight wood. Supernaturally based inquiry, whether real necromancy or Gothic fiction, falsely sends us to ruins and negation.

In her 1831 introduction to *Frankenstein*, Mary Shelley, distanced from Percy's influence by his death and recalling the ghost-story challenge of the summer of 1816, wrote that "Shelley, more apt to embody ideas and sentiments in the radiance of brilliant imagery, and in the music of the most melodious verse that adorns our language, than to invent the machinery of a story, commenced one founded on the experiences of his early life" (7). At the same time that she recalls and excuses her husband's failure, Mary Shelley points to the crucial element of supernaturalism in "Hymn to Intellectual Beauty." Beginning a ghost story by thinking of his early life experiences, Percy Shelley must quickly have realized that he could not use those experiences in a conventional Gothic narrative; his early literary experiences had already taught him the limitations of that form. There was nothing left but to offer his understanding of the supernatural, to explain why he could not write a ghostly narrative, and "Hymn to Intellectual Beauty," although it certainly has other implications as well, is the result.

In light of the aesthetic sketched here, it should come as no suprise that Percy Shelley's 1818 preface to *Frankenstein* in many ways runs counter to the novel's interests and themes, a fact that makes the preface characteristic of Percy's response to his wife's novel, as Mellor recently demonstrated (57–65, 219–24).[7] Percy begins by minimizing the supernatural, which is appropriate since the creature's making is the result of science, but he goes on to create a series of smoke screens that serve (among other functions) to indicate his own distance from his wife's use of the literary supernatural.

There is no question *Frankenstein* involves some of "the elementary principles of human nature" (13), although the references to Homer, Shakespeare, and Milton seem a bit forced. Percy begins his serious dissembling in the third paragraph of his preface: "I am by no means indifferent to the manner in which whatever moral tendencies exist in the sentiments or characters [the novel] contains shall affect the reader; yet my chief concern in this respect has been limited to the avoiding the enervating effects of the novels of the present day, and to the exhibition of the amiableness of the domestic affection, and the excellence of universal virtue" (13–14). Of course familial and domestic bonds are central to the novel, but their "amiableness" is noticeable principally in its absence or destruction, as Kate Ferguson Ellis notes in her study of the family in *Frankenstein,* in which she also remarks on Percy Shelley's "selective" reading of the novel's theme (123–24). The novel's "chief concern" is a supernaturally sublime horror arising from the perversion of familial and natural affections, but as this is the sublime trope Shelley rejects in his "Hymn," we should not expect, only one year later, that he can be in agreement with the basic horror of the novel, especially given that, as Mellor explains, he seemed blind to the novel's critique of paternal irresponsibility, of which he himself was monstrously guilty. This likewise rendered opaque to him the novel's redemptive vision of family and community.

Percy Shelley continues: "The opinions which naturally spring from the character and situation of the hero are by no means to be conceived as existing always in my own conviction; nor is any inference justly to be drawn from the following pages as prejudicing any philosophical doctrine of whatever kind" (14). Here speaking in his own voice, he is distancing himself from the metaphysical implications of what he sees as his wife's horror sublime. (I would point out also that Percy Shelley, who preferred "terror" in his Gothic fictions, refers in the preface to "supernatural *terrors*" (13; emphasis added); Mary Shelley almost always uses "horror" when speaking of the supernatural, "terror" when speaking of the conventional sublime.)

The last two paragraphs of the preface sketch briefly the circumstances of the novel's composition, ending with the observation that the two other participants (he has apparently forgotten Polidori) "left me on a journey among the Alps, and lost, in the magnificent scenes which they present, all memory of their ghostly visions" (14). We have seen that the dismissal of "ghostly" interests is the result of Percy Shelley's literary and intellectual development, as he finds the natural sublime to obviate supernaturalism's horrors, but such a statement would be a very odd statement were it actually written by the author of *Frankenstein*. The central scene in the novel, after all, occurs in one of the most sublime locales in the Alps—the very spot in and about which Percy Shelley wrote "Mont Blanc"—but there is nothing of the positive in Mary Shelley's mountaintop sublime. Losing one's ghostly visions in the Alps is what Percy Shelley did; Victor went to Chamounix and encountered the greatest horror of his life. Further suggestive of Percy Shelley's evasions is the fact he is being slightly misleading (or simply mistaken) regarding the events of that summer (unless by "journey among the Alps" we should understand a boat trip around the lake): he and Byron set off a few days after the ghost-story pact, it is true, but for a sailing tour of Lac Leman, not a journey among the Alps. A tour of the Alps was conducted that summer but not by the two poets: on 21 July, approximately one month after the ghost-story session, the two Shelleys and Claire Clairmont set off on a tour of Chamounix and Mont Blanc (Marchand 243–45). *Frankenstein*'s preface, finally, is much more useful for what it tells us about Percy Shelley than for what it says about the novel.

*I*n his own rendering of mountaintop supernatural sublimity, Byron both comments on the Shelleys' attitudes toward the supernatural and declares his own distance from Gothic supernaturalism. A lifelong interest in the supernatural peaked in the summer of 1816.

Manfred—although not begun until three months after the ghost-story sessions, after both an August visit by Matthew Lewis and a September tour of the Bernese Alps with Hobhouse—is the most direct result of the summer's literary supernaturalism, a work configured as a polemical response to the literary supernaturalism of the Shelleys. Although Byron could not have seen much of *Frankenstein* before its publication, his intimacy with the Shelleys during this summer more than accounts for the correspondences noted below and makes significant influence a virtual certainty. Indeed, so close are *Manfred* and *Frankenstein* in their general concerns, even when they reach contrary conclusions, that one critic remarked, "It seems almost as likely that first drafts of *Frankenstein* influenced the poem [*Manfred*] as the other way around" (Small 55).

Byron would have sympathized with Percy Shelley's rejection of Gothicism's radical horror, yet he was unable to adopt the countering strategy of Percy's positive sublime. In a passage markedly similar to that which opens *St. Irvyne,* Manfred ascends the Jungfrau to declare his unwillingness to live:

> And you, ye crags, upon whose extreme edge
> I stand, and on the torrent's brink beneath
> Behold the tall pines dwindled as to shrubs
> In dizziness of distance; when a leap,
> A stir, a motion, even a breath, would bring
> My breast upon its rocky bosom's bed
> To rest forever—wherefore do I pause? (I.ii.13–19)

Manfred does pause, however, and like Wolfstein is saved by the intervention of others. But here the poem parts company with Percy Shelley's novel; while Manfred shares Wolfstein's self-assessment of superiority to his rescuer (II.i.38), he does not join forces with him. Manfred is too far beyond the chamois-hunter, too intense in his energy and too absorbed in his guilt, to dissemble among humans regardless of how thoroughly their condition may emblematize marginality or alienation. Even the chamois-hunter, one of the few who dares the mountain's greatest heights and who has little interaction with even remote mountain villages, is too much a part of humanity for Manfred. This solipsism will prove the key by which Manfred (and therewith Byron) rejects the horror of radical Gothicism.

In the poem's next scene, Byron extends his comment on Percy Shelley's literary supernaturalism, in effect rewriting "Mont Blanc" so as to counter that poem's claim that through imagination humanity gains awareness of and solace from unseen universal powers. Percy Shelley figures the imagination as the "witch of Poesy"; Manfred pays a visit to the "Witch of the Alps"; both witches dwell in Alpine river valleys noted for rainbows and rushing cataracts. Manfred has already sought the aid of lesser spirits—those of earthly elements and his own "star"—but they cannot grant him the oblivion he seeks. He turns then to a higher power, the witch, but where in "Mont Blanc" the poet's "own separate phantasy" receives solace from its witch—imagination's connection to "the clear universe of things around"—the Witch of the Alps can do nothing for Manfred but elicit from him an impassioned lament of alienation: "From my youth upwards / My spirit walked not with the souls of men, / Nor looked upon the earth with human eyes . . ." (II.ii.50–52). For Manfred, the imagination is unable to console the restless and autonomous spirit.

But Kant argues that where imagination fails reason may triumph, and Byron reports Manfred's early intellectual-rationalist inquiries into the nature of things in terms that leave no doubt he is thinking of the Shelleys, not only of the "Hymn to Intellectual Beauty" but also of *Frankenstein*:

> And then I dived,
> In my lone wanderings, to the caves of death,
> Searching its cause in its effect; and drew
> From withered bones, and skulls, and heaped up dust,
> Conclusions most forbidden. Then I passed
> The nights of years in sciences, untaught
> Save in the old time; and with time and toil,
> And terrible ordeal, and such penance
> As in itself hath power upon the air
> And spirits that do compass air and earth,
> Space, and the peopled infinite, I made
> Mine eyes familiar with Eternity,
> Such as, before me, did the Magi . . .
>   and with my knowledge grew
> The thirst of knowledge, and the power and joy
> Of this most bright intelligence . . . . (II.ii.79–91, 94–96)

Byron here conflates the two Shelleys' modes of supernatural investigation in order to prepare his own conclusions. Percy Shelley's youthful necromantic inquiries, both personal and literary, came to naught as he rejected both the easy answers and the radical horror that Gothicism promulgated. Mary Shelley modified that Gothicism, making it natural rather than supernatural, scientific rather than superstitious, but an element of horror remained nonetheless, appearing, literally, as a new form of being, a hideous shadowing self beyond the pale of those rules that shape and order human experience.

Byron brings both of these metaphysical paradigms together in Manfred's important autobiographical speech in order to exploit elements of both while confirming neither. The necromancy of the young Percy Shelley proves successful for Manfred; the poet of "Hymn to Intellectual Beauty" never held converse with the departed dead, but Manfred routinely summons spirits and parleys with the mighty Arimanes. Byron uncovers a certain degree of horror in his universe—Manfred's life is anguished, his "solitude is solitude no more, / But peopled with the Furies," (II.ii.130–31) and a spirit comes for him in the end—but there is none of Victor Frankenstein's emotional incapacity in *Manfred,* none of Wolfstein's acquiescent death when the devil sweeps Ginotti off to hell. The horror that plagues Victor is grounded in his own failure of responsibility; Manfred too has transgressed social and natural limits and has attempted to rid himself of his burden by suicide and madness, yet he fully accepts his responsibility. Manfred is anguished not so much that Astarte has died as that she has suffered for his actions: "Her faults were mine—her virtues were her own— / I loved her, and destroyed her!" (II.ii.116–17). When her spirit is summoned, Manfred declares his willingness to suffer for them both, in contrast to Victor's refusal to accept the responsibilities and duties of the secular father-god he sought to become.

Manfred accepts these, most evidently in his refusal to give himself over to the power of the spirits. Byron makes the rejection of metaphysical subordination symmetrical by having Manfred also refuse the offer of religious consolation tendered by the Abbot, whose piety mirrors Manfred's occult researches. In the Abbot's offer, Manfred finds nothing that can ameliorate the intensity of his spiritual self-torment:

> Old man! there is no power in holy men,
> Nor charm in prayer—nor purifying form
> Of penitence—nor outward look—nor fast—
> Nor agony—nor, greater than all these,
> The innate tortures of that deep despair,
> Which is remorse without the fear of hell,
> But all in all sufficient to itself
> Would make a hell of heaven—can exorcise
> From out the unbounded spirit the quick sense

Of its own sins, wrongs, sufferance, and revenge
Upon itself. . . . (III.i.66–76)

A titanic solipsism is both Manfred's greatness and his downfall; like Prometheus, Manfred triumphs over his punishment because of it.

Manfred's greatest act of self-assertion occurs at the poem's conclusion, where he bids a heroic defiance to the "dusk and awful figure" that comes to claim him. Unlike Ginotti or Faustus, Manfred has achieved his powers not through a compact with the devil but "by superior science—penance—daring— / And length of watching— strength of mind—and skill / In knowledge of our fathers . . ." (III.iv.115–17). While such self-reliance makes him akin to Victor Frankenstein, Manfred's defiance is of a different order than Victor's, whose threats and pistols have no effect on his creature. Manfred, "creating out of his despair a meaningful framework within which to die" (Gleckner 257), does so without succumbing to horror: "Old man! 'tis not so difficult to die" (III.iv.151). Byron was right to complain to John Murray that dropping the line destroyed "the whole effect and moral" of the poem, for Manfred's deliberate acceptance of his fate, so unlike Victor's tormented and half-unwilling death and Wolfstein's abrupt dissolution, is necessary if his metaphysics are to retain their integrity, if his death is to be consistent with his life. Manfred indeed defies the spirit who has come for him: "I bear within / A torture which could nothing gain from thine: / The mind which is immortal makes itself / Requital for its good or evil thoughts, / Its own origin of ill and end . . ." (III.iv.127–31). There is no horror beyond the self, for Manfred as for Milton's Satan; that which Victor Frankenstein thought he had created in the world was really within. Byron's supernaturalism is like that of both Coleridge and Hawthorne in its interiority—"these eyes but close / To look within," Manfred declares in his opening soliloquy—although neither of these writers would have countenanced Byron's repudiation of Christian solace.

Percy Shelley's early Gothic supernaturalism was more in sympathy with Byron's supernaturalism than anything the younger poet later developed; the optimistic sublime of "Mont Blanc" fails for Byron, for whom the hell within cannot be transcended so blithely. Leslie Marchand quotes a passage from Byron's journal in which the poet records the limitations of the sublime: "neither the music of the Shepherd, the crashing of the Avalanche, nor the torrent, the mountain, the Glacier, the Forest, nor the Cloud, have for one moment lightened the weight upon my heart, or enabled me to lose my own wretched identity . . ." (252). The failure of sublimity's trademark suspension of self testifies to the truth of Marchand's assessment that Byron's "real quarrel with life was that he could not transcend the bounds of morality; the 'half deity' did not compensate for the 'half dust' " (254). Such inescapable selfhood denies the transcendent optimism that enabled Percy Shelley to repudiate Gothic horror.

Yet neither is the moral horror that so dominates Mary Shelley's novel sufficiently final for Byron, for it supposes a failure of will and resolve. Manfred uses Victor's science in combination with occult arts but is never troubled by the ghosts or spirits he summons, which are never his punishment or avatars of his failure. Manfred's trouble is within, not externalized in some projection like Victor's creature. There is too much of weakness, for Byron, in the projection of *Frankenstein*; Victor's problem is that he has given his own failings so much power they have become autonomous and reach back to destroy him. Manfred's failings are not those of inadequacy but of excess. Both protagonists die but for profoundly different reasons. Victor is worn out from chasing his creature, his own divided self, across the icy waste. Manfred's titanic insistence on the sufficiency of self makes such self-division impossible. He may, like Byron himself, have felt the "fundamental split between skepticism and the impulse to believe and belong" (Marshall 15), but his interview with the Abbot reveals that Manfred's mind is decided: belief and belonging are not possible, and Manfred recognizes and accepts this. In contrast to Victor, Manfred dies in peace because he dies intact. The ironically named Victor, although eagerly anticipating union with the spirits of his dead family, finds the moment of his death troubled because his creature still lives.

There is an implicit ethical code informing the action and philosophy of *Manfred*, to be sure, and since it is the violation of this code that torments Manfred, the inference that the work has some element of ethical conservatism is just. Byron is not, despite his rejection of Percy Shelley's positive sublimity, a radical Gothicist; his supernatural inquiry uncovers no failings in the universe at large. As William Marshall notes:

> By 1817 . . . [Byron] had largely accepted imperfection in the Self and in Man's consciousness as an end in itself rather than as an obstacle in one's view of life that somehow had to be got around. He had become . . . an ironist, one aware of the limits of human capacity and the absurdity of many forms of human activity, but in exposing these he was offering no suggestion for an ideal substitute in human behavior. (16)

In the Byronic universe it is humanity that fails, whether through timidity or excess, and Byron deplores the former while recognizing a redemptive heroism in the latter.

Byron's works from the summer of 1816 demonstrate ambivalence about the Gothic and the ability of the literary supernatural to investigate the human condition. He rejected Percy Shelley's cosmic optimism; Robert Hume speculates that perhaps it was Byron's "Augustan affinities which so severely undermine his faith in the transcendent power of imagination, but Byron's cosmic despair is not offset even by his glorying in the mysterious grandeur of heroes modeled on himself" ("Gothic" 289). It is very much the point of *Manfred*, which offers no conventionally redemptive vision, that "only the final and total isolation of the Self, which (psychologically as well as philosophically) renders death necessary, constitutes reality" (Marshall 109); given such visions of the human condition the poem must share at least some of the protonihilist implications of radical Gothicism. (This, I take it, is what Hume is thinking of when he sees Byron, philosophically speaking, as more of a Gothic writer than a Wordsworthian or Keatsian Romantic.) Yet Byron will not recognize the universal horror of the yawning gulf, denying the unknown the power to debase through terror. The "half-deity" scorns what the "half-dust" fears.

In these general contours, Byron exhibits qualities that will become more pronounced in the supernaturalist fiction of his fellow ironist Poe. Although he will work without Byron's Old World supernaturalism for the most part, Poe will find a universe that threatens and even destroys, yet its horror will be of our own making, a necessary condition of our being.

Chapter Seven

''Wonders are No Wonders''

Keats and the Supernatural

Keats's greater receptivity to the literary supernatural led to a deeper involvement in his era's "high culture" reassessment of Gothic supernaturalism than was the case for any of his major contemporaries except Coleridge. In keeping with the aesthetic revisionism of high Romanticism, Keats came to deploy the familiar tropes of sublimity against Gothic supernaturalism.

Albrecht notes that Keats used "sublime" only rarely and then usually in the alchemical sense, signifying "a process of separating out some desirable quality or product from grosser materials" (*Pleasures* 136). This process becomes, aptly, a metaphor for the Keatsian sublime as regards his supernaturalism, since for Keats the supernatural partakes neither of Gothic horror nor of conventional religious consolation but was instead an adjunct to the visionary poetics that informed all of his major work.

Keats found Gothic sublimity, with its reliance upon either conventional Christian metaphysics or radical nihilist horror, antithetic to his secular optimism, yet he did not take the Wordworthian tack of (largely) renouncing the supernatural. Like Coleridge, Keats seized on supernaturalism's metaphoric possibilities, finding in Gothic tropes a metaphoric capacity that had been neither exhausted nor irredeemably tainted by prior deployments. But where Coleridge seized upon super-naturalism's psychological aspect, Keats (like Percy Shelley) turned the Gothic supernatural outward rather than in, heavenward rather than down. The supernatural still figures predominantly as a form of sus-pension for Keats but not as soul-freezing moment of terror or awe-struck incapacity before the divine. Rather, supernaturally impelled suspensions become moments of near-ecstatic elevation, fleeting but nonetheless gesturing at unguessable potential and immutable truth.

Keats's fundamental poetic desire follows the contours of the sub-lime experience; as Jack Stillinger explains, the basic structure of a Keatsian poem is a rising movement toward a transcendent state fol-lowed by a return to the empirical world with greater insight and hope. For Keats, transcendence ultimately is be denied to mortals, but knowledge of its possibility is not, and in this knowledge is little room for terror.

At the same time, Keats's assessment of the supernatural and its aesthetic value was far from unambiguous; the following, in a letter to his publisher John Taylor (17 November 1819), reveals how Keats was drawn in two directions by the simultaneous promise and insuffi-ciency of the literary supernatural:

> As the marvellous is the most enticing and the surest guarantee of har-monious numbers I have been endeavouring to persuade myself to un-tether Fancy and let her manage for herself—I and myself cannot agree about this at all. Wonders are no wonders to me. I am more at home amongst Men and women. I would rather read Chaucer than Ariosto.
> (*Letters* II: 234)

Obviously such sentiments must be balanced with the fact that a num-ber of Keats's most important poems employ the supernatural, nor can we forget that Keats read Spenser as avidly as he turned the pages of Chaucer.[1] Recognizing this comfortable duality in Keats, the peace-ful—indeed, symbiotic—coexistence of the fancy loving and the in-tensely real, we arrive at the foundational premise of Keatsian supernaturalism. Keats struck a balance between Chaucer and Ariosto by rejecting not the forms of romance or the language of supernatural-ism but by reconfiguring these external elements so that his supernatu-ralism might take on new meaning and a more human focus, although not always in the Coleridgean psychological sense. Supernaturalism is inherently the language of the extra-rational, the beyond-nature, and

Keats exploited this basic fact so that he might consider the potential of human artistic and imaginative reach, the aesthetically represented spiritual longing for contact with the transcendent.

The present chapter concentrates on Keats's four best-known supernatural poems: "Isabella" (1818), "The Eve of St. Agnes" (January–February 1819), "La Belle Dame sans Merci" (April 1819), and "Lamia" (July–August 1819). The dates of composition are significant because this group comprises a progressive supernaturalist probing of the ability of the human spirit to make contact with and participate in the transcendent, and much of the significance of Keats's supernatural treatments of this theme inheres in the developmental pattern mapped by these four texts.[2] In all of these supernatural poems, love relationships metaphorically encode human/supernature contact, and desire becomes emblematic of "the combined self-surrender and self-possession that one finds at the heart of the complete visionary experience" (Ende 71). Keats's aesthetic of course also included negative capability, another expression of his desire for slipping the shackles of self; the supernatural poems, and the aesthetic of supernaturalism they endorse, I take to be complementary to this aesthetic. Keats's trope of confident self-negation in turn links these four poems with his major nonsupernatural works of the same time, particularly the great odes. Stillinger's declaration that Keats's "significant poems center on a single basic problem, the mutability inherent in nature and human life, and openly or in disguise they debate the pros and cons of a single hypothetical solution, transcendence of earthly limitations" (100) can be applied with equal legitimacy to the supernatural poems, validating the appraisal of Keats's supernatural works as central to and deeply expressive of the poet's lifelong artistic concerns.

*L*ike Keats's later supernatural works, "Isabella" finds human passion capable of dissolving the natural/supernatural barrier and discovers as well that the crossing of that barrier is problematic and ephemeral. As Keats's earliest study of supernaturally figured transcendence, "Isabella" does not develop the intellectual sophistication of the later poems, working through its Boccaccian story without fully engaging the theme that dominates the later works: the role of the visionary imagination in transcendence. Unlike "Lamia," which also brings with it a foundation in Continental literature, "Isabella" remains primarily a love story tinted at times with a Gothic atmosphere. It is a tentative consideration of the metaphoric power of literary supernaturalism, one surpassed by the later poems. But precisely because of this contrast with the later works and because it is a beginning point, "Isabella" merits notice here.

The first appearance of Lorenzo's ghost makes clear the poem will forsake Gothic horror for love. Describing "the pale shadow" in terms that make rather explicit the decomposed state of Lorenzo's body, Keats is quick to back off from this tantalizing suggestion of Gothicism and declare that the love empowering the ghostly visitation denies the moment any share of horror: "Its eyes, though wild, were still all dewy bright / With love, and kept all phantom fear aloof / From the poor girl by magic of their light . . ." (289–91). This is an early strategy for suppression of Gothic horror, an inversion of Burger's "Lenore" that shows the natural/supernatural union to be mutually desired; it is an obvious step in making the supernatural signify the object of transcendent desire. Keats easily succeeds: Lorenzo, like many of Poe's heroes, is heartened by the paleness of his lover (the physiological token that the supernatural experience has affected Isabella), and his response indicates the ability of love successfully to breach the nature/supernature barrier: "Thy beauty grows upon me, and I feel / A greater love through all my essence steal" (319–20).

Keats verges toward the Gothic again when Isabella seeks her lover's forest grave:

> Who hath not loiter'd in a green church-yard,
>   And let his spirit, like a demon-mole,
> Work through the clayey soil and gravel hard,
>   To see scull, coffin'd bones, and funeral stole;
> Pitying each form that hungry Death hath marr'd,
>   And filling it once more with human soul?
> Ah! this is holiday to what was felt
>   When Isabella by Lorenzo knelt. (353–60)

Yet even such morbid Gothicism is turned to good account. From the moment Isabella begins the exhumation, an act of movement toward and alliance with the extramortal realm of experience that Lorenzo now represents, she begins to lose her connection with the human, natural world. Unearthing one of Lorenzo's gloves and kissing it "with a lip more chill than stone," Isabella deposits it in the bosom of her dress, "where it dries / And freezes utterly unto the bone / Those dainties made to still an infant's cries . . ." (372–74). The immediate effect of her love is to deny her place in humanity's march of generations, to negate the procreativity of her body. This negation prefigures her own death, but her passing is redeemed not only by the desirability of death but by the equation of death with another sort of fecundity: Lorenzo's decomposing head nourishes Isabella's basil so that it grows with unsurpassed luxuriance (425–27). The multiple implications here are not evidence of Keats's uncertainty regarding the virtues of this tentative and simple troping of transcendence, for the references to fertility (the luxuriant basil) and to its loss (Isabella's preoccupation with the dead) are linked by their affirmation of love's transcending power. Isabella's devotion to the plant, the embodiment now of her love-object, was strong enough "to wean / her from her own fair youth, and pleasures gay, / And even remembrance of her love's delay" (462–64), and to remove her almost completely from participation in the larger world of nature:

> And she forgot the stars, the moon, and sun,
>   And she forgot the blue above the trees,
> And she forgot the dells where waters run,
>   And she forgot the chilly autumn breeze;
> She had no knowledge when the day was done,
>   And the new morn she saw not. . . . (417–22)

Keats pushes Isabella's alienation from life and nature further still with his invocation of the "Lethean" Muses (Echo, Melancholy, and Music) who will celebrate her love with "syllables of woe" (441). But love is linked with death not out of perverse and horrid fascination, as in *The Monk,* but because Keats is working, however simply, with death and the supernatural as elements of an image cluster testifying to the human capability of sublimation in the alchemical sense, of a purging of the "grosser materials." The process is not without pain and has a necessary connection with death, but it is impelled here by love, that most positive of human emotions. Isabella's denial of her own generativity and her alienation from her brothers (who, after all, are murderers) must be understood accordingly.

Given such a context, it might at first be surprising that the poem ends not with a "Lenore"-like union of the lovers in the afterworld but with the death of Isabella, driven to insanity by the loss of her beloved basil pot. "Isabella" may indeed owe something to Burger's "Lenore" and the ballad tradition behind that poem, but Keats circumscribes that tradition's influence at a crucial juncture. Lorenzo returns, as the wronged or demonic lovers always do, but not to ravish his bride back to a shadowy supernatural world; rather, he wishes only to explain his long absence, lament his loneliness, and reaffirm

his love, a necessary development that both informs the poem's tragedy and constitutes its redemption. Love is the nexus binding spirit to
flesh, and it is a positive, benevolent love: Lorenzo is hardly the
demon-knight of "Lenore" or the slave of perverse lusts as is Ambrosio. At the same time, Keats cannot condone a blissful union of the
lovers after death. The prospect may exist, certainly, but "Isabella"
must end without entering the afterlife; the transcendent realm simply
is not accessible. Isabella finally dies "a death too lone and incomplete," and when she does the poet has nothing further to say. Love's
reach and power are sufficient to penetrate the barrier between life
and death, but as for the actual consequences, all we have is Isabella's
lament: "O cruelty, / To steal my basil-pot away from me!" Her cri de
coeur has nothing to do with the transcendent, but this lack of relation
is precisely the point. In "Isabella" all we know on earth is love and
sadness.

At the same time, Louise Smith's claim that the poem is one in
which "impassioned sexuality must yield to the damnation of the real
world's fierce destruction" (311) is an overstatement, for the poem is
not, at its core, about the destruction of love but about its transformative capabilities and power. The supernatural dimension reveals love's
purer register, a more idealized form allied to our desire to sublime
ourselves, to leave behind what Byron called our "half dust" so that
the "half deity" may realize its true nature. But as to what that nature
is, "Isabella" holds no clue. Even our brief glimpse into the Other-
world is of no help: Lorenzo's ghost appears in the aspect of Lorenzo's
rotting body. The half-dust confounds us again, and our imaginations
fall back to earth.

The poem hardly qualifies as a profound reflection on the transcendent power of human passion and the relationship between the natural
and the numinous. At the same time, as the first in a series of supernatural poems, it establishes the basic Keatsian premise that while the
passions of the human heart may be strong enough to assail the
boundary between mortal and transcendent realms, these passions
must eventually fail. Isabella, the knight, Lycius—all fail to achieve in
this world the object of their quest.

*I*sabella" is something of a dark meditation, then, a poem of
discovery in which Keats learns that the effort involved in penetrating the barrier of human limitations consumes us. Keats's next major

supernaturalist poem, "The Eve of St. Agnes," serves as a partial corrective to this discovery, for it posits a love that, while partaking of the transcendent, does not founder on the necessarily limited perception of the extramortal experience, as it does in "Isabella." In order to realize this optimism, "Eve" moves away from the more Gothic atmosphere of the earlier poem.

"The Eve of St. Agnes" is less supernatural than its title suggests, for its concern is as much with literary traditions—"old romance" and Miltonic and Coleridgean echoes—as with anything else, as Robert Kern effectively demonstrates in "Keats and the Problem of Romance." Indeed, the poem contains little if anything of the supernatural, unless we consider as such a domestic superstition only one character takes seriously, or the seemingly agentless opening of doors and sliding of bolts, the "magicality" of which may be attributed as much to grammar as to ghosts. Yet the poem is crucial to the progression traced here, for in it Keats considers closely the ability of intense emotional experience to transcend human limitations, a matter that will be at the heart of the more supernatural "La Belle Dame" and "Lamia." As with these later poems, Keats here links the visionary imagination with passion, but in this second of the four works he has not yet raised his sights as high as he will, for the very human Porphyro and Madeline have taken as their love objects not fairies or spirits but each other. The poem is even, in one sense, a step back from "Isabella," with its mortal/ghostly passion; "St. Agnes" is, in effect, an attempt by Keats to redeem human passion. The poem's inherent optimism also serves to distance the work from Keats's later, more supernatural works.

Keats's deliberate manipulation of audience reaction in "St. Agnes" has been convincingly documented;[3] his authorial self-consciousness is further evident in his playful flirtation with the pseudosupernatural descriptions applied to his characters when first introduced. That these supernaturalist hints always disappear, never to return, testifies not so much to Keats's reluctance fully to engage the supernatural as to his sense of authorial control: he introduces these descriptive elements to raise our expectations only that he might deflate or confound them.

Such a technique is very much in keeping with Keats's general approach to the poem, an approach involving both a "heightened awareness of the tenuousness of the imaginative world into which he was withdrawing and . . . a view of the poet's role as conjurer that was at times ironic" (Sperry 201). Indeed, Keats's use of the Gothic here is almost sportive, appropriately so given his personal view of the genre.

Yet "Eve" is not, as Sperry argues, "parody or burlesque" (201), and that Keats employs a "beguiling inconsistency" with his characters does not mean he did not take them seriously. The poem's softly ironic tone serves a different end, and that Keats's characters "lay claim at various times to different levels of existence or reality that continually play off against, challenge, or modify each other" (Sperry 211) is evidence of Keats's reconfiguration of basic Gothic structures and expectations.

Consider the case of Angela, a menial in the intellectual as well as occupational sense of the word, who is first seen "Shuffling along with ivory-headed wand" (92). Yet with or without this traditional magic prop she works no magic, and after this one mention the wand disappears from the poem. She is, after all, a "Gossip dear"—no sorceress, simply a Keatsian version of the loquacious, superstitious servant common in Gothic romances (typified by Annette in *The Mysteries of Udolpho*). Angela's timidity and reluctant cooperation with Porphyro are equally components of a stock characterization. The poem's most supernatural description of Porphyro is put by Keats into her mouth precisely because we are not to take it seriously, rather as a deliberate and self-conscious manipulation of the audience/narrative relationship, as well as evidence of Angela's unsophisticated character.

Porphyro's indignation at the thought of "Madeline asleep in lap of legends old" (135) further evidences Keats's self-conscious use of romance elements, one paralleled by Porphyro's considered (and successful) attempt to manipulate the St. Agnes' Eve superstition to his advantage. Porphyro proves to be a conjuror, certainly, but the magic he employs is that of the poet, not the sorcerer.[4] Angela's distress at his "stratagem" is appropriate for her limited, tradition-bound "way," and her reproof of Porphyro—"I deem / Thou canst not surely be the same that thou did'st seem" (144)—is hardly objective evidence of the young lover's supernaturalism. Angela registers disappointment here, not surprise or fright, for she has realized that this ordinary mortal man is out to seduce her young mistress. It is true she laughs with apparent skepticism when she mentions that "the conjuror plays / This very night" (124–25), but her repeated references to the saint's day suggest that, even if the domestic superstition of the occasion means nothing to her (and it certainly would not at her age), it being a holy day is enough to make Porphyro's stratagem unsavory and improper. But a little emotional manipulation by Porphyro secures Angela's reluctant cooperation (again, a Gothic commonplace).

Her assistance is remarkably efficacious, for it permits Porphyro to spy on Madeline as she undresses, Angela here substituting for *The Monk*'s diabolic mirror. Her last words—"Ah! Thou must needs the lady wed, / Or I may never leave my grave among the dead" (179–80)—further confirm her traditionality, for such a tryst, she believes, must properly end in the social sanctification of a wedding, and the reference to her afterlife suggests that superstition holds a larger place in Angela's mind than even she suspects.

It becomes clear that the moral and social structures endorsed by Angela do not hold sway over the lovers when Madeline escorts "the aged gossip" down the stairs; they descend from the level on which consummation is imminent to "a safe level matting"—down, in other words, to the world of the cold asceticism of the Beadsman and the gross sensual indulgence of the revelers, a world of physical extremes (denial and indulgence) where transcendent experience remains unknown, where passionate intensity is, like the Beadsman, "aye unsought for."

The reader's introduction to Madeline, like that to Porphyro, hints at supernaturalism: she is "like a mission'd spirit" (193), "all akin / To spirits of the air, and visions wide" (202). Yet Keats makes it clear something is lacking in the condition: "her heart was voluble, / Paining with eloquence her balmy side; / As though a tongueless nightingale should swell / Her throat in vain, and die, heart-stifled, in her dell" (204–7). Alone in her chamber, Madeline is silenced, her passion voiceless and her desire unexpressed. Her world, like Langdale Hall, is "a self-enclosed, stagnant Eden, which, while it may protect us from pain, denies us joy" (Wiener 121). It will be only by intrusion, by contact with the external and the Other, that the empowering potential of her passion will be realized.

Understanding that Coleridge made much the same point in "Christabel," Keats describes Madeline's room in terms similar to those used for Christabel's at the point where the innocent maiden leads Geraldine, that poem's embodiment of experience, into her virginal chamber.[5] At the corresponding moment in his own poem, Keats underscores the necessity of external intrusion:

> Full on this casement shown the wintry moon,
> And threw warm gules on Madeline's fair breast,
> As down she knelt for heaven's grace and boon;
> Rose-bloom fell on her hands, together prest,
> And on her silver cross soft amethyst,
> And on her hair a glory, like a saint:

> She seem'd a splendid angel, newly drest,
> Save wings, for heaven. . . . (217–24)

The moon, like Porphyro and like Geraldine, is an external agency penetrating into the young woman's "chaste" chamber. Foreshadowing Porphyro's effect, the intrusive moon ("pallid" outside the chamber) effects a change in Madeline, for suddenly the white and cold of virginal association are replaced by "warm gules" and "rose-bloom," the silver of her cross vanquished by "soft amethyst."

The effect of this encounter of innocence with experience is considerable. Though the moment only foreshadows the change she will undergo in her union with Porphyro, Madeline even now becomes "like a saint" and "a splendid angel." She had not before been described in such terms, but despite the apparent promotion from spirit to angel, something crucial is lacking. In terms of Keats's own metaphor, she is without wings; just as an angel cannot ascend to heaven without them, Madeline cannot begin her own transcendent experience without the agent of her own ascent: the intense emotionalism of Porphyro, the poem's embodiment of that experience necessary to complement her innocence. Porphyro's weakening at the sight of Madeline in the transforming rays of the moon is not evil faltering in the face of good; rather, it is his realization of the transforming power of the visionary experience.

Incomplete without the vital component of intimate human contact, Madeline retires alone to her bed, the "chilly nest" in which she is not so much protected as "Blinded alike from sunshine and from rain, / As though a rose should shut, and be a bud again" (242–43). These lines sketch a movement toward isolation and denial—a movement ironically expressed in natural imagery, for it is participation in the world of nature, both physical and human, that Madeline has shunned. We see her only indoors prior to her encounter with Porphyro, just as the overprotected Christabel must venture from Langdale into the "midnight wood" to begin her initiation into experience. Madeline is equally unfulfilled within her enclosing space; the revellers are drunken boors, and that Madeline "danc'd along with vague, regardless eyes" (64) among them clearly marks their inability to affect her.

So it is appropriate that Porphyro, the lover from across the moors, comes to her bed "Noiseless as fear in a wide wilderness" (250). He sets a feast (the first stage in the pleasure thermometer progression), but the too-close connection between such sensuality and the baseness of the revelers is emphasized when "the boisterous, midnight, festive clarion, / The kettle-drum, and far-heard clarionet, / Affray [Porphyro's] ears" (258–60). This first step, the invocation of sensuous nature, proves ineffective (as does wine in "Ode to a Nightingale"), for despite Porphyro's incantation—"And now, my love, my seraph fair, awake!" (276)—Madeline remains deep in the "midnight charm" of her "steadfast spell."

Music (one step higher on the ladder of intensities, equivalent to "the viewless wings of Poesy" in the "Nightingale" ode) proves partially effective. So close and so immanent is the presence of her completing lover that Madeline partially awakens, understandably frightened, into a halfway world, much like the Coleridgean dreamer in the hypnagogic state: "Her eyes were open, but still she beheld, / Now wide awake, the vision of her sleep: / There was a painful change, that nigh expell'd / The blisses of her dream so pure and deep . . . " (298–301). The description of Porphyro as "pallid, chill, and drear" (311) is not due to his finding himself "momentarily isolated from the sustaining warmth and vitality of [Madeline's] dream" (Sperry 214) but rather a result of his being (unlike Geraldine) as human and as powerless to achieve transcendence alone as Madeline is, even though he is the vitalizing power in her circumscribed world. This I believe is the point Keats wishes to make by describing his previously fiery hero as "pale" twice within fifteen lines.

Confronted with the possibility of a transcendent experience a chieved in a passionate lover's union, Porphyro asserts himself, and the lovers consummate their passion as the moon sets, the earlier agent of penetration and infusion of energy and experience no longer necessary; innocence and experience have met and melded, completing each other in the realm of the human.

With the "magic" of their union marked by the arrival of the "elfin storm," the lovers readily slip from the "castle foul" and the stultifying life it represents. Supernatural references return in abundance at the poem's conclusion: twice in two lines the lovers are said to be "like phantoms," and no explicit agent is mentioned in those lines that describe the opening of doors and sliding of deadbolts. There is no basis for supposing the presence of supernaturals where none have been discovered earlier; the grammatical ambiguity here is further deliberate flirtation on Keats's part with a Gothicism he will not endorse.

A larger ambiguity is raised by the famous tense shift in the last stanza: "And they are gone: ay, ages long ago / These lovers fled away into the storm" (370–71). The sense of deception readers sometimes feel upon encountering these lines was something Keats wanted in the poem (Bate 443, fn), but in the very contrast of these lines with the body of the narrative lies the redemption of the lovers, not a sense that they are forever lost "to the depths of time and mortal experience" (Kern 187). The contrast of the very real and immediate Porphyro and Madeline in the narrative and the "long ago" lovers of the concluding stanza serves to make us aware of the effect of this tale of "old romance" on us in our moment. The shock does not produce "the illusion that the momentary can be made permanent" (Atkins 129) but is instead a challenge to readers to acknowledge that the just-read story of love's triumph has a very real significance for us, that the part of the tale that affects us most is not its surface Gothicism or "old romance" but its essential humanity. Madeline and Porphyro may have fled into the storm and died "ages long ago," but in their effect on the reader they endure, and if, as Wasserman suggests, the ending places the lovers in a "spaceless, timeless, selfless realm of mystery" (*Tone* 123), it also forces us to apprehend the immediacy of their mutually enhancing passion. Desire, after all, is the agent empowering them to face the elfin storm, the world of dynamic forces outside the placid sterility of the castle.

In the supernatural poems that were to follow in the same year, Keats raised the metaphysical stakes by insisting on a more immediate link between the human and transcendent realms; Madeline and Porphyro escape inhibiting tradition, but the scenario considered in "St. Agnes" was not, for Keats, an adequate or final test of the transformative power of desire. Such a test would come only by measuring the power of the intense visionary experience against the highest human aspirations. The visionary realm, accessible only to sublimed spirits, continued to beckon insistently, and in his next two supernatural poems Keats was directly to consider attempts to engage and apprehend this realm.

*L*a Belle Dame sans Merci" is Keats's first supernaturalist attempt to consider sustained human contact with the transcendent or numinous, a possibility only hinted at in the more thoroughly human poems just considered. Compared to "Lamia," the treatment in "La Belle Dame sans Merci" is schematic, focusing almost exclusively on the emotional devastation that follows in the aftermath of the failed visionary experience. "La Belle Dame" opens with a quick sketch of a nature that has become the objective correlative of the knight-visionary's anguished state. Colored by suggestions that the moment of richness and plenitude is past—"The squirrel's granary is full / And the harvest's done" (78)—the ordinary world has become the site of decay and emptiness, as unfulfilling as the castles of "Christabel" and "Eve of St. Agnes." The sense of waste and death is inescapable: the sedge has dried; the birds are silent; even the knight himself "fast withereth." The images—lily and rose—that describe him link him not with the forces of nature but with the decay that surrounds him. The poem's only gesture of communality, the presence of the unknown questioner who abruptly disappears, serves primarily to underscore the essential isolation of the knight.

Like "Lamia," "La Belle Dame sans Merci" signals a participation in the numinous by means of a love relationship between a human male and supernatural female, a relationship that necessarily proves incapable of sustaining itself. Yet while the association of the "fairy's child" with a numinous nature is clear, her moral status is not. Some critics have regarded la belle dame, like Lamia, as evil or demonic (Evert 245; Clapp 90–92; Perkins 263), but such assessments evade the question of where responsibility for the human failure in these poems lies. Charles Patterson points out a moral fact about la belle dame that we must not ignore:

> She is a nonmortal, daemonic creature of Celtic origins, and she is neutral as to good and evil because she is outside the human pale and all its restrictions. There is no context of good and evil in the particular daemonic matrix of the poem. (*Keats* 138)

There is nothing overtly malevolent about either Lamia or la belle dame, or Geraldine for that matter; the evil we register in them is simply a projection of our own inadequacies, the very limitations of our humanity that so haunted Keats.[6]

There are two other significant characteristics the fairy shares with Lamia. Both magic women have an ability to draw the men they seek out of the social world: Lycius, returning to Corinth with Lamia, enters a city that to his altered perception appears dreamlike and insubstantial; the knight-at-arms, having "set [the fairy] on [his] pacing steed," becomes so detached from the ordinary world that he "nothing else saw all day long" (21–22). Both women conduct the objects of their desire to an isolating enclosure: Lamia's magic-built dream palace, la belle dame's "elfin grot."

Parallels between the male characters also obtain: the knight, like

Lycius, cannot resist that part of himself which binds him to the world of humanity. Like the thrill of trumpets that destroys Lycius's tentative participation in a world of higher perception, the dream of the knight-at-arms (a dream of men, the mortality of men, and their inability to find psychic nourishment in a world not truly theirs) calls him out from the spell of the woman and her elfin grot, which, in the penultimate stanza, is seen itself to *be* "the cold hill's side." What has changed is not the knight's location, but his perception of and participation in those aspects of nature that lie beyond the purview of the five senses.

Like his counterpart in "Lamia," the knight finds that his experience with the transcendent—a world not available to him in his mortal condition—has rendered him unfit for (or incapable of enduring) existence in the quotidian world. The more dramatic "Lamia" delivers this point with greater impact, for the exorcism of Lamia is immediately (and, the implication is, necessarily) followed by the death of Lycius. "La Belle Dame" makes the same point but less urgently, with considerable gain in pathos and elegiac mood.

The poem concludes by returning to the language of its opening, but there is no sense of hope or renewal attending this circularity, for it is a return to the language of discontinuity and decay. Indeed, as Patterson points out, the final stanza serves to remind us, ironically, of the unnamed speaker and the "fruitful and propitious nature" he represents (*Keats* 134–35)—a nature now inaccessible to the knight-at-arms:

> And this is why I sojourn here
> Alone and palely loitering,
> Though the sedge is wither'd from the lake
> And no birds sing. (45–48)

Bereft of his visionary insight, the knight discovers the grot to be simply a cold hillside, a bleak wasteland reifying and reaffirming, as Wasserman remarks, the loss of transcendence (*Tone* 77). Return to the real world is a resumption of self-identity, an isolation in self that "is the opposite of a fellowship with essence which absorbs the proper self . . ." (*Tone* 77). Cut off from both the human and the natural (in both its physical and numinous manifestations), the knight is fated to linger without hope, to wither amid the symbols of his own devastation.

*L*ike Percy Shelley's early novels, "Lamia" (1819) was a calculated attempt to appeal to the popular tastes fostered by Gothic fiction. As Keats wrote to George and Georgiana on 18 September of that year, "I am certain there is that sort of fire in ["Lamia"] which must take hold of people in some way—give them either pleasant or unpleasant sensation. What they want is a sensation of some sort" (*Letters* II: 189). What Keats offered was nothing like a Gothic thriller but rather his most elaborate and trenchant scrutiny of Gothicism's supernatural suspension.

Keats proceeds deliberately, establishing in the poem's prefatory section a thematics of interpenetration, a mingling of two distinct realms of experience: real and visionary, natural and supernatural. Here Keats invokes a remote setting and atmosphere, an idealized and fanciful Greek classical world of possibility and purity:

> Upon a time, before the faery broods
> Drove Nymph and Satyr from the prosperous woods,
> Before King Oberon's bright diadem,
> Sceptre, and mantle, clasp'd with dewy gem, Frighted
> away the Dryads and the Fauns
> From rushes green, and brakes, and cowslip'd lawns. . . .
>   (I: 1–6)

This fairy-tale invocation begins the greatest interpenetration of realms in the poem, for it immerses the reader in the magic world of the text. It presents for our consideration a world patently not our own—indeed, a world twice removed from ours, for we must reach back through the medieval realm of faery to the classical age of Olympian deities—but it is a world that, with its "charm" beginning and strong narrative voice (free of the deliberate self-interrogation of "The Eve of St. Agnes"), demands our surrender, our willing suspension not only of disbelief but of distance. This suspension will prove crucial at the poem's conclusion, where the utter dissolution of the textual world will have its implications made more insistent and immediate by reader involvement.

More directly engaging the theme of movement from one level of existence to another is the descent of Hermes "From high Olympus" to the "sacred island" of Crete—a descent, in Northrop Frye's terms, from the realm of the divine or numinous to the realm of ideal or unfallen human nature (23ff), an Edenic world where the presence of the numinous in nature may still be directly felt and carries with it a vitalizing power. The amorous Hermes, empowered by Lamia to see the invisible nymph who is the object of his passion,

> towards her stept: she, like a moon in wane,
> Faded before him, cower'd, nor could restrain
> Her fearful sobs, self-folding like a flower
> That faints into itself at evening hour: But the God fostering
> her chilled hand,
> She felt the warmth, her eyelids open'd bland . . .
>
> . . . .
>
> Into the green-recessed woods they flew;
> Nor grew they pale, as mortal lovers do. (I: 136–41, 144–45)

These last two lines emphasize the character of this transcendent realm, marking it as distinct from the next rung down on the ladder of experience, the fallen world of physical nature as humans know it. The latter is the Romantics' world of traumatic self-consciousness, a world in which awareness of our status as autonomous actors on the universal stage separated humanity from its original intimacy with nature, from the consolations of the numinous with which nature was believed ultimately to connect. In three well-known lines that precede those quoted above, Keats provides another important characterization of the difference between the realms of gods and humans: "It was no dream; or say a dream it was, / Real are the dreams of Gods, and smoothly pass / Their pleasures in a long immortal dream" (I: 126–28). At this ideal level, with no distinction between the real and the imaginary, participation in a transcendent nature is absolute. Here is the Romantics' lost Eden, and the main part of the poem addresses the signature Keatsian theme of human participation in this more intense, fuller existence.

Strangely enough, it is Lamia who must penetrate to the human world of physical nature, suggesting, as did Hermes' descent, that movement down the hierarchy of realms is much easier than movement up. But such descent is not casually effected. Lamia, moving to the fallen world from a numinous supernatural one, must literally change her being. Her shape-changing has mortified some critics— Douglas Bush, for example, finds that "Lamia from the start is not a very sympathetic figure, and she still is less so when she undergoes a convulsive metamorphosis into a beautiful woman" (157)—but it is essential; the violence done to Lamia is symptomatic of the violence done to human perception and to the world of nature in the fall into self-consciousness and alienation.[7]

Yet Lamia's essential nature has not changed, as the poem doubly emphasizes: first, by pointing out her ability to recall "how she could muse / And dream, when in the serpent prison-house" (I: 202–3) just after she finds herself in the woods near Corinth; second, by emphasizing upon her human manifestation the powerful capacity for love with which she was associated in her previous form. Given the importance of her role in the amorous adventure of the messenger-god, it is not too much to identify Lamia, as Gerald Enscoe does, as "the very spirit of human love" (152); her explanation of and motivation for her own desired change (her "swooning love" for Lycius) confirms such a reading. Love, and the transcending power it represents for Keats, is clearly made to serve here, as in the earlier poems, as metaphor for the human desire that both seeks and empowers the movement from one realm to the other. Love motivates Hermes for his descent, impels Lamia to slough off her serpent form and go to Corinth, and permits Lycius temporarily to participate in the attenuated numinous Lamia's desire represents.

The introduction of Lycius establishes the final point of contrast between the human and supernatural worlds, a contrast that turns on the role and efficacy of rationality in human existence. At Lycius's entrance, rational faculties are notable by their absence: "Over the solitary hills he fared, / Thoughtless at first, but ere eve's star appeared / His phantasy was lost, where reason fades, / In the calm'd twilight of Platonic shades" (I: 233–36). Even when his mind is active, it is so "where reason fades." A few lines further on, we see Lycius so unattuned to his surroundings that "shut up in mysteries, / His mind wrapp'd like his mantle" (I: 241–42) he walked right past the alluring Lamia. He is, in other words, off his intellectual guard; his rational faculties—those which have most contributed to humanity's fall into self-consciousness and away from nature—in abeyance, Lycius is most susceptible to the charms of Lamia. He is now almost as close to the unfallen realm of nature as the unaided mind can get. Only the poet's visionary reverie would be closer, as Coleridge discerned in the preface to "Kubla Khan." In this halfway state, Lycius falls under the influence of Lamia, who herself has come halfway—indeed, further—to meet him.

Some have taken the lovers' initial encounter to conclude with Lycius "trapped . . . in the world of illusion" (Bernstein 180) or with his falling under a spell (Stillinger 56), but such readings slight the theme of interpenetration of realms so central to the poem. If we can indeed say Lycius is entrapped, it is not by Lamia but by the (desirable) experience and higher perception she represents. The Orpheus/Eurydice reference that occurs here (I: 248) confirms that their meeting is emblematic of the tentative mingling of these two realms, as does the narrator's suggestive statement that after the exchange of a kiss Lycius "from one trance was wakening / Into another" (I: 296–97).

The conversation preceding the kiss reveals Keats's ontological suppositions in the poem, first among which is that the conditions operative in one world are irrelevant in the other, evidenced by Lycius's reaction to Lamia's first words: "so delicious were the words she sung, / It seem'd he had lov'd them a whole summer long" (I: 249–50). When a moment seems a season, perception has lost its mooring in reality, and indeed Lycius has now become suspended, in a sense, from his usual world. But this particular detachment is not simply a separation from nature; it is instead a movement toward—but not *to*—the supernatural or transcendent world that is Lamia's natural abode.

Even such limited movement has begun to attune Lycius's perceptions to the subtleties of that higher realm, something evident in his praise of Lamia:

> Ah, Goddess, see
> Whether my eyes can ever turn from thee!
>
> . . . .
>
> Stay! though a Naiad of the rivers, stay!
> To thy far wishes will thy streams obey:
> Stay! though the greenest woods be thy domain,
> Alone they can drink up the morning rain:
> Though a descended Pleiad, will not one
> Of thine harmonious sisters keep in tune
> Thy spheres, and as thy silver proxy shine? (I: 257–58, 261–67)

Lycius's hesitant identifications of Lamia's mythological status, however inaccurate, are valid in their implication that Lamia's ties to the world of nature are much more intimate, even numinous, than those of human beings.

Lamia herself, coyly flirting with Lycius, confirms his intuitive perceptions, although nothing indicates that Lycius is sufficiently self-possessed to recognize the confirmations:

> Thou canst not ask me with thee here to roam
> Over these hills and vales, where no joy is,—

Empty of immortality and bliss!
Thou art a scholar, Lycius, and must know
That finer spirits cannot breathe below
In human climes, and live: Alas! poor youth,
What taste of purer air hast thou to soothe
My essence? (I: 276–83)

Lamia is literally correct in maintaining that Lycius's world, "below" her own, is devoid of the "joy" associated with her existence in the realm closer to nature, yet her suggestion that life for beings such as herself is impossible in the coarser world, while perhaps true, nonetheless hints that she will in fact be able to live at least for a time in the fallen world: "finer spirits cannot *breathe* below / In human climes, and live" (emphasis added). The prefatory section of the poem contains important uses of "breathe" or "breath," always in conjunction with the love pursuit of Hermes (see lines 28, 121, and 124 in part one), and Lamia's use of the word here, suggesting that breath is the vital component, indicates that a requiting of her love may enable her to remain with Lycius, just as Hermes's desire for and success with the nymph were essential to his descent from Olympus and his blissful sojourn on Crete.

This breath imagery is repeated a few lines later, again with telling implications: "[Lamia] began to sing, / Happy in beauty, life and love, and every thing, / A song of love, too sweet for earthly lyres, / While, like held breath, the stars drew in their panting fires" (I: 297–300). The suggestion of suspension here ("held breath") characterizes quite effectively what is happening to Lycius, for his involvement with Lamia, itself emblematic of a tentative, transcendent participation in nature, is attended by a suspension both of his normal activities in the world and of the operations of that world. Time, we have seen, has lost its normal reference; space will do the same when Lamia reduces the journey to Corinth to just a few steps, after which she creates an opulent palace out of nothing. All these phenomena have their root and possibility in the suspension of Lycius's rational, analytic faculties; prompted by a "supernatural" encounter, this suspension may be structurally cognate with the soul-freezing experience of the Burkean sublime, but it is profoundly different in its motive impulse and its implications. Lycius experiences not petrification of his faculties but extension of them, a nonrational transcendent reach toward expanded possibility and engagement. Here is Keats's positive sublime, a secularized reading of the religious sublimes of Dennis and others, and a de-terrorized reading of the Gothic sublime.

The sublime suspension of Lycius accounts for some incidents that have incorrectly been taken as evidence of Lamia's malevolence. Lamia lies to her lover on a couple of matters, but these untruths need not be read as the sinister weavings of a vampiric enchantress; they are, rather, an effort to minimize the trauma of Lycius's suspension, to reduce the dislocation of supernatural sublimity. It is evident that Lycius is caught in a cycle of ontological uncertainties: "Lycius from death woke into amaze, / To see her still, and singing so sweet lays; / Then from amaze into delight he fell / To hear her whisper woman's lore so well" (I: 322–25). Lamia astutely realizes that not only will the twilight world she and Lycius now inhabit demand both concession and careful manipulation if its precarious existence is to be maintained but also that Lycius himself must be carefully handled:

> Thus gentle Lamia judg'd, and judg'd aright,
> That Lycius could not love in half a fright,
> So threw the goddess off, and won his heart More pleas-
> antly by playing woman's part,
> With no more awe than what her beauty gave (I: 334–38)

Gothicism's traumatic supernaturalism is hereby muted, subordinated to the Keatsian aesthetic. Indeed, Keats extends the need for controlled deception even to the audience (which after all was implicated in the narrative from its opening): "Let the mad poets say whate'er they please / Of the sweets of Fairies, Peris, Goddesses, / There is not such a treat among them all, / Haunters of cavern, lake, and waterfall, / As a real woman, lineal indeed" (I: 328–32). Lycius, living at the juncture of two realms, discovers that neither is fully available to him. Corinth has become a dream-world, without immediacy for Lycius, a place of murmurs and shadows:

> all her populous streets and temples lewd,
> Mutter'd, like tempest in the distance brewed,
> To the wide-spreaded night above her towers.
> Men, women, rich and poor, in the cool hours,
> Shuffled their sandals o'er the pavement white,
> Companioned or alone; while many a light
> Flared, here and there, from wealthy festivals,
> And threw their moving shadows on the walls,
> Or found them cluster'd in the corniced shade
> Of some arch'd temple door, or dusky colonnade. (I: 352–61)

So removed is Lycius from the ordinary world that even his usual social contacts are forsaken as he passes through Corinth "Muffling his face, of greeting friends in fear" (I: 362)—and no one does he less desire to meet than Apollonius, his mentor and the poem's embodiment of those rational faculties antithetical to the world and experience of Lamia—faculties that are, as Wasserman notes, an inherent part of Lycius himself (*Tone* 168). It is natural, therefore, that Apollonius has gone from being Lycius's "trusty guide / And good instructor" to "the ghost of folly haunting [his] sweet dreams" (I: 375–77). The Apollonian world of reason and logic, philosophy and empiricism, is incompatible with that world of transcendent participation which is the generative world of Lamia.

The lovers briefly find respite and solace in the hybrid world of Lamia's dream temple, but for Keats the demands of empirical life cannot long be ignored. Such is the lesson of the "Ode to a Nightingale," where the bird's "plaintive anthem" fades into the natural landscape away from the forlorn poet, whose visionary flight toward transcendent participation in the natural ends with his own ontological uncertainty: "Was it a vision, or a waking dream? / Fled is that music:—Do I wake or sleep?" (79–80). Examining this halfway condition, with its ambiguity and tacit optimism, Keats finds, characteristically, that the transitional realm the lovers inhabit cannot withstand the pressures on its fragile boundaries. In one moment's wavering of Lycius's intensity, the integrity of the dream-suspension begins to decay:

> from the slope side of a suburb hill,
> Deafening the swallow's twitter, came a thrill
> Of trumpets—Lycius started—the sounds fled,
> But left a thought, a buzzing in his head.
> For the first time, since first he harbour'd in
> That purple-lined palace of sweet sin,
> His spirit pass'd beyond its golden bourn
> Into the noisy world almost forsworn. (II: 26–33)

Lycius, elevated by his love for Lamia to a tentative participation in the numinous, falls back into rationalist self-consciousness, and "knowing well / That but a moment's passing thought is passion's passing bell" (II: 38–39), both Lamia and the reader realize that the poem's tragic denouement is now inevitable and imminent. Without the support of a constant and engaged passion, Lamia cannot exist in human climes, and her cry "You have deserted me;—where am I now?" (II: 43) is doubly accurate, for indeed she has lost a *place* as surely as she has lost a lover. The same is true for Lycius; only in their fusing of two realms of experience did the lovers fully live; the dissolution of their emotional symbiosis resolves their hybrid world into its component elements and the lovers to return to solipsistic being, only to discover that the world is no longer a haven for the sort of beings they have become. Their supernatural suspension has been broken; all that remains is intellectual and emotional aftermath.

Some commentators have identified Lycius's pride as the cause of his destruction, and certainly Lycius's desire to let his "prize . . . pace abroad majestical" (II: 57–59) is instrumental in the disastrous wedding celebration. But Lycius makes his declaration only after passionate intensity falters—after the thrill of trumpets—and it is more in the nature of symptom than cause. Douglas Bush recognizes that the statement raises issues beyond self-aggrandizement when he writes that the lovers' final incompatibility is evidence of "Keats's long-continued awareness of the different and sometimes opposed kinds of truth open to the poetic senses and imagination and to philosophic reason" (159). The poem documents a fiercer antagonism than such words suggest, one that may not be between Apollo and Dionysus as much as it is between Apollo and Pan.

Having been penetrated by the rationalist world, the "meanwhile" realm of Lamia's dream-temple deteriorates as Lycius struggles to preserve what he has recently experienced. But his efforts are cast in forms learned in that rationalist world, and his ill-considered desires to parade his "Prize" and "entangle, trammel up and snare / [Lamia's] soul" (II: 52–53) in his own by means of marriage (a social institution of the fallen human world) have the expected effect. Involved deeply in an experience beyond the pale of his Apollonian training, Lycius reverts to traditional paradigms of thought, to rationalist principles of intellectual containment, and the inevitable result is that the experience, now antithetical to his reactivated rational perception, must come to a crushingly tragic end.

Lamia's reluctant preparation for the wedding, coupled with Lycius's new "Fierce and sanguineous" (II: 76) manner, recall Hermes and the nymph in the poem's opening section. But Hermes and the nymph were essentially of the same order of being; their transcendent love could not grow pale. An important boundary is crossed with Lamia's descent to Corinth, and in the world of human action, love indeed grows pale and dreams fade into nothingness. Needing love but helpless to control how her love is received, Lamia can only wait for events to roll to their ineluctable conclusion.

By the time of the wedding Lycius has almost completely returned to the rationalist world, as his attempt to pledge Apollonius indicates. The extent to which the worldview represented by Apollonius is antithetical to that embodied in Lamia is made clear in the famous passage following the crowning of Apollonius with "spear-grass and the spiteful nettle":

> Do not all charms fly
> At the mere touch of cold philosophy?
> There was an awful rainbow once in heaven:
> We know her woof, her texture; she is given
> In the dull catalogue of common things.
> Philosophy will clip an Angel's wings,
> Conquer all mysteries by rule and line,
> Empty the haunted air, and gnoméd mine—
> Unweave a rainbow, as it erewhile made
> The tender-person'd Lamia melt into a shade. (II: 229–38)

Although it may well be, as Bush notes, that Keats did not unreservedly endorse such a view (58–59), it is at the same time certain that "there is little doubt that Keats meant the victory of Apollonius to be seen as a hollow one" (Enscoe 162). After all, Apollonius is, as Bate remarks, not a representative for Keats of that philosophy that facilitates a " 'disinterested' openness to the diverse amplitude of fact . . . [but of] the reductive uses of analytic philosophy, the essence of which is to reduce a thing to certain elements and then to substitute the simple interpretation for the complex reality. What is not susceptible of such reduction is merely denied" (559). Whether Keats himself endorsed such a view is, finally, less important than the fact that these lines present the Lycian/Apollonian world from Lamia's perspective; they express a fundamental antagonism between the world of fallen human existence and the transcendent world of unfallen nature. Lycius's apparent cursing of both Lamia and his teacher may be evidence of Keats's own ambiguity on these matters, and modern critical consensus is that none of the characters in this drama represent an adequate or balanced viewpoint (Sperry, 308–9; Bate 557). It is difficult to disagree with such a claim, but at the same time the incontrovertible fact of the poem is that Lamia is driven from the world of human nature, by the insufficiency of human visionary capabilities and, subsequently, by Apollonian reason—and we cannot overlook the fact that Lycius, forever affected by his brief sojourn in a shadow of that higher world, can no longer live fully in this one. Stillinger sees the poem as Keats's "fullest and most pessimistic exposition of the dangers of dreaming, of overinvestment in illusion, and the impossibility of escape from the realities of the human condition" (53), but the issues, while they include these, are larger, for Keats is commenting on the inability of humanity to regain, in a renewed contact with nature and the numinous powers hidden in nature's extrarational corners, a long-lost Eden.

When we understand "Lamia" as the culmination of a progressive analysis of the supernatural sublime, we cannot escape, entirely, Stillinger's assessment quoted just above, although to see Keats as poet of pessimism is of course impossible. The exuberance of his quest and his unflagging belief in the vitality of the imagination combine with his empathic imaginative powers to more than compensate for his belief that the human spirit is destined to forever fail in its attempt to forsake the "vale of soul-making"—to always return, in a pattern Stillinger finds common in the Romantics, from a brief foray into a higher realm where even imaginative existence cannot, for humans, endure. Keats is not a poet of limits but of exuberant effort. In these revisions of Gothic supernaturalism is evidence that for Keats, as for Wordsworth, there was no horror lurking in the far corners of experience just beyond the horizons of the phenomenal universe.

Chapter Eight

Allegory and Fantasy

The Short Fiction
of Hawthorne and Poe

The project of American romance, like that of British Romantic supernaturalism, was shaped to a significant degree by its desire to revise and reconfigure traditional Gothic supernaturalism, appropriating it for an increasingly distinct cultural milieu while owing much to the revisionist efforts of British Romantic writers. The most obvious departure effected by the Americans was topographical: the Old World landscapes of medieval castles, ruined abbeys, and blasted heaths was a foreign and indifferent terrain for American romancers. Even Hawthorne, with his acute historical sensitivity, lamented America's stultifying lack of historical depth. It was, appropriately, in the preface to *The Marble Faun* that Hawthorne sketched the dilemma of the American romancer: "No author, without a trial, can conceive of the difficulty of writing a romance about a country where there is no shadow, no antiquity, no mystery, no picturesque and gloomy wrong, nor anything but a commonplace prosperity. . . . Romance and poetry, ivy, lichens, and wallflowers need ruin to make them grow" (IV: 3). Denied a repertoire of ruin, American romancers turned native elements—forests, frontiers, Indians—to Gothic purpose and thereby

produced a different sort of romance, a different supernatural literature that was both less supernatural than much British Gothic fiction
and, in some hands at least, more disturbing.

To return to Frederick Frank's term, American Gothic is a "factual"
Gothic: not "realistic" but an anchoring of the Gothic in the world of
the ordinary, an effect Hawthorne repeatedly achieves by combining
his historicism with an insistently near-allegorical symbolism, effectively grounding his work in historical and moral reality. Poe is a different case. Whereas his tales may be closer to the real than, say, *The
Monk,* his revision of Gothicism moves beyond that of Hawthorne,
who by reconciling the supernatural with history and Christian morality rejected a radical vision. Poe deliberately intensified the radical potential of the Gothic by severing Gothicism's links to morality and
place, thereby producing the first works of English-language fantasy
that are recognizably "modern" in their engagement with ontological
and philosophical anxieties still extant today.

Poe and Hawthorne produced their "romances" in what was, given
the continued influence in America of Scottish Common Sense, a cul-
turally "hostile climate" (Bell, *Development* 13–14). Such a climate
was unavoidable, for Scottish Common Sense regarded even the realistic novel as suspect in its deviation from actuality (Martin 73). Indeed
a moral basis was claimed for the condemnation of all fiction: since
the order of the actual was inherently good, the order of the merely
possible must be "delusive, distorted, dangerous" (Martin 76). This
philosophy condemned fiction in no uncertain terms: "The order of
possibility is subordinate, dependent, inferior, incomplete, imperfect,
insufficient of itself, whereas the order of actuality is the antithesis of
all of these things" (Martin 92).

To some extent the principal American romancers—Brown, Irving,
Cooper, Hawthorne, Poe, Melville—saw as part of their literary task
the repudiation or qualification of Common Sense stringency, and to
varying degrees all embraced what Clara Reeve, in *The Progress of
Romance,* termed "what never happened nor is likely to happen." As
one critic explains, Poe "shrewdly mined the Gothic vogue in an artistic quest to describe forces often held in check because they were alien
to the nineteenth-century vision" (Shelden 75). Poe himself was fully
aware of the reactionary element in his aesthetics. In a review of de la
Motte Fouqué's *Undine,* Poe remarks on "our antiromantic national
character," and noting that the republication of *Undine* is "an experiment well adapted to excite interest," he charges "every lover of literature for its own sake and spiritual uses, to speak out, and speak boldly,

against the untenable prejudices which have so long and so unopposedly enthralled us" (*Essays* 252). The project of American romance, at least one of its most memorable gestures, was to break this enthrallment.

Poe pursued the most extreme course, insisting in his work on an uncompromising revelation of the deeper and subjective actualities inherent in the realm of imaginative possibility, those "psychological realities, those complex areas that refuse to be contained by any single vision" (Shelden 75). Poe is the chief American subject in this final chapter because his literary project most clearly and dramatically advances a revision of Gothic supernaturalism while at the same time endorsing some of its most radical findings. It is because of Poe's radical stance that one may confidently speak of his "fierce resistance to his culture's almost universal claims for the overriding values of common sense" (R. Pearce, *Continuity* 143). For Poe, even more than for Hawthorne, "the truth of the human heart" was more readily approached and analyzed through other means:

> In Poe's fantasies . . . the protagonist must bear witness to, even be the agent of, the destruction of the "real" world, just so that a "surreal" world, that of the hypnagogic imagination, may be brought into view. At once to demonstrate the need to bring that world into view and actually to do so—this was Poe's driving concern. His situation drove him to believe that it was in the end the only, or the ultimately, real world. (R. Pearce, *Continuity* 148)

The American romance is often understood in contrast to the novel, an approach encouraged by Hawthorne's famous definitions. His most complete distinction between the two forms comes in the preface to *The House of the Seven Gables:* the novel aims at "a very minute fidelity, not merely to the possible, but to the probable and ordinary course of events"; the romance has much more freedom, although Hawthorne mandates that it may not "swerve aside from the truth of the human heart" and should "mingle the Marvellous rather as a slight, delicate, and evanescent flavor, than as any portion of the actual substance of the dish offered to the Public" (II: 1).[1] In "The Custom House," Hawthorne claims the primary concern of the romance writer is with "a neutral territory, somewhere between the real world and fairyland, where the Actual and the imaginary may meet, and each imbue itself with the nature of the other" (II: 36). This territory, for

Hawthorne as for Coleridge, is an "intermediate space," the conceptual and ontological interstices at the furthest reaches of human experience.

Hawthorne points the direction in "The Haunted Mind," in which the dreamer stirs at two A.M. to find himself halfway between sleep and waking, a state of "conscious sleep" much like that which Coleridge posits for Luther during the confrontation with Satan. In this altered state vision is privileged and enhanced; one sees the "ghostly inhabitants" of dreams "with a perception of their strangeness, such as you never obtain while the dream is undisturbed" (IX: 304). This heightened vision occurs only in the neutral territory of the half-dream, a place where daytime structures lose their rigidity and the mind turns inward, able at last to peer beyond "the lights, the music and the revelry" of daily life and scrutinize the "tomb and dungeon" that lie within "the depths of every heart" (IX: 306). Gillian Beer, among others, believes that for the Romantics "the romance expressed a world permanently within all men: the world of the imagination and of dream" (7). This power of introspection given "outness" (Coleridge again) was the source of romance's deep fascination for both Poe and Hawthorne. Both authors understood that to abandon rationalist boundaries for their fiction was not tantamount, as Scottish Common Sense would have it, to an abandonment of fiction's value by dissolving the close tie between narrative and the real. Instead it served to assign new values to words and the fictional constructs made of them.

*H*awthorne was much more cautious in this regard than Poe, for while he invoked "romance" more consistently and more seriously than did, say, Irving, his tendency to moralize romance elements, to link them closely with Christian tradition, results in a corpus less insistent on the inadequacy of received wisdom and the unfathomability of the human heart, less troubled by the apparent unknowability of the universe. In Hawthorne, failures are most often failures of the human spirit, the consequence not of a malevolent cosmos but of the insufficiency of human moral integrity. Dimsdale suffers and dies because his spirit has been weakened by Puritan guilt and moral cowardice; Judge Pyncheon embodies not moral or metaphysical chaos but the human spirit perverted and made petty by the lust for material wealth and influence. The list of Hawthorne's failed protagonists could be extended considerably.

It has been well argued that "Hawthorne's sense of depravity—his power of blackness—is rightly apprehended only as a consciously historical recognition of the Puritan 'Way' in which America had begun" (Colacurcio 14); the sweep of this statement makes evident that such historical vision includes Hawthorne's supernaturalism. Indeed, while it is difficult to separate Hawthorne's historical interest from his supernaturalism, this chapter will concern itself with appraising Hawthorne's supernaturalism not so much as a reflection of his interest in Puritanism or other historical phenomena but as it locates him in a tradition of Romantic supernaturalism. Such an approach requires certain assumptions and a declaration of limitations. In order to conduct his literary enterprise, Hawthorne had to become what Roy Harvey Pearce identifies as the "symbolist as historian." While in no way denying the importance of Hawthorne as a "moral historian," to use Michael Colacurcio's phrase, my study of Hawthorne and of his modifications of Gothic supernatural suspension necessarily requires an emphasis on the "symbolist" side of Pearce's equation.

The relationship between Hawthorne's supernaturalism, historicism, and morality is complex and shifting: it is obvious in tales such as "The Grey Champion" and "Legends of the Province House," less so in pieces such as "My Kinsman, Major Molineux." At times the connection disappears altogether: Colacurcio uses the essentially ahistorical "Hollow of Three Hills" to show that "a significant historicism was no more a given for Hawthorne than was any sort of vital familiarity with Puritan faith and experience" (46). In some of Hawthorne's most supernatural tales—"Hollow," "Feathertop," "The Snow-Image"—the historical dimension is either absent or superficial. At other times all three elements compete: "Alice Doane's Appeal," which Pearce sees as "an experiment in the direct communication of a sense of the past" ("Sense" 338), is also supernatural in its embedded narrative of murder, wizardry, and ghosts. Yet Hawthorne does not balance these elements: the embedded supernatural story is an attempted supernatural suspension, but it elicits only laughter from its auditors. Only when the young writer begins to speak of the real horrors on Gallows Hill do the young women exhibit the fright he was seeking to evoke. History triumphs over supernaturalism; more than once Hawthorne himself demonstrated that supernaturalism had greater affinity for morality than history. Hawthorne's deep interest in Salem witchcraft and in Puritan religious supernaturalism is obvious, but he wrote no learned treatises as a result of this interest. He instead wrote tales and romances, literary fictions marked by a pervasive didacticism. His interest in the supernatural had very real, very evident roots in New England history, but he was most concerned—as were Reeve, Radcliffe, and Walpole, but not Poe—to provide moral edification: "The imaginary in Hawthorne does not represent an occult reality, as it does for many Romantics. Nor is superstition a form of higher knowledge. . . . Hawthorne used the imaginary to supplement history with a moral" (Siebers 161). Although there are occasions when Hawthorne's supernaturalism is free from history, it is never entirely free from morality.

Subordination of the fantastic to moral considerations accounts for Hawthorne's circumscribed supernaturalism, his assiduous exploitation of fantasy's symbolic value in tales that claim as their narrative center the known and knowable world of human experience and history. For Hawthorne, "the familiar resources of the Gothic romancer are not used primarily to awaken terror or wonder but to embody a moral—not to induce an intense psychological state in the reader but to make imaginatively concrete a truth of general and permanent significance or to symbolize a condition of mind or soul" (Doubleday 250). "P.'s Correspondence" is a perfect example: in Hawthorne's hands, the Gothic motif of madness leads not to daemonic solipsism but to a revisionist history that reconciles Romanticism's greatest rebels, Byron and Shelley, to orthodox Christianity and conventional behavior. The anarchic energy of insanity is harnessed, made to affirm rather than deny morality, to sabotage radical speculation.

The consequent necessity of close fidelity to real-world experience requires that Hawthorne rarely employ as a narrative element the characteristic suspension of Gothic fiction. Poe follows the English Romantics in the use of suspension as a comment upon or extension of Gothicism's horror; Hawthorne's moral concerns make him reluctant to engage a structural device of separation.

Consideration of some of Hawthorne's supernaturalist tales provides confirmation.[2] Even in tales as fully supernatural as "The Hollow of the Three Hills" or "Feathertop" the supernatural is never the thematic point of the tale. The second of these tales is representative of Hawthorne's most metaphoric, and thereby moral, supernatural tales, a group that includes "A Select Party," "The Hall of Fantasy," and "A Visit to the Clerk of the Weather," among others. Such tales invoke no suspension, for they have no ordinary or real world to leave behind, operating as they do almost entirely in the realm of the supernatural. These tales are more "fantastic" than they are "supernatural," for they have no quotidian world against which the supernatural may be perceived as such.

"Feathertop," tellingly subtitled "A Moralized Legend," concerns the social dissembling attendant upon human vanity; Mother Rigby's witchcraft transforms the "jumble of sticks, and tattered clothes, and a bag of straw, and a withered pumpkin" (X: 235) into a well-dressed dandy, but although the magical construction of Feathertop occupies a fair portion of the story, it is involved more with Hawthorne's moral purpose than with any use of the supernatural to suggest the inadequacy of conventional worldviews. Even the presence of the invisible attendant spirit, Dickon, contributes only to the allegoric component of the tale: he is associated with Mother Rigby's pipe, bringing coals and tobacco, and it is through the agency of the pipe that the scarecrow becomes animated and maintains his false appearance during his foray into the village. Hawthorne uses the pipe and its associations with the diabolic (its bowl is carved with animated demons) as the token for what in real life is unknown: the mysterious means or agency by which some humans become corrupt, duplicitous, exploitive. When Feathertop, having almost won the heart of Polly Gookin, catches sight of himself in one of Hawthorne's ubiquitous mirrors, he sees "the sordid patchwork of his real composition, stript of all witchcraft" (X: 244) and returns to Mother Rigby's cottage to surrender the pipe, whereupon he collapses into "a medley of straw and tattered garments" (X: 245). The tale earns its subtitle when Mother Rigby—the witch, the supernatural being, of the tale—remarks that "There are thousands upon thousands of coxcombs and charlatans in the world, made up of just such a jumble of worn-out, forgotten, and good-for-nothing trash, as he was! Yet they live in fair repute, and never see themselves for what they are. And why should my poor puppet be the only one to know himself, and perish for it?" (X: 245). It would be hard to imagine Anna Barbauld complaining of Hawthorne's works, as she did of Coleridge's "Rime," that they had too little of the moral in them.

Less fantastic than "Feathertop," and therefore more able to invoke supernaturalism's suspension, is "The Hollow of the Three Hills," a tale that nonetheless maintains a clear distance from the Gothic supernatural. "Hollow" is no more about witchcraft and magic than is *The House of the Seven Gables;* it is, rather, about the price humans pay for the evasion of moral and communal responsibilities. The tale finds its emotional center not in the witch's magical summoning of voices and sounds but in the terrible pathos of which those sounds speak, the tragedy they signify. The adulteress's meeting with the witch in the "symbolic hell" of the hollow (Pandeya 179) is a form of suspension, a temporary disengagement from the tangible world of quotidian existence. "In those strange old times, when fantastic dreams and madmen's reveries were realized among the actual circumstances of life . . ." the story begins (IX: 199), but the implications of this suspension are moral rather than metaphysical. One critic, examining the degree to which "Hollow" reflects biblical understandings of witchcraft, concludes that these elements "function along with dreams and reveries to clarify and order experience, to define the limits of man's power, and to suggest that his responsibilities are set in a universal moral context rather than in a purely personal one" (Stock 32–33). The witch is not an avatar of chaotic or hostile forces, as is Lucifer in *The Monk;* she is not the dreaded antagonist of Hawthorne's Puritan ancestors. She is instead an objectification of human conscience, an agent bringing us to awareness of our failures, not those of the universe in which we live. The problem for Hawthorne is not that the universe is disordered but that humanity is often unable to live up to those moral demands humanity (through religion and through history) places upon itself. The witch's participation in the knowledge she reveals does not, then, suggest that "she shows herself [to be] beyond the pale of mercy and the power of redemption" (Colacurcio 45). She indeed provides vision ironically and mockingly, but the irony attends Hawthorne's mirror imagery: the realization that we are not what we seem, that we are the agents of our own undoing.

"Hollow" and tales such as "Graves and Goblins" reveal most clearly the nature of supernaturalism's appeal for Hawthorne. In such works the supernatural provides, as it did for Coleridge,[3] a lexicon of interiority and self-scrutiny, a linguistic mirror that, while it holds the human world at arm's length, nonetheless functions as mirrors always do in Hawthorne, to provide glimpses into the self. Romance was, for Hawthorne, the narrative means by which an artist obtained the psychological distance necessary for any literary scrutiny of the human condition.

One of the darkest of Hawthorne's visions of human capacity is "Young Goodman Brown," which presents a world seemingly predicated upon hypocrisy and deceit. Brown abandons his wife—his Faith—on that sabbath night because of the failure of his trust and, on his way to the devil's convocation, discovers that little is or has been what it seemed. His father and grandfather were violent and intolerant men; old goodwife Cloyse is intimately acquainted with the devil, much to Brown's dismay: " 'That old woman taught me my catechism!' said the young man; and there was a world of meaning in this simple comment" (X: 80). His prior world of meaning, humanly constructed, becomes oppressive for Brown with his discovery that virtually the entire population of his town has turned out to reveal and share their moral deformity at the witches' sabbath.

As critics have long observed, the suggestion is strong that the devil is within Brown as well: "the elder traveller exhorted his companion to make good speed and persevere in the path, discoursing so aptly, that his arguments seemed rather to spring up in the bosom of his auditor, than to be suggested by himself" (X: 80). Believing Faith to have died, Brown becomes "maddened with despair" and rushes along the forest path "with the instinct that guides mortal man to evil" (X: 83). That "he himself was the chief horror of the scene, and shrank not from its other horrors" (X: 83) indicates the interiority of evil; the presence of his townsfolk at the sabbath suggests that this evil is also within others, regardless of their apparent sanctity. His suspension from his prior, known world is here fully effected. Taking up the devil's staff, Brown overcomes the last of his scruples and gives himself over to belief in an evil universe: "There is no good on earth; and sin is but a name. Come, devil! for to thee this world is given!" (X: 83).

Of all the American romancers, Hawthorne "most overtly adopted the Puritan wilderness as his central symbol" (Mogen 341) and nowhere more famously than in "Brown"; the forest is not only the site of the narrative's central episode but corresponds also to the center or heart of Brown's moral self as he comes to acknowledge ambiguity and the impossibility of moral certitude. The forest episode is doubly destructive for Young Goodman Brown. It first undermines his belief that he understood his village-world, that its surface reflected its heart; the forest scene also obviates any future possibility that Brown may derive comfort or consolation from those who constitute this unknowable humanity. We are left with something of a moral tautology, to be sure, but this serves Hawthorne's meaning. The human moral world Brown perceives cannot be trusted because humans deceive and dissemble; because humanity is not what it appears, one's world cannot fully be known—one cannot, if one is at all like Young Goodman Brown, get one's moral bearings. Thus Brown is never released from the moral suspension initiated by his contact with the devil in the forest—a suspension more enduring than the tale's epistemological question: "Had Goodman Brown fallen asleep in the forest, and only dreamed a wild dream of a witch meeting? Be it so, if you will. But, alas! it was a dream of evil omen for young Goodman Brown" (X: 89). Dreams are never merely dreams in Hawthorne; the reality of the experience is insignificant next to its subjective power and the "psychomoral response" it evokes (Colacurcio 295). Whether dream or actuality, the experience has altered Brown's understanding of human nature. His life is forever poisoned by the recognition of evil within the human heart; even "his dying hour was gloom" (X: 90). For Brown, whose story "dramatizes the final failure of all 'visible' moral evidence" (Colacurcio 310), no recovery is possible.

Such a reading is not intended to suggest Hawthorne is, like Lewis or Maturin, a writer of radical disposition, although elements of this tale tend in that direction. In "Young Goodman Brown," as in Reeve's *Old English Baron,* didacticism severely circumscribes the implications of any supernaturalism, itself contained by Hawthorne's gestures of ambivalence and uncertainty. The implicit and insistent morality of Hawthorne's romances ultimately makes his universe an ordered one, even if it is not quite the same unsullied cosmos of Radcliffe or Reeve. Never accepting the protoexistentialist gloom of radical Gothic, Hawthorne, with his "Calvinistic sense of the 'dread necessity' of sinning" (Donahue 200), is acutely aware of the shadows within the human heart and of the need to recognize and address, rather than defy, them. Maule's curse resides not in the house but in the heart of the Pyncheons; Phoebe, unlike Emily in *Udolpho,* must do more than merely endure the evil until it vanishes. The darkness in Hawthorne never simply goes away: Maule's curse has lingered for 160 years. Phoebe must confront the darkness; her marriage to Holgrave is not so much the sign that all wickedness is past, as is Emily's marriage to Valancourt, but rather the necessary acknowledgment of the shadows within. Radcliffe insists on what is for us a decidedly unmodern disavowal of the heart's gloomy interior; Hawthorne's romance supernaturalism recognizes and accepts the shadowed heart as a necessary part of humanity.

Hawthorne's ordered cosmos has implications beyond those of morality. James Walter claims that for Hawthorne "the primary falsehood of his age . . . was a spirit of abstraction which divorced man from those natural movements in his own soul which tell him of his kinship with the earth and his own kind" (277). "The New Adam and Eve" makes this clear in the most literal sense, and other stories comment on other aspects of alienation. Forsaking or forgetting the kinship Walter identifies is the unpardonable sin of Aylmer, Rappacini, and Reuben Bourne, to name only a few. In the more famous tales, this failure is often represented as the desire to refigure nature ("Rappacini's Daughter"), extend the limits of mortality ("Ethan Brand"), or overvalue the rational, an act strikingly exemplified in what may be Hawthorne's most radical tale, "The Snow-Image."

Here, Hawthorne presents what seems to be a genuine supernatural element, the "snow-girl" that comes to life, in order to suggest the inadequacy of a rationalist world view. Invested with life by the "simplicity and good faith" of Violet and Peony, the snow-image embodies imaginative and artistic energy, the fantastic made real by human belief not yet hardened by the principles of empirical thought. Only the children possess this transforming and magical simplicity in full measure; the mother retains a trace of her youthful imaginative purity, but it fades before the rationalist onslaught of Mr. Lindsey. The practical father, an "exceedingly common-sensible" man, insists on bringing the snow-image into the house and setting her before the stove, unthinkingly destroying the magic created by the innocence and imaginative exuberance of his children.

In its repudiation of desensitized rationalism, "The Snow-Image" perhaps approaches closest of all Hawthorne's tales to the subversive aspect of the Gothic so frequently encountered in Poe, but even this tale restrains its interrogation of the received boundaries of knowledge and being. Perhaps precisely because the tale is antithetical to rationalist, Common Sense dogma, Hawthorne appends an explicit moral that channels the tale's implications in such a way that its potential radicalism is defused. While recognizing that the tale is one in which "common-sense finds itself at fault," Hawthorne explains that it is "nevertheless capable of being moralized in various methods":

> One of its lessons, for instance, might be, that it behooves men, and especially men of benevolence, to consider well what they are about, and, before acting on their philanthropic purposes to be quite sure that they comprehend the nature and all the relations of the business in hand. What has been established as an element of good to one being, may prove absolute mischief to another. (XI: 25)

As a result, "The Snow-Image" is not about the utter failure of rationality, although in other hands it may have carried precisely that message. Like Coleridge with his prefaces, Hawthorne here actively guides our reading of his work, limiting the play of his signifiers so his readers will take from the tale only the intended message. His characteristic moralizing, linked with a general metaphysical optimism, denies to Hawthorne's *oeuvre* the radical cast of Poe's. Explicit moral equivalences must necessarily restrict the implications of a work's symbols;

tales intended to point morals depend upon a fixed and stable epistemological and ontological background—on such a basis is founded
the greatest difference between Poe and Hawthorne.

The use of the supernatural for didactic or allegorical purpose limits the supernatural element's signifying power, of necessity referring
the supernatural to existing intellectual and moral constructs. Only
when freed from explicit moralization may the supernatural be radical, as we have learned from our study of Reeve's *The Old English
Baron*. Employed even quasi-allegorically in what is otherwise a realistic text, supernaturalism or fantasy becomes, as T. E. Apter expressed it, "inessential to the work's themes and ideas, however
appropriate it may be to their presentation" (2). Such is the case with
both Reeve and Hawthorne, for whom Gothicism was a vehicle for
serving traditional thematic purposes.

Rosemary Jackson's assessment of Hawthorne's fantastic turns
upon this issue of didacticism: "The result of an inveterate allegorizing
tendency in Hawthorne is an insistence upon clearly articulated
'meaning,' which produces . . . 'petrified fantasies' " (110). Edward
Davidson seems to be making much the same point when he notes that
"Hawthorne, as Poe himself quite correctly pointed out, had a tendency to lapse into allegory and thereby reduce and delimit those
imaginative exercises that, with the purity of his tone, made the Hawthorne tale itself an act of the imagination" (181). An allegoric fantastic cannot readily partake of the essentially subversive nature of the
unrestrained (or "genuinely") fantastic, which Jackson characterizes
as

> an art of estrangement, resisting closure, opening structures which cate-
> gorize experience in the name of a "human reality." By drawing atten-
> tion to the relative nature of these categories the fantastic moves toward
> a dismantling of the "real," most particularly of the concept of "charac-
> ter" and its ideological assumptions, mocking and parodying a blind
> faith in psychological coherence and in the value of sublimation as a
> "civilizing" activity. . . . From Hoffmann and German Romanticism to
> the modern fantastic in horror films, fantasy has tried to erode the pil-
> lars of society by undoing categorical structures. (175–76)

The radical mode of Gothic supernaturalism is the progenitor of the
fantastic Jackson here champions; conservative Gothicism attempts to
shore up those eroding pillars.

The point merits brief elaboration. Fantasy has an inherently
greater potential for radical implication than does supernaturalism—

there are many more conservative than radical Gothic fictions—for the fantastic operates within the real, forsaking ghosts or haunted castles to suggest the insufficiency of received wisdom. Supernaturalism needs these and, in its Gothic manifestations at least, often had to labor mightily in order to "get away with" ghosts and demons. Such things, after all, are not encountered in ordinary life, so Gothic novels must be set in the past and/or in remote locales where life as we know it cannot intrude upon the narrative integrity of a life we do not know. Even Coleridge, using the supernatural as a primitive psychological lexicon, needed to elaborate theories of suspended disbelief and then still call his works dreams and reveries in order to be comfortable with his supernaturalism.

The fantastic operates much closer to the real and ordinary world, usually within it, throwing into doubt the integrity of the suppositions and assumptions with which we structure the workaday world. Hawthorne and Poe knew each other's work,[4] and their tales share a movement away from Gothic supernaturalism, but Hawthorne's revision of the Gothic was much more restrained than Poe's. For reasons both many and complex, Hawthorne softened the radical impact of his Gothic revisionism by allegorizing, and thus moralizing, the supernatural.

*T*he value of allegory constitutes the most well-known point of difference between the two and serves as point of entry into this chapter's consideration of Poe's work. Poe's views on the use of allegory seem clear: "In defense of allegory . . . there is scarcely one respectable word to be said," he wrote in a review of Hawthorne's *Twice-Told Tales* and *Mosses from an Old Manse* (*Essays* 582). With such pronouncements Poe seems to reject the mode, primarily on the grounds that it interferes with "that unity of effect which, to the artist, is worth all the allegory in the world" (*Essays* 583). Certainly Poe found such failings in Hawthorne, who was "infinitely too fond of allegory" (*Essays* 587).

Hawthorne's allegorizing troubled Poe because it brought a work's moral dimension into prominence. Poe never used allegory or romance to point morals in the same sense Hawthorne did, but Poe was, despite his well-known dictum, not entirely averse to at least one form of allegorizing. In the same review, Poe wrote that "Where the suggested meaning runs through the obvious one in a *very* profound under-current, so as never to interfere with the upper one without our own volition, so as never to show itself unless called to the surface, there only, for the proper uses of fictitious narrative, is it available at all" (*Essays* 582–83). While rejecting Hawthorne's obtrusive reliance on allegory, Poe has high praise for another writer's approach to the allegorical: "Of allegory properly handled, judiciously subdued, seen only as a shadow or by suggestive glimpses, and making its nearest approach to truth in a not obtrusive and therefore not unpleasant *appositeness,* the 'Undine' of De La Motte Fouqué is the best, and undoubtedly a very remarkable specimen" (*Essays* 583).

Poe always thought highly of *Undine,* a work that for him transcended the limitations of most allegory: "Beneath all there runs a mystic or under-current of meaning, of the simplest and most easily intelligible, yet of the most richly philosophical character" (*Essays* 256). A few lines on, Poe refers to "that objectionable under-current of meaning," but finds that de la Motte Fouqué has so "elaborately managed" it that he "nearly succeeded in turning the blemish into a beauty" (*Essays* 257). Indeed, Poe writes of *Undine* that it is "a model of models, in regard to the high artistic talent which it evinces. . . . Its unity is absolute—its keeping unbroken" (*Essays* 257). Poe objects to allegory precisely because it destroys unity of effect, but it is apparently possible for allegory to be handled in such a way—as a kind of insistent symbolism, it seems—that compromise of artistic principle is avoided. And while the review of *Undine* initially appeared seven years before that of Hawthorne's collections, the praise of *Undine* in the Hawthorne review suggests that Poe had not changed his mind regarding *Undine*'s artistic merit and achievement. Indeed, Poe's work on occasion bodies forth this same sense of the allegorical that Poe found in *Undine.*

A further point of difference between Poe and Hawthorne was the latter's dependence upon his New England past: we need only compare "Young Goodman Brown" to "The Snow-Image" to understand the effects of Hawthorne's historicist vision on Gothicism's radical impulse. Poe, eschewing the moralizing historicism of Hawthorne, brought the Gothic more closely in line with the real—that is, away from the blatantly supernatural—while pursuing the radical Gothic's metaphysical implications to their extremes.

Poe was able to effect this because, as Daniel Hoffman recognizes (327), he relied on an extremely pure form of the Gothic. He extracted from radical supernaturalism little more than atmosphere and attitude in order to reveal not the need for or wisdom of complying with extant moral or political paradigms but to reveal absence. In this way he demonstrated that post-Enlightenment Western culture harbors the seeds of profound dislocation and anxiety concerning humanity's place and vitality in any scheme of cosmic order—should there prove to be one. J. Gerald Kennedy highlights just this function of a certain strain of Gothicism when he writes that the Gothic "enacts the radical uncertainty of an epoch of revolution in which nearly all forms of authority—neoclassicism, Right Reason, religious orthodoxy, and aristocracy—came to be seen as constricting systems. . . . Alone in a landscape of nightmare, the Gothic hero experienced the dark side of Romantic freedom: existential disorientation, wrought by the loss of defining structures" (40). Freer than Brown and Hawthorne from a lingering anxiety over the American Puritan tradition (Poe is, significantly, the only Southern writer among the major American romancers), Poe is able to carry the radical "supernatural" project to new intensities.

Joel Porte observes of American romance that it "grows out of dark meditations on guilt, sin, suffering—passionate experience of all kinds—and its value lies precisely in its ability to bring out of the shadows and make available for us those ordinarily shunned emotions that deepen and humanize us" (*Romance* 98). Hawthorne and Irving were very much concerned to deepen and humanize; theirs was a literature of moral correction, one that ventured into the "neutral territory between the real world and fairy land," in Hawthorne's phrase, in order to gain a perspective on human moral failings. Poe also relied upon romance's distancing and defamiliarizing effect but for more drastic purpose. In his hands, and perhaps partially as a result of his abandonment of the historical or fabulist modes employed by Hawthorne and Irving, the romance begins to explore the subversion, the questioning, of traditional modes of knowing that are rooted in radical Gothic and are now so much a part of modern fantasy. As Todorov and Jackson have suggested, Poe's work must be considered on a par with the most troubling fantastic literature of the twentieth century, a claim supported by David Ketterer's assessment that Poe is "in many ways the most contemporary" of classic American writers (277). Michael Davitt Bell, examining this *ne plus ultra* of the romance spectrum, identifies the nexus between Poe and modern consciousness:

> To admit the claims of romance was to open the doors to nihilism. If, for romance, subjective states could become valid objects of mimesis, if no subjective state was certifiably more true than any other, and if the

> truth could only be known subjectively, then the chaos of psychological relativism was just around the corner. (*Development* 145)

Poe is the only American Romantic who steps boldly through those doors, taking firm strides into the darkness.

G. R. Thompson correctly observes that American Romantic Gothic seeks to embody the "ontological, epistemological, and axiological concerns central to the Romantic dilemma of subject and object" ("Apparition" 92); in the nineteenth century this dilemma is most powerfully engaged by Poe, who in his work attempts a comprehensive examination of the legitimacy and value of the prevailing worldview. Although he employs techniques that may seem antithetical in execution and intent—Gothic and supernatural themes alongside quasi-scientific discourse—Poe's fiction, as Thompson demonstrates, is all of a piece. It seeks to interrogate the reality posited by Scottish Common Sense philosophy and American frontier pragmatism. Poe's most troubling fiction possesses the central trait of Jackson's "subversive" fantastic, for it "focuses upon the unknown within the present, discovering emptiness inside an apparently full reality" (158). Thompson extends the unsettling implications of Poe's work even further; for him, "Poe's ironic vision has, as its philosophical basis, the 'question' of epistemology: the ambiguity of human experience suggests a meaningless or absurd universe, but this apprehension is itself ambiguous" ("Paradox" 338). For the timid, this suspicion of the text is a way out, a denial of the fantastic's ability to discover philosophical dread and terror. For more sophisticated readers—and in *Poe's Fiction* Thompson argues convincingly it is these whom Poe is most concerned to address—the uncertain ground onto which the fantastic opens is accepted as the foundation of (modern) existence. In such explorations Poe went beyond the more secure—because they were historically or allegorically grounded—moral investigations conducted by Hawthorne and raised to a greater intensity the dark vision of Charles Brockden Brown.

As a result Poe produced "a literature of overwhelming negative possibility: the possibility that beyond the elaborate act of the game there is nothing" (Thompson, *Fiction* 191). Poe was never concerned to offer or even seek an answer: traditional theological consolations meant little to him; he mocked the Transcendentalists and all they represented (though there are some points of affinity). Like Blake, Poe in *Eureka* invented his own system, one that took "matter" as its central cosmological principle and could muster nothing but an "ambivalent skepticism" of the possibility of meaning in the universe (Thompson, *Fiction* 191ff). Poe concerned himself primarily with a world of uncertainty, and it may be that those critics who see Poe as a failed Transcendentalist—as is true of those who see Gothic novelists as failed Romantics—are more effectively revealing their own preconceptions. Poe is the first American author of the fantastic to use and surpass the machinery of the Gothic for the expression of discontent with a society being shaped so unqualifiedly by empiricist thought and industrial capitalism. Such an assessment requires that we understand Poe as the proponent of a vision not universally shared, although Poe was not the first to recognize the cultural and intellectual anxieties taking shape in the aftermath of the American, Industrial, and French Revolutions. As Leo Marx indicates, recognition of these anxieties emerged from "the stream of post-Kantian idealism" and was especially furthered by Hegel's concept of "self-estrangement" (176). Friedrich Schiller and Thomas Carlyle, whose works Poe knew, helped disseminate these notions in England and America, and that these views were not widely accepted (machine-induced progress often being hailed with what sometimes approached rapture) may help to account for Poe's inability to find a sympathetic readership.[5] Other American writers were aware of these concerns, of course; even Ralph Waldo Emerson and Henry David Thoreau expressed some uneasiness over the effects of industrialization on the human psyche. But their sensibilities were profoundly different from Poe's, and the resultant sense of terror so strong in Poe is absent in the Transcendentalists. Indeed, as Marx shows, the concern of Emerson and Thoreau for the negative effects of industrial development was outweighed by what they saw as the expanded potential and promise the new technologies would bring. Unable to get beyond the grave, as some critics have put it, Poe found little consolation in transcendence. For us his greatest value is in the sense of horror that accrues from the realization that the romance, as practiced and extended into the fantastic by Poe, can uncover the emptiness not only in reality but in our schemes to rise above that reality. In an increasingly secular age, Poe exaggerated the normal tendency of the romance to uncover "something nihilistic and untamable" (Frye 305) and in that exaggeration found an uncertainty, both ontological and epistemological, that for many characterizes the modern world.

Certainly Poe himself laid claim to a universal validity for his project. As he noted in the preface to the 1840 edition of *Tales of the Grotesque and Arabesque,* responding to those who saw too much of the influence of "Germanism" in his work, "If in many of my productions terror has been the thesis, I maintain that terror is not of Germany, but of the soul,—that I have deduced this terror only from its legitimate sources, and urged it only to its legitimate results" (II: 473). These "legitimate sources" are not the ghosts and goblins of childhood terror but the very things upon which the rationalists based their hopes for infinite progress: the human mind and its rational abilities. One of the most horrific aspects of Poe's work is the implied failure of sense perception and intellection in apprehending the totality of human existence; horror emerges as Poe reveals the inadequacy of that which we have long believed adequate.

"Berenice" (1835) is a tale with such a purpose. It features that most characteristic of Poe's narrative devices, the mad or otherwise liminal narrator, a trope employed frequently by Poe because such a narrator's perspective enables insights that the rest of humanity (for whom Poe's frequent term was "the mob") lacks. In his priviledging of the marginal, Poe was very much the Romantic artist. As E. J. Hobsbawm reminds us, the representative myth-heroes of the age were figures such as Satan, the Wandering Jew, "and other trespassers beyond the ordinary limits of life" (306). Egaeus is such an antihero: descended from a family that "has been called a race of visionaries" (II: 209), Egaeus declares that "the realities of the world affected me as visions, and as visions only, while the wild ideas of the land of dreams became, in turn,—not the material of my everyday existence— but in very deed that existence utterly and solely in itself" (II: 210). Dissociation from the real is here insisted upon completely as the objective surrenders to the subjective.

The disjunction between Egaeus and the real produces a strange misalignment of his intellectual priorities: he reads strange apocalyptic treatises and suffers from a "monomania" in which his complete attention is absorbed for hours or days on end by the most trivial of details. It is both expected and significant that these "pernicious vagaries . . . bid defiance to anything like analysis or explanation" (II: 212). Egaeus exists, we can already see, in a world where conventional intellectual operations and priorities have diminished vitality, even though Egaeus is in some regards the epitome of intellectuality. Born in a library, he "loitered away [his] boyhood in books" (210), virtually living in the library, leaving it only once to visit Berenice's corpse, and even this passage was excised by Poe in later publications of the tale. Yet his intellectuality fails Egaeus, for his disease inverts and devalues normal mental processes. His monomania is not, Egaeus explains, the mere exaggeration of a daydreamer's reverie, "but [is] primarily and essentially distinct and different" (II: 212). The daydreamer uses the first object of attention as the point of departure for a process of comprehensive, assimilative intellection; Egaeus, on the other hand, cannot escape the object: "Few deductions, if any, were made; and those few pertinaciously returning in upon the original object as a centre" (212). Contrary to conventional experience, the universe collapses for Egaeus into a single meaningless point, an intellectual black hole from which no meaning escapes.

Further evidence of reason's insufficiency is discovered in Egaeus's relationship with the comely Berenice, to whom he feels attraction only after her wasting illness strikes; during her years of health and vitality, Egaeus "had never loved her":

> In the strange anomaly of my existence, feelings with me had *never been* of the heart, and my passions *always* were of the mind. . . . I had seen her—not as the living and breathing Berenice, but as the Berenice of a dream—not as a being of the earth, earthy, but as the abstraction of such a being—not as a thing to admire, but to analyze—not as an object of love, but as the theme of the most abstruse though desultory speculation. (II: 214)

In his strangely altered fashion, Egaeus (named after the father who, in *A Midsummer Night's Dream*, cannot understand love) can perceive Berenice only as an object of intellectual contemplation; he fails to appreciate not only Berenice's allure but her very humanness as well. He proposes marriage only after her vitality no longer threatens his intellectual containment of her—and it is still "an evil moment" when he proposes—and only on occasion can Egaeus find his wife's physical decay a cause for anguish. It is rather a cause of fascination for him, and even then only in regard to "the physical frame of Berenice—in the singular and most appalling distortion of her personal identity" (II: 213). Perversely, Egaeus's intellectuality leads him to equate Berenice's identity only with her observable physical appearance; it is as though deprived, by overdevelopment of the intellectual, of any means of intuitively or emotionally understanding Berenice, he is reduced to dealing with her only as an empirical construct. Even when his monomania comes upon him and he is completely absorbed in contemplation of her teeth, the occurrence has for him only intellectual significance:

of Berenice I more seriously believed *que tous ses dents étaient des idées. Des idées!*—ah here was the idiotic thought that destroyed me! *Des idées!*—ah *therefore* it was that I coveted them so madly! I felt that their possession could alone ever restore me to peace, in giving me back to reason. (II: 216)

When it appears she has died, Egaeus violates Berenice's grave in order to possess those ideas, those teeth—to appropriate for himself, in his gruesomely misdirected way, the "significance" of Berenice.

Intellect fails Egaeus more profoundly than merely in its inability to keep him from being a grave robber: he cannot perceive that Berenice has been put into the grave alive, nor can he recall the actual exhumation and violation itself. Both of these aspects of the tale have their psychoanalytic exegeses (see Bonaparte 213–19) but signify further: Egaeus's intellect and his obsession do not allow him to perceive, as a more humanly sensitive fiancé might have done, that Berenice was only in a deep cataleptic trance, not dead, when put into her coffin. In a passage Poe removed after the first two publications of the work (apparently finding it too morbid), Egaeus visits Berenice's coffin and thinks he sees her finger twitch. This might have prompted him to save her, but he immediately raises his eyes to her face and, perceiving her teeth, rushes "forth a maniac from that apartment of triple horror, and mystery, and death" (II: 217). His narrow intellectuality determines that all things outside of intellectual experience—sexual vitality, horror, mystery, death—are to be a source of fear or revulsion. He must eliminate or avoid these in order to face existence, which means he must reduce and emotionally sterilize his experiences in order to deal with them. The final inadequacy of his excessive intellection is manifested in the amnesia that affects Egaeus after the awful deed, an amnesia symbolic, as David Halliburton explains, of consciousness cut off from external reality and even from "the intentionality of its own acts" (206). Reason and intellect fail to provide Egaeus a field of reference large enough for dealing with a full range of human experience, and so he is lost in self-indulgent despair: "Misery is manifold. The wretchedness of earth is multiform" (II: 209).

Poe's modification of supernatural suspension intensifies the questioning of rationality's preeminence. Egaeus's periods of monomaniacal contemplation are similar to supernaturally induced suspension, indeed akin to Raymond's fascination with the Bleeding Nun. The terror in "Berenice," however, is all the more effective for its proximity to the ordinary world. The events of the story are sufficiently horrific that Poe felt constrained to apologize to its first publisher for the tale's brush with bad taste (Mabbott II: 207), but most terrifying is that these events are in and of the real world. In a sense, ghosts make Gothic terror comfortably distant, for few of us expect ever to meet with spirits. And while few will be subject to Egaeus's fits of absorption, the real-world basis of these fits—they are, after all, a perverted form of rationality and have a physiological cause—makes the terror of the story immediate. Egaeus's suspension cannot not be ended in this world, for it is *of* this world and ineluctable. There is no Bleeding Nun to be exorcised and laid to rest; life in the world of the ordinary and the actual is terror's cause and point of origin. Egaeus reminds us, in the tale's opening words, that "evil is a consequence of good" and that "out of joy is sorrow born" (I: 209), and the same indissoluble bond connects Egaeus's life in the real world to the experience of shadow and mystery. He writes of a prenatal "remembrance which will not be excluded; a memory like a shadow, too, in the impossibility of my getting rid of it while the sunlight of my reason shall exist" (I: 210). As Coleridge did in "Christabel," Poe reminds us that light does not exist without casting shadow, that good is linked with evil and life with some measure of pain and horror. Poe has gone further, however, insisting more on the existentialist horror than on the redemptive good.

"Berenice" is also of interest in that it glances at another important motif in Poe, that of the dead returned. Berenice of course was not dead, nor was Madeline in "The Fall of the House of Usher," and so these tales remain, however precariously, in the realm of the uncanny. But the same is not true for "Ligeia" and "Morella," where the dead women return in spirit if not in (original) body.[6] These tales, along with the colloquies and mesmeric pieces, by advancing the possibility that death is not an absolute and impermeable barrier against which life terminates abruptly, serve a subversive function in their "opening out" of reality and, by avoiding rationalist explanations in favor of emotional intensity, question the implicit claim of rationality to be the only mode of comprehending the boundaries and possibilities of experience.

"The Fall of the House of Usher" is one of the most powerful articulations of Poe's concern with the inadequacy of traditionally privileged modes of perception, an inadequacy revealed primarily in "Usher"'s refiguring of both the Burkean and Kantian sublimes. Since I have already discussed this tale's critique of sublimity in detail elsewhere,[7] I would only point out here that Poe's hostile interrogation of sublimity has as its motive impulse not merely the shortcomings of

Burkean and Kantian theory, but his recognition of the fundamental inability of the sublime, which is at its heart an aesthetic of transcendence and compensation, to address what we now identify as a Dark Romantic understanding of the human condition. "Usher" confronts the theories of both Burke and Kant with the sort of terror Poe felt to exist in the universe—those terrors that know no redemption—and it is emotion, not theory, that triumphs. The aesthetic containment of sublimity's turbulent energies championed by Burke is shattered by a terror that consumes; Kant's rationalist rescue of the mind from sublimity's power is shown to be inadequate in the face of terrors too vast for reason to master.

Poe's unsettling vision of the limitations of a rationalist perspective is made doubly potent by his ability to invoke science, the intimate ally of intellectuality and a rational worldview, as a vehicle for radical meaning. Employing the tropes of science and scientific discourse, Poe is able to breach the limits that scientific thought has imposed on human knowledge and experience. "Sonnet—To Science" is in much the same spirit as the lament in Keats's "Lamia" that "cold philosophy" has undone the magic inherent in the natural world—but it is much more serious. Poe here assails the stultifying effects of the "dull realities" that "preyest . . . upon the poet's heart" (3) and sap his artistic vigor, but the poem insists so strongly on these effects that they seem to assume, at least in the profundity of their impact upon the poet, a power and a presence even in the world of the ordinary:

> Science! true daughter of Old Time thou art!
> Who alterest all things with thy piercing eyes.
> Hast thou not dragg'd Diana from her car?
> And driv'n the Hamadryad from the wood
> To seek a shelter in some happier star?
> The gentle Naiad from her fountain flood?
> The Elfin from the green grass, and from me
> The summer dream beneath the shrubbery? (I: 91)

The difference between objective and subjective realities is blurred; what not even Poe himself accepted as actualities—elves, hamadryads, mythic deities—are here equated with the poet, placed in syntactic parity with him, as though his privileged vision of or participation in a world that contains such beings grants them an ontological validity equal to his own.

Poe, like Yeats, does not much concern himself with elves and naiads and other traditional trappings of the magical in his later work, but he returns again and again to the effect here created, that of registering dissatisfaction with the self-assured claims of the Common Sense philosophers and their valorization of objective reality and the limitations it imposes on human experience. Yet Poe's relationship with "science" is more complex than this youthful condemnation suggests. Like Wordsworth, who could lament the loss of an intimate contact with Nature in works such as "The World Is Too Much With Us" and "On the Projected Kendal and Windermere Railway" and yet also write "Steamboats, Viaducts, and Railways," Poe found in scientific exploration and invention some cause for celebration. "The Thousand-and-Second Tale of Scheherezade," while satirizing the popular appetite for Oriental tales, is also an appreciation of scientific inquiry's ability to comprehend increasingly complex natural wonders and make discoveries that seem as "marvellous" as anything in the *Arabian Nights.* Of even greater moment are the ratiocinative tales and essays, in which Poe champions the rational thinking that is both cause and consequence of a scientific worldview. How to account for the presence of such works in the canon of a man who spends much of his time tearing down the barriers erected by science? Marie Bonaparte and Harry Levin have seen the ratiocinative tales as Poe's attempts to counter or deny the madness he felt creeping up on him (Bonaparte 93–96; Levin 142), but much more satisfying is Roy Harvey Pearce's assessment that such works are attempts to push common sense and rational thinking into or at least close to the realm of fantasy (*Continuity* 147–48); such an explanation takes into full account Poe's ambivalence toward science, the suspicions of what Poe termed its "psychal" costs and effects that go hand in hand with its intellectual and practical success.

Much of Poe's importance lies precisely in this ambivalence, in the collision between the Romantic exploration of the human condition and the scientific demand for empirical knowledge and understanding—and limits. Yet Poe does, without doubt, come down finally on the side of the poetic and intuitive: "As a citizen of his age, Poe held steadily to the view that the supersensual and imaginative faculties of man might be guides to truth and understanding far superior to the formal, divisive logic of rationalists like Descartes and Locke, or Alexander Pope" (Davidson 99). Pieces such as "The Colloquy of Monos and Una" (1841) support such a view. The disembodied spirits discussing their lives (and deaths) from their privileged vantage point make clear that, given the present course of things on Earth, human progress through science is impossible, for knowledge has outstripped humanity's sense of "taste" and morality, and "the price of highest civilization" can be nothing less than "widest ruin" (II: 611). The transcendent possibilities humanity could realize must begin with a purification and elimination of all "Art" (by which Poe means something like "artifice"), its "rectangular obscenities" and the power it has given humans to exercise dominion over Nature (II: 612).

The colloquy goes on to deny immateriality and the belief that death entails a complete loss of sentience. This notion is explored further in the late prose poem *Eureka* (1848), as well as in "Mesmeric Revelation" (1844), an interesting expression of Poe's ambiguity because it invokes the latest "scientific" discovery, mesmerism, to "prove" that "there is no immateriality" (III: 1033), that all souls and even God are only finer forms of matter. The complexities (and confusions) of these ideas are outside the scope of this study; suffice it to say Poe was employing a scientific veneer—in his language, tone, and atmosphere—in order to advance what could only be called, according to the scheme established here, radical tenets. Writing of *Eureka*, Thompson explains that "The universe [Poe sees] is deceptive; its basic mode seems almost to be a constant shifting of appearances; reality is a flux variously interpreted, or even created, by the individual human mind" (*Fiction* 165). Although he writes of God, Poe constructs a universe without spiritual consolations, one that "is much like a gigantic hoax God has played on man" (Thompson, *Fiction* 165). Poe's is a cosmos deeply shadowed by metaphysical darkness, for *Eureka* affirms not a belief in design but in void.

Poe's insistence on the void has hardly gone unnoticed. R. P. Adams, invoking Morse Peckham, locates Poe within the tradition of "negative Romanticism," the proponents of which "inhabit a universe without purpose or meaning" (430). Edward Davidson argues a similar case. Positing a Romantic "journey of the mind," a sort of epistemological quest regarding the place of humankind in the universe, Davidson argues that Poe never got past the first stage of such a quest, a stage Davidson characterizes as "an act of destruction or renunciation: the real world was abandoned or reduced to the conditions imposed by the self as mind" (50). Such assessments are largely true but not because of some inherent failing of Poe's artistry: such "renunciations" are the end of the line. Poe's tales, like the texts of radical Gothicism, effect the dismantling of real-world moral and intellectual constructs by using the fantastic to peer behind them and reveal absence and hollowness, to demonstrate that these constructs are not all-sufficient explanations of the operations, power, or scope of the human psyche and the universe it inhabits. This assessment of the human condition was one Poe was advancing as complete in itself, not as a first stage in some later critic's schema of metaphysical progression.

Schiller wrote that "Man is more than a match for any of nature's terrors once he knows how to give them form and convert them into an object of his contemplation," but it is unlikely Poe would agree. It is true he attempted some of what Schiller suggests, for Poe certainly used horror as a

> means to externalize, in vivid physical objects, inner states of being and a method of portraying the mind's awareness of itself. . . . Specters, images of death and the dead, the terror of the unknown—these and others became means not just for excitement but for the quest of the imagination toward a further understanding. (Davidson 126)

Yet when the quest went far enough, as it always did with Poe, the discoveries, although they gave terror form, could not provide any means for dealing with it, through contemplation or otherwise. The revealed anxieties and uncertainties were too vast and too fundamental to be apprehended or contained by any intellectual system, and so the verbalization of that anxiety was—and remains—task enough.

The possibility of moral virtue redeemed the romances and tales of Hawthorne, but Poe had less faith in humanity's innate goodness. As an exploration of the psyche, "The Cask of Amontillado" (1846) discovers dark primal forces eluding the restraints of reason and propriety. The descent into the Montresor family vaults is the central event of the story, one rich in its implications. It is a descent into a place innately unhealthful—the catacombs are "insufferably damp" and the nitre "hangs like moss upon the vaults"—and this atmosphere is clearly a threat to the health of the ironically named Fortunato. (It is necessary that Fortunato is to be punished for an unnamed transgression against Montresor: Poe's concern is with vengeance and hatred as basic human impulses, not as responses to specific situations.) Yet the vaults ultimately present a far greater threat, for a descent into them is, in a sense, a descent into the historical depths of the species, into the primal, subconscious mind. What is revealed there is disturbing: the Montresor family arms—the social icon (re)presenting them to the world at large—concern vengeance (*"Nemo me impune lacessit"*), and the catacombs are lined with bones. Fortunato proposes a toast to "the buried that repose around us" (III: 1259) but does not realize they repose there because of the vengeance-lust that seems almost part of the protagonist's genetic inheritance or that he has put himself in the way of that lust. It endures in the very blood and spirit of the Montresors; the past reaches into the present to deliver the terrible message that humanity is never free from inherited darkness.

Ironically, Poe here approaches close to Hawthorne as we see him in *The House of the Seven Gables,* where the past also configures the present, particularly as regards a specific building and the family associated with it. But the difference between the two writers proves greater than the similarity, for in Hawthorne the past exacts a retributive vengeance, and the Maule/Pynchon feud is resolved; in Poe, there is no final retribution, only the enduring fact of vengeance. Fortunato is entombed alive and Montresor's evil deed goes unpunished: there is no final arbitration or equalization, none of the balancing of the scales that obtains for Hawthorne.[8] The unfathomable hatred and the impulse toward revenge in Montresor are victorious and exalting, and there is no sense that Providence or any other moral agent will serve to check him or to permit Fortunato to be avenged.

The moral vacuum at the tale's conclusion generates a fantastic terror greater than that of Gothic supernaturalism. Poe invokes the journey underground, as do many Gothic writers, but in Poe's rendering of that topos there is no eventual re-emergence. *The Monk*'s sepulcher scenes are temporary suspensions for most of the novel's characters: Lorenzo, Virginia, Agnes, and even Ambrosio return to the surface; the first three return even to the world of ordinary human community. Poe begins with a descent, but it is one that, in a sense, never ends. Fortunato is entombed alive, and the tale's final words emphasize the reach and endurance of vengeance across time. Even Montresor's exit from the vaults is omitted from the tale. Poe characteristically truncates the structure of suspension, leaving his readers in the vaults as well, confronting forever a terror greater than that of a summoned demon, greater because the desire for vengeance, symbolic here of human evil, is human in origin and impulse. A devil that departs after the conditions of its contract are fulfilled is less terrifying than the unrestrained yet calculated demonic energy of malevolent purpose displayed by Montresor.

"The Black Cat" (1843) pushes this dark view further in its declaration that human nature holds within it the potential for the most perverse communal betrayals. Unlike most narrators of Poe's serious Gothic tales, this one begins by insisting on his sanity and announces that he is reporting a purely objective reality: "Yet, mad am I not—and very surely I do not dream" (III: 849). Nor are we ever presented with evidence to the contrary. The "mere household events" (III: 849) that constitute the tale are just that, and yet, as the narrator insists, "they have presented little but Horror" (III: 849–50). The conclusion is inescapable: the world of objective reality is as capable of bodying forth a debilitating horror as is the subjective reality of the witch-haunted dreamer, a point not made again with comparable force until Henry James and Franz Kafka. Poe here inverts the usual suspension and distancing of Gothic supernaturalism, depicting horror not as something exotic or as suspended from real life but as an integral part of real life, a consequence of "household events."

"The Black Cat" 's narrator, noted for the "docility and humanity" of his disposition, is possessed not by demons but by "the Fiend Intemperance," aided by "the spirit of PERVERSENESS" (III: 852), the latter identified as "one of the primitive impulses of the human heart—one of the indivisible primary faculties, or sentiments, which give direction to the character of Man" (III: 852). In the face of a human psyche so constituted, how may stability be achieved? Clearly, the tale answers, it cannot. The narrator is thoroughly debased by intemperance and perverseness; eventually he kills the cat he had once loved so deeply. The resonances of his deed prove ineluctable, the responsibility unavoidable; a near-double of the dead Pluto mysteriously appears and takes to the narrator instantly, even as he recoils from the beast, finding the cat a source of "absolute dread," of "terror and horror" (III: 855)—a negative and unfulfilling sublime. From this time on, the narrator tells us, "Evil thoughts became my sole intimates—the darkest and most evil of thoughts" (III: 856). Hatred of the cat is transferred to his wife only momentarily, but that is sufficient and she is killed. Her corpse is hidden in a wall of the basement, the house's foundation, as though by going deep enough the narrator believed he could bury the evidence of his deed, just as the conscious mind seeks to bury unacceptable drives in the primal id, foundation of the psyche. But perversity, embodied literally in the second cat, proves self-revealing; when the basement is full of policemen the entombed cat yowls its "wailing shriek, half of terror and half of triumph" (III: 859), and the narrator is undone.

The impossibility of containing the irrational and destructive impulses of the mind is the subject of two more works of the same period, "The Imp of the Perverse" (1845) and "The Premature Burial" (1844). "Imp" is also in that line of Poe's works that finds suspect the assumption that by reason alone humans may understand and order their world. The tale begins by emphasizing the difficulty of believing in the operation or existence of things nonrational but, with an increasing firmness, insists there is some aspect of the human psyche that makes us "act, for the reason we should *not*" (III: 1220). Here "Imp" joins its voice with "The Black Cat" and other works that, in their collective dark register, speak of an ineluctable shadow on the soul: "Nor will this overwhelming tendency to do wrong for the wrong's sake, admit of analysis, or resolution into ulterior elements. It is a radical, a primitive impulse—elementary" (III: 1221). From such deeply encrypted and irresolvable features of the psyche it is impossible to escape, especially if Ketterer is correct in his claim that the narrator "is at his most perverse in supposing that the imp of the perverse lies outside of man's reason, whereas it is, in one sense, a consequence of it" (108). Reason is the source of the irrational, just as light is the source of shadow, as life is the source of death and mystery.

The second of these tales, "The Premature Burial," is often regarded as one of Poe's lesser pieces. The Levines, for example, locate it among the "Slapstick Gothic" set of works (294–95); Paul Lewis, writing on the humorous in Gothic fiction, finds it the ludicrously funny story of "one of the few Poe characters who either learn from misfortune or have therapeutic experiences" (319). I claim greater consequence for the tale. The narrator begins by invoking "the severity and majesty of truth" (III: 995), and while it is easy to see how such language has led critics to read the tale as a hoax, it should not shape the final evaluation of a tale that, having discussed actual cases of premature burial, moves on to study the horror of such an event in one fictive case. The burden of the latter part of the story is that "no event is so terribly well adapted to inspire the supremeness of bodily and of mental distress, as is burial before death. . . . We know of nothing so agonizing upon Earth—we can dream of nothing half so hideous in the realms of the nethermost Hell" (III: 961). The events in which the narrator becomes involved examine this terror: his cataleptic trances, his profound fear of being mistaken for dead, his elaborate precautions to avoid being prematurely interred. The fact that his fears prove baseless (one is tempted to say "ungrounded") when he discovers that his "coffin" is only the closeness of a ship's bunk suggests not so much a levity of tone as a temporary—and only temporary—escape from the horrors that attend human existence. It may be that some readers see a "lightness" in the fact that the narrator's survival effects positive change in him:

My soul acquired tone—acquired temper. I went abroad. I took vigorous exercise. I breathed the free air of Heaven. I thought upon other subjects than Death. . . . I read no "Night Thoughts"—no fustian about churchyards—no bugaboo tales—*such as this*. In short, I became a new man, and lived a man's life. From that memorable night, I dismissed forever my charnel apprehensions. (III: 969)

Yet his escape from the horrors of the grave has not been as successful or as final as the above passage might suggest. He may not read "bugaboo tales such as this," but he certainly took the trouble to write one, and we need turn only to the final paragraph to realize that the narrator has not so much vanquished terror as effected an uneasy truth with it:

There are moments when, even to the sober eye of Reason, the world of our sad Humanity may assume the semblance of a Hell—but the imagination of man is no Catharsis, to explore with impunity its every cavern. Alas! the grim legion of sepulchral terrors cannot be regarded as altogether fanciful—but, like the Demons in whose company Afrasiab made his voyage down the Oxus, they must sleep, or they will devour us—they must be suffered to slumber, or we perish. (III: 969)

Slumber they must if we are to live at all in the world of quotidian concerns and experience—and this principle explains the action taken by Montresor—but Poe's canon suggests that the sleep of demons is decidedly uneasy, for the possibility of being devoured, of perishing in the unknowable abyss behind our comforting constructions, remains, for Poe, very real.

The narrator of "The Premature Burial" faces his demons alone, which makes him representative of Poe's protagonists. The epistemological terrors with which his works are concerned assume their fullest gravity and significance when their assault encircles the individual, insulating and cutting him or her off from the consolations normally provided by communal belonging. The effect of such isolation apparently was to be the concern of "The Light-House," unfinished at Poe's death.

The narrator of the fragment, sent to operate an isolated lighthouse, records the fear that seems to define the entire experience: "there is no telling what may happen to a man all alone as I am" (III: 1390). He tries to put a good face on his isolation—"My spirits are beginning to revive already, at the mere thought of being—for once in my life at least—thoroughly alone"—but a greater complexity regarding his solitude seems to be building. Having reflected on the social intrigue by which he obtained his position, the narrator returns to the specter of his isolation: "Besides, I wish to be alone. . . . It is strange that I never observed, until this moment, how dreary a sound that word has—'alone'! I could half fancy there was some peculiarity in the echo of these cylindrical walls" (III: 1390–91).

The remainder of the fragment is taken up with the narrator's efforts to see something, anything, from his vantage point: "A few seaweeds came in sight but besides them absolutely *nothing* all day—not even the slightest speck of cloud. . . . Nothing to be seen, with the telescope even, but ocean and sky, with an occasional gull" (III: 1391). The almost overpowering sense of isolation here is Poe's compressed statement of an increasingly real fact of existence. The isolated narrator, cut off from "society" (a word Poe stresses in the first paragraph) is enclosed in a solitary tower, the very existence of which is a solipsistic battle-cry bidding defiance to the external environment, here perceived as potentially hostile and destructive: "and yet I have heard seamen say that, occasionally, with a wind at South-West, the sea has been known to run higher here than any where with the single exception of the Western opening of the Straits of Magellan" (III: 1392). The solitary self confronting such empty hostility is enclosed in a structure believed inviolable, but the very tone in which this conviction is presented and our awareness of Poe's usual strategies conspire to suggest that Mabbott is correct when he claims "That Poe's lighthouse was doomed to fall cannot be doubted . . ." (III: 1388–89). The motif of the "building destroyed" suggests a parallel with "The House of Usher," but here the implications are different if not graver, for the threat is now external, proceeding not from the disturbed mind but from the environment, from the world at large.

In his studies of nightmarish marginality Poe proves very much the progenitor of the Western fantastic tradition, which consistently has been a literature of isolation and alienation. Jackson explains that fantasy derives ultimately from *menippea*, an essentially "carnivalesque" form, differing from it principally in that fantasy, unlike the earlier genre, is not communal but has evolved in such a way as to become a literature of alienation and disjunction (14–17). These are the essential traits of Poe's canon, distinguishing his work sharply from that of Hawthorne, whose consistent appeal to a moral system demands a sense of community, however discontent with that community his narrators or heroines may be. With Poe, the opposite is true: his protagonists are always solitary or isolated men—"A Man of the Crowd" is an "external" study of just such a liminal figure—and this motif of isolation shapes the subversive and unsettling effect of Poe's fantastic, one that foregrounds the problematic and increasingly tentative consolations, the fragility, of community and meaning. In the West, Enlightenment sensibilities have isolated the individual, shifting the power and burden of self-identity away from the corporate body, whether church or political system, where it most frequently rested in previous ages. It is because of such factors that the fantastic does not emerge as a consistently subversive mode or genre until the Romantics, when art began to assess the impact of alienation, industrialization, and revolution on the human psyche. Poe turned the relatively crude impulse and form of the Gothic into the modern fantastic.

Thompson, in *Poe's Fiction,* argues a position that has direct bearing on the claim that Poe is the first English-language fantasist. Thompson writes that the ironic is "the dimension that explains how Poe was able to protect himself from the despair to which such immersion as his in the nightside vision must normally lead. . . . Irony was the device that allowed him to contemplate his obsession with death, murder, torture, insanity, guilt, loss and fear of total annihilation in a meaningless universe, and also to detach and protect himself from the obsession" (8–9). This very modern irony is what permitted Poe to indulge his dark vision to the degree requisite to make him our first fantasist. Turning "an inadequate Gothicism" into "the literary vehicle for his own double and triple vision" (Thompson, *Fiction* 17), Poe turned the outworn literary tropes of his age into tales that gave expression to fears and anxieties very familiar still. Poe's voice reverberates strongly in our own age, for his "momentary transcendence of the dark chaos of the universe" (*Fiction* 117) by means of ironic mockery is the same trope we today employ to obtain the chief (hollow) consolation left to us.

Notes

Chapter 1: The Supernatural Sublime

1. In addition to those studies of the sublime cited in the text, other useful works include James B. Twitchell, *Romantic Horizons: Aspects of the Sublime in English Poetry and Painting, 1770–1850;* the first chapter of Angela Leighton, *Shelley and the Sublime: An Interpretation of the Major Poems;* Neil Hertz, *The End of the Line: Essays in Psychoanalysis and the Sublime;* Morton D. Paley, *The Apocalyptic Sublime;* the five essays comprising "The Sublime: A Forum" in *Studies in Romanticism* 26 (1987); the issue of *New Literary History* (16 [1985–1986]) devoted to the sublime; and Peter de Bolla, *The Discourse of the Sublime—Readings in History, Aesthetics, and the Subject.*

2. A provocative study of the relationship of the "fantastic" to Western culture's evolving dominant worldviews is provided by James D. Ziegler in "Primitive, Newtonian, and Einsteinian Fantasies: Three Worldviews." Of related interest in the same volume are Peter Cersowsky, "The Copernican Revolution in the History of Fantastic Literature at the Beginning of the Twentieth Century," 19–26; and John M. Lipski, "The Literature of the Unknowable," 113–21.

3. Otto notes the correlation between the artistic representation of sublimity and the lived experience of what he calls the *mysterium tremendum,* "the deepest and most fundamental element" in religious emotion (12). See esp. p. 27 and pp. 41–42. For direct application of Otto's work to Gothic fiction, see S. L. Varnado, "The Idea of the Numinous in Gothic Literature"; Varnado's fuller treatment of the subject in *Haunted Presence;* see also Devendra Varma, *The Gothic Flame,* esp. 206–33; and Judith Wilt, *Ghosts of the Gothic: Austen, Eliot, and Lawrence,* 12–24. The relation of the numinous to Gothic fiction is discussed in the opening section of part I of this study.

4. Recent book-length studies of Gothic or fantastic fiction that examine Todorov's theory include Rosemary Jackson, *Fantasy: The Literature of Subversion;* Christine Brook-Rose's *The Rhetoric of the Unreal: Studies in Narrative and Structure, Especially of the Fantastic;* Tobin Siebers, *The Romantic Fantastic;* Margaret L. Carter, *Specter or Delusion? The Supernatural in Gothic Fiction;* and Terry Heller, *The Delights of Terror: An Aesthetic of the Tale of Terror.* In addition to developing a Todorov-based typology of terror literature, Heller briefly considers the relation between his categories and the aesthetic of the Kantian sublime, suggesting that "it may . . . be true that all tales of terror seek in various ways to produce" the aesthetic effect of

the sublime" (206). Introduced only in his conclusion, this idea does not shape Heller's categories.

PART I: GOTHIC FICTION AND THE SUPERNATURAL SUBLIME

1. Fuller discussion of this point is found in Jerome J. McGann, *The Romantic Ideology: A Critical Investigation,* and many of his subsequent writings.

2. Much of the sublime's oppressive nature may be attributed to the fact that it is conceived, in Burke and elsewhere, as a masculinist aesthetic, in contrast to the passive/submissive femininity of the beautiful. See W. J. T. Mitchell's chapter on Burke in his *Iconology: Image, Text, Ideology,* esp. pp. 129–31; and Isaac Kramnick, *The Rage of Edmund Burke—Portrait of an Ambivalent Conservative,* 92–98. For a treatment of sublimity that both agrees with and departs from this view, see Mellor, *Romanticism and Gender,* 85–106.

3. Gothicism as a self-subversive enterprise is examined from a formalist perspective in George Haggerty, *Gothic Fiction/Gothic Form.* David Punter, examining the Gothic tradition from another angle, identifies two modes of inherent doubleness in the genre. The first is "a blend of indulgence and moral rectitude" (41); the other is that tales of both explained and real supernaturalism "work by having it both ways: by persuading to belief while withholding full authorial confirmation of that belief" (76).

CHAPTER 2: DIDACTICISM AND ROMANTIC ERROR

1. The edition of Reeve's *The Progress of Romance* cited here is a facsimile of the first edition; I have modernized the orthography.

CHAPTER 3: THE YAWNING GULF

1. For discussion of Gothic fiction and its political milieu, see the works by Astle, Brooks, Frank, Morse, and also Ronald Paulson, "Gothic Fiction and the French Revolution," and his book *Representations of Revolution,* which also includes a chapter on "The Sublime and the Beautiful."

2. For a study of *Wieland* as Brown's analysis of "his relation to historical time and place" and the interplay of Old and New World intellectual forces, see Axelrod's chapter on the novel (53–96).

3. For a survey of Gothic elements in Brown, see Donald Ringe, *Gothic,* 41–45.

4. For the influence of Scottish Common Sense thought on early American intellectual life, see Terence Martin, *The Instructed Vision.* Discussion of the effect of SCS thinking on Brown may be found in Michael Davitt Bell, " 'The Double-Tongued Deceiver,' " 145–46, an article that also examines Brown's general suspicion of the literary imagination.

CHAPTER 4: DRAMATIC TRUTH

1. These footnotes are not those Coleridge himself included in the *Biographia* but interpolations from elsewhere in his writings supplied by the editors of the Princeton-Bollingen series of Coleridge's works.

2. Wlecke demonstrates that Coleridge and Wordsworth had similar understandings of the sublime (94–105), although Clarence Thorpe argues that Coleridge was more insistently religious in his understanding of sublime experience than was Wordsworth (206–7). For a detailed discussion of both Coleridge's and Wordsworth's understandings of sublimity and their debts to prior theories of sublimity, see Raimonda Modiano, *Coleridge and the Concept of Nature*, 101–37. Coleridge's debt to Kant is also traced by Clarence Thorpe; D. M. MacKinnon, "Coleridge and Kant"; and John Simon, "Coleridge and the Sublime."

3. On Coleridge's understanding of "daemons" as objectifications of inner states, see Kramer; J. B. Beer, *Coleridge the Visionary*, 99–132; and Patterson's essay on "Peter Bell." Some further light is shed by Charles I. Patterson, "The Daemonic in *Kubla Khan*: Toward Interpretation."

4. *"Quid agunt?"* Coleridge adds; *"quae loca habitant?"* (p. 186). See also *Coleridge's Verse: A Selection*, 55–56, 119.

5. The most famous source-study of the supernatural in "Christabel" is Arthur Nethercot, *The Road to Tryermaine: A Study of the History, Background, and Purposes of Coleridge's "Christabel."* Surveys of the poem's folkloric elements include Elizabeth M. Liggins, "Folklore and the Supernatural in 'Christabel' "; and John Adlard, "The Quantock *Christabel.*" The poem's debts to Gothic fiction and the ballad revival are traced by Donald Reuel Tuttle, " 'Christabel' 's Sources in Percy's *Reliques* and the Gothic Romance"; Edward Dramin, " 'Amid the Jagged Shadows': *Christabel* and the Gothic Tradition"; and Elizabeth Chadwick, "Coleridge's Headlong Horsemen: Insinuating the Supernatural."

CHAPTER 5: "INQUIRE NOT IF THE FAERY RACE"

1. The major studies of Wordsworth and the sublime are those by Wlecke and Albrecht. Other valuable treatments include Raimonda Modiano, "The Kantian Seduction: Wordsworth on the Sublime"; Eve Walsh Stoddard, "Flashes of the Invisible World: *The Prelude* in the Context of the Kantian Sublime"; and two essays by W. J. B. Owen, "The Sublime and the Beautiful in *The Prelude*," and "Wordsworth's Aesthetics of Landscape." The Wordsworthian sublime is treated by James Scoggins in *Imagination and Fancy: Complementary Modes in the Poetry of Wordsworth*, but Scoggins's discussion is hampered by the then-unavailable fragmentary essay by Wordsworth on the sublime.

2. Campbell and Mueschke point specifically to Anna Barbauld, *Sir Bertram* (1773), as well as to Radcliffe, *Romance of the Forest* (1792) and

244 Notes to Pages 145–165

The Mysteries of Udolpho (1794) ("Study" passim). A general discussion of the influence of Gothic and German "horror-romantic" on Wordsworth is to be found in Sukumar Dutt, *The Supernatural in English Romantic Poetry,* 155–56 and 217–88. Wordsworth owned copies of *The Romance of the Forest, The Old English Baron,* and *The Castle of Otranto,* conservative Gothics all; see Chester L. Shaver and Alice C. Shaver, *Wordsworth's Library: A Catalogue.*

3. For a comparison of the supernatural elements in these two poems, see Kathleen Coburn, "Coleridge and Wordsworth and 'the Supernatural,' " esp. pp. 122–25. The relationship of these works is also discussed by Mary Jacobus, who finds that " 'The Ancient Mariner' explores all that is irrational in our experience of the world: *Peter Bell* affirms normality; its laws are stable and its values unambiguous. One poem disturbs, the other reassures . . ." (272). She also points out that "Peter Bell" and "The Idiot Boy" constitute a Wordsworthian parody of the conventions of Gothic balladry (Jacobus 250–61 and passim). For these works as Gothic parodies, see also J. E. Jordan, "Wordsworth's Humor," esp. 88–89; R. F. Storch, "Wordsworth's Experimental Ballads: The Radical Uses of Intelligence and Comedy"; Stephen Maxfield Parrish, "Dramatic Technique in the *Lyrical Ballads,*" esp. 87–88.

4. The poems I am discussing here have been analyzed as a group by W. Strunk Jr., "Some Related Poems of Wordsworth and Coleridge"; he finds "The Three Graves," "The Thorn," "The Danish Boy," and "Hart-Leap Well" to constitute a study of the curse.

5. For a reading that centers on the personal importance of the poem to Wordsworth, see W. J. B. Owen, " 'The Thorn' and the Poet's Intention."

CHAPTER 6: THAT SUPERNATURAL SUMMER

1. The events of summer 1816 are recalled in the standard biographies of the principals involved, as well as in their journals. Valuable critical studies include Christopher Small, *Ariel Like a Harpy,* esp. 30–36 and 48–67; Radu Florescu, *In Search of Frankenstein,* esp. 95–127; Ernest J. Lovell, Jr., ed., *His Very Self and Voice: Collected Conversations of Lord Byron,* 185–86; and David Ketterer, *Frankenstein's Creation: The Book, the Monster, and Human Reality.* For a succinct account of the ghost-story sessions and the works they produced see James Rieger, "Dr. Polidori and the Genesis of *Frankenstein,*" originally published in *Studies in English Literature* and included, in revised form, as an appendix to *The Mutiny Within.* M. K. Joseph also discusses these matters in appendix A to his Oxford UP edition of *Frankenstein.*

2. An excellent discussion of science in *Frankenstein* is by Anne K. Mellor, "A Feminist Critique of Science" (89–114) in her book on Mary Shelley.

3. On the subject of mountains in the 1816 works of the Shelleys and Byron, see Fred V. Randel, "*Frankenstein,* Feminism, and the Intertextuality of Mountains," and "The Mountaintops of English Romanticism."

4. For the Shelleys' understanding of the mountainscapes of the Alps

as desolate and horrific, see Ronald Tetreault, "Shelley and Byron Encounter the Sublime: Switzerland, 1816."

5. Valuable readings of the novel's political dimension are by Lee Sterrenburg, "Mary Shelley's Monster: Politics and Psyche in *Frankenstein,*" and Ronald Paulson, "Gothic Fiction and the French Revolution."

6. Both Shelleys were greatly influenced by Brown's novels: see M. K. Joseph, vii; Christopher Small, 91–99; F. C. Prescott, "Wieland and *Frankenstein*"; Eleanor Sickels, "Shelley and Charles Brockden Brown"; and Mervin T. Solve, "Shelley and the Novels of Brown." The Shelleys were also attuned to the Gothic tradition in general: Mary's yearly lists of works read by her and her husband include, for 1814–1816, *The Monk, Caleb Williams, Edgar Huntly, The Italian, Wieland, St. Leon, The Mysteries of Udolpho,* and Maturin's play *Bertram* (see *Mary Shelley's Journal,* ed. Frederick L. Jones). See also John V. Murphy, *The Dark Angel: Gothic Elements in Shelley's Works;* Steven Behrendt, viii–xv; Devendra Varma, 197–99; and Radu Florescu, 173–80.

7. Other critics have noted the complicated psychodynamics of Percy's relationship to the characters in *Frankenstein.* See Peter Dale Scott, "Vital Artifice: Mary, Percy, and the Psychopolitical Integrity of *Frankenstein,*" in Levine and Knoepflmacher, 172–202; and Christopher Small, 100.

Chapter 7: "Wonders are No Wonders"

1. For the influence of Gothic literature on Keats, see Martha Hale Shackleford, " 'The Eve of St. Agnes' and *The Mysteries of Udolpho*"; M. R. Ridley, *Keats's Craftsmanship,* 96–190; Robert Gittings, *John Keats,* 255–56; Devendra Varma, *The Gothic Flame,* 195; Robert H. O'Connor, "Keats' 'The Eve of St. Agnes' and Ballad Gothicism"; and Stuart Peterfreund, "Keats's Debt to Maturin." Keats's knowledge of the romance fantastic is noted by Karen J. Harvey, "The Trouble about Merlin: The Theme of Enchantment in 'The Eve of St. Agnes.' "

2. Miriam Allott also notes a development in three of Keats's supernatural poems—"Isabella," "The Eve of St. Agnes," and "Lamia"—in the chapter of that name. She remarks "the increasing care which is taken to limit 'wonders' and 'luxuries' and to penetrate 'sensation' by 'thought' " (51).

3. See Marion H. Cusac, "Keats as Enchanter: An Organizing Principle of *The Eve of St. Agnes*"; Robert Kern, "Keats and the Problem of Romance"; and Stuart Sperry, 200–3, 218–19.

4. In contrast to the famous denunciations of Porphyro as rapist (Stillinger's assessment) or as "a destroyer" (Twitchell 94), a more balanced view of Porphyro as a sincere lover who adapts romance to reality in his quest for Madeline's love is provided by Leon Waldoff, *Keats and the Silent Work of the Imagination,* 62–81. I am most in accord with David Wiener's assessment

of Porphyro, whom he finds a "Satanic hero removing his heroine from pristine innocence out into a fallen, but superior, world of experience, a vale of soul-making" (122).

5. The pertinent lines from "Christabel" are I: 175–89. On the similarities between the two poems, see Rosemarie Maier, "The Bitch and the Bloodhound: Generic Similarity in 'Christabel' and 'The Eve of St. Agnes.' "

6. For a discussion of similarities between Keats's fairy woman and other mediating female figures in Romantic poetry, see Judith Weissman, " 'Language Strange': 'La Belle Dame sans Merci' and the Language of Nature."

7. Representative negative readings of Lamia's character may be found in Twitchell; Stillinger; Warren Stevenson, "Lamia: A Stab at the Gordian Knot"; and Bernice Slote, *Keats and the Dramatic Principle,* esp. 152–53. My position accords with those of Patterson, who sees Lamia to be "a neutral daemonic female with lovable qualities and no malicious intent" (191); Bate, who finds that "she intends anything but harm to the mortal she loves" (555); and Barbara Fass, who observes "It is not that [Lamia] is evil, but that she is attempting the impossible" (*La Belle Dame sans Merci and the Aesthetics of Romanticism* 80).

CHAPTER 8: ALLEGORY AND FANTASY

1. Hawthorne's caution here is close to that offered by Walter Scott (whom Hawthorne admired) in his 1827 essay "On the Supernatural in Fictitious Composition." On Hawthorne's careful use of fantastic tropes see Terence Martin, "The Method of Hawthorne's Tales."

2. I have chosen to examine the tales since they are the most supernatural parts of Hawthorne's canon and most readily enable comparison with Poe. For a detailed study of Gothic elements in Hawthorne's romances see Frederick Frank, 398–467; and Jane Lundblad, *Nathaniel Hawthorne and European Literary Tradition,* 81–149. An earlier version of Lundblad's study, concentrating more upon Hawthorne and the Gothic, was published as *Hawthorne and the Tradition of Gothic Romance.*

3. For the influence of Coleridge on Hawthorne, see Richard Harter Fogle, "Nathaniel Hawthorne and the Great English Romantic Poets"; a condensed version appeared in the *Nathaniel Hawthorne Journal.* See also Fogle, "Art and Illusion: Coleridgean Assumptions in Hawthorne's Tales and Sketches."

4. On the literary relationship of Poe and Hawthorne, see D. M. McKeithan, "Poe and the Second Edition of Hawthorne's *Twice-Told Tales.*"

5. Poe was hardly unknown in his time, of course, although his often vitriolic literary criticism was the main cause of what reputation he did gain. Still, it is hardly likely that his "considerable local fame" as the author of "gruesome and fantastical tales" (144; Killis Campbell, "Contemporary

Opinion of Poe") indicates the same perceptive evaluation of his achievement that Poe has gained in the past half-century.

6. For studies of the vampire motif in Poe, see Liahna Babener, who undertakes an exhaustive examination of "Berenice," "Morella," "Ligeia," "The Oval Portrait," and "The Fall of the House of Usher," examining in detail the ways in which Poe incorporates intellectual or moral vampirism (184–273). See also Lyle H. Kendall, Jr., "The Vampire Motif in 'The Fall of the House of Usher' "; Lee J. Richmond, "Edgar Allan Poe's 'Morella': Vampire of Volition"; and James B. Twitchell, *The Living Dead,* 59–66, 124–29, 166–71. For the argument that the narrator has fallen in love with a Siren who has conquered death in order to come back and kill him, see Daryl E. Jones, "Poe's Siren: Character and Meaning in 'Ligeia.' "

7. "The Power of Terror: Burke and Kant in the House of Usher."

8. For the view that Montresor has suffered fifty years of anguished remorse over his deed, see Thompson, *Poe's Fiction,* 13–14; Hoffman, *Poe,* 223–24; William H. Shurr, "Montresor's Audience in 'The Cask of Amontillado' "; and Charles A. Sweet, Jr., "Retapping Poe's 'Cask of Amontillado.' "

Works Cited

Abrams, Meyer H. *Natural Supernaturalism: Tradition and Revolution in Romantic Literature.* New York: Norton, 1971.

Adams, R. P. "Romanticism and the American Renaissance." *American Literature* 23 (1952): 419–32.

Adlard, John. "The Quantock *Christabel.*" *Philological Quarterly* 50 (1971): 230–38.

Albrecht, W. P. *The Sublime Pleasures of Tragedy: A Study of Critical Theory from Dennis to Keats.* Lawrence: UP of Kansas, 1975.

———. "Tragedy and Wordsworth's Sublime." *Wordsworth Circle* 8 (1977): 83–94.

Allot, Miriam. *John Keats: A Reassessment.* Ed. Kenneth Muir. Liverpool: Liverpool UP, 1959.

Apter, T. E. *Fantasy Literature: An Approach to Reality.* Bloomington: Indiana UP, 1982.

Arensberg, Mary. "Introduction: The American Sublime." *The American Sublime.* Ed. Mary Arensberg. Albany: State U of New York P, 1986. 1–20.

Ariès, Phillippe. *Western Attitudes toward Death: From the Middle Ages to the Present.* Tr. Patricia M. Ranum. Baltimore: Johns Hopkins UP, 1974.

Astle, Richard Sharp. "Structures of Ideology in the English Gothic Novel." Diss. U of California San Diego, 1977.

Atkins, G. Douglas. "The Eve of St. Agnes Reconsidered." *Tennessee Studies in Literature* 18 (1973): 113–32.

Axelrod, Alan. *Charles Brockden Brown: An American Tale.* Austin: U of Texas P, 1983.

Babener, Liahna Klenman. "Predators of the Spirit: The Vampire Theme in Nineteenth-Century Literature." Diss. U of California Los Angeles, 1975.

Bate, W. Jackson. *John Keats.* 1963. Cambridge: Belknap-Harvard, 1982.

Baym, Nina. "A Minority Reading of *Wieland.*" *Critical Essays on Charles Brockden Brown.* Ed. Bernard Rosenthal. Boston: G. K. Hall, 1981. 87–103.

Beer, Gillian. *The Romance.* New York: Methuen, 1970.

Beer, J. B. *Coleridge the Visionary.* London: Chatto and Windus, 1959.

Behrendt, Stephen C. Introduction. *Zastrozzi and St. Irvyne.* By Percy Bysshe Shelley. New York: Oxford UP, 1986.

Bell, Michael Davitt. *The Development of American Romance: The Sacrifices of Relation.* Chicago: U of Chicago P, 1980.

———. " 'The Double-Tongued Deceiver': Sincerity and Duplicity in the Novels of Charles Brockden Brown." *Early American Literature* 9 (1974): 143–63.

Bernard, J. H., trans. Introduction. *Critique of Judgement.* By Immanuel Kant. New York: Hafner, 1951.

Bernstein, Gene. "Keats' 'Lamia': The Sense of a Non-Ending." *Papers on Language and Literature* 15 (1979): 175–92.

Bewell, Alan. *Wordsworth and the Enlightenment: Nature, Man, and Society in the Experimental Poetry.* New Haven: Yale UP, 1989.

Bhalla, Alok. "Shades of the Preternatural: Thematic and Structural Essays on the Gothic Novel." Diss. Kent State, 1978.

Birkhead, Edith. *The Tale of Terror: A Study of the Gothic Romance.* 1921. New York: Russell and Russell, 1963.

Blair, Hugh. *Lectures on Rhetoric and Belle-Lettres.* 1783. Ed. Harold F. Harding. 2 vols. Carbondale: Southern Illinois UP, 1965.

Bolla, Peter de. *The Discourse of the Sublime—Readings in History, Aesthetics, and the Subject.* Oxford: Blackwell, 1989.

Bonaparte, Marie. *The Life and Works of Edgar Allan Poe: A Psychoanalytic Study.* Trans. John Rodker. London: Imago, 1949.

Boulton, J. T. Introduction. *A Philosophical Enquiry into the Origin of Our Ideas of the Sublime and the Beautiful.* By Edmund Burke. 1757. 2nd ed. 1759. New York: Columbia UP, 1958.

Bradley, A. C. "The Sublime." *Oxford Lectures on Poetry.* London: Macmillan, 1909. 37–65.

Brisman, Leslie. "Coleridge and the Supernatural." *Studies in Romanticism* 21 (1982): 123–59.

Brook-Rose, Christine. *The Rhetoric of the Unreal: Studies in Narrative and Structure, Especially of the Fantastic.* New York: Cambridge UP, 1981.

Brooks, Peter. "Virtue and Terror: *The Monk.*" *English Literary History* 40 (1973): 249–63.

Brown, Charles Brockden. *Edgar Huntly; or Memoirs of a Sleep-Walker.* 1799. Kent: Kent State UP, 1984. Vol. 4 of *Bicentennial Edition of the Novels and Related Works of Charles Brockden Brown.* Ed. Sydney Krause and S. W. Reid. 6 vols.

———. "On the Cause of the Popularity of Novels." *Literary Magazine and American Review* 7 (June 1807): 410–12.

———. *Wieland and Memoirs of Carwin.* 1798. Kent: Kent State UP, 1977. Vol. 1 of *Bicentennial Edition of the Novels and Related Works of Charles Brockden Brown.* Ed. Sydney J. Krause, S. W. Reid, and Alexander Cowie. 6 vols.

Brown, Marshall. "A Philosophical View of the Gothic Novel." *Studies in Romanticism* 26 (1987): 275–301.

Buchen, Irving H. "Wordsworth's Gothic Ballads." *Genre* 3 (1970): 85–96.

Burke, Edmund. *A Philosophical Enquiry into the Origin of our Ideas of the*

Sublime and Beautiful. 1759. Ed. J. T. Boulton. 2nd ed. New York: Columbia UP, 1958.

Bush, Douglas. *John Keats: His Life and Writings*. New York: Collier, 1966.

Butler, Marilyn. *Romantics, Rebels, and Reactionaries: English Literature and Its Background, 1760–1830*. Oxford: Oxford UP, 1981.

Byron, George Gordon, Lord. *The Complete Poetical Works*. Vol. 4. Ed. Jerome J. McGann. Oxford: Clarendon, 1986.

Campbell, Killis. "Contemporary Opinion of Poe." *PMLA* 36 (1921): 142–66.

Campbell, Oscar James, and Paul Mueschke. "*The Borderers* as a Document in the History of Wordsworth's Aesthetic Development." *Modern Philology* 23 (1926): 465–82.

———. " 'Guilt and Sorrow': A Study in the Genesis of Wordsworth's Aesthetic." *Modern Philology* 23 (1926): 293–306.

Carter, Margaret L. *Specter or Delusion? The Supernatural in Gothic Fiction*. Ann Arbor: UMI, 1987.

Castle, Terry. "The Spectralization of the Other in *The Mysteries of Udolpho*." *The New Eighteenth Century: Theory, Politics, English Literature*. Ed. Felicity Nussbaum and Laura Brown. New York: Methuen, 1987. 231–53, 307–10.

Cersowsky, Peter. "The Copernican Revolution in the History of Fantastic Literature at the Beginning of the Twentieth Century." Collins and Pearce. 19–26.

Chadwick, Elizabeth. "Coleridge's Headlong Horsemen: Insinuating the Supernatural." *Wordsworth Circle* 8 (1977): 47–55.

Clapp, Edwin R. "La Belle Dame as Vampire." *Philological Quarterly* 27 (1948): 89–92.

Clark, David Lee. *Charles Brockden Brown: Pioneer Voice of America*. Durham: Duke UP, 1952.

Cleman, John. "Ambiguous Evil: A Study of Villains and Heroes in Charles Brockden Brown's Major Novels." *Early American Literature* 19 (1975): 190–219.

Coburn, Kathleen. "Coleridge and Wordsworth and 'the Supernatural.' " *University of Toronto Quarterly* 25 (1955–1956): 121–30.

Colacurcio, Michael J. *The Province of Piety: Moral History in Hawthorne's Early Tales*. Cambridge: Harvard UP, 1984.

Coleridge, Samuel Taylor. *Biographia Literaria*. 1817. Ed. James Engell and W. Jackson Bate. 2 vols. Vol. 7 of *The Collected Works of Samuel Taylor Coleridge*. Princeton: Bollingen-Princeton UP, 1983. 16 vols.

———. *Coleridge's Verse: A Selection*. Ed. William Empson and David Pirie. New York: Schocken, 1973. 55–56, 119.

———. *Collected Letters of Samuel Taylor Coleridge*. Ed. Earl Leslie Griggs. Vol. I. Oxford: Clarendon, 1956. 2 vols.

———. *Complete Poetical Works of Samuel Taylor Coleridge*. Ed. Ernest Hartley Coleridge. 1912. Vol. I. Oxford: Clarendon, 1957. 2 vols.

————. *The Friend.* Ed. Barbara E. Rooke. 2 vols. Vol. 4 of *The Collected Works of Samuel Taylor Coleridge.* Princeton: Bollingen-Princeton UP, 1969. 16 vols.

————. *Lay Sermons.* Ed. R. J. White. Vol. 6 of *The Collected Works of Samuel Taylor Coleridge.* Princeton: Bollingen-Princeton UP, 1972. 16 vols.

————. *Marginalia.* Ed. George Whalley. 2 vols. Vol. 5 of *The Collected Works of Samuel Taylor Coleridge.* Princeton: Bollingen-Princeton UP, 1984. 16 vols.

Collins, Robert A., and Howard D. Pearce, eds. *The Scope of the Fantastic—Theory, Technique, Major Authors.* Selected Essays from the First International Conference on the Fantastic in Literature and Film, 1980. Westport: Greenwood, 1985.

Cooke, Michael G. *The Romantic Will.* New Haven: Yale UP, 1976.

Cowie, Alexander. Historical Essay. *Weiland and Memoirs of Carwin.* By Charles Brockden Brown. 1798. Kent: Kent State UP, 1977. Vol. 1 of *Bicentennial Edition of the Novels and Related Works of Charles Brockden Brown.* Ed. Sydney J. Krause, S. W. Reid, and Alexander Cowie. 6 vols. 311–48.

Crowther, Paul. *The Kantian Sublime: From Morality to Art.* Oxford: Clarendon, 1989.

Cusac, Marion H. "Keats as Enchanter: An Organizing Principle of *The Eve of St. Agnes.*" *Keats-Shelley Journal* 17 (1968): 113–19.

Davidson, Edward H. *Poe: A Critical Study.* Cambridge: Harvard UP, 1957.

Day, William Patrick. *In the Circle of Fear and Desire: A Study of Gothic Fantasy.* Chicago: U of Chicago P, 1985.

DeLamotte, Eugenia C. *Perils of the Night: A Feminist Study of Nineteenth-Century Gothic.* New York: Oxford UP, 1990.

Delson, Abe. "The Function of Geraldine in *Christabel:* A Critical Perspective and Interpretation." *English Studies* 61 (1980): 130–41.

Dennis, John. *The Grounds of Criticism in Poetry.* 1704. Menston, England: Scholar, 1971.

Donahue, Alice McNeill. *Hawthorne: Calvin's Ironic Stepchild.* Kent: Kent State UP, 1985.

Doubleday, Neal Frank. "Hawthorne's Use of Three Gothic Patterns." *College English* 7 (1945–1946): 250–62.

Drake, Nathan. *Literary Hours, or Sketches Critical and Narrative.* 2nd ed. 1800. 2 vols. New York: Garland, 1970.

Dramin, Edward. " 'Amid the Jagged Shadows': *Christabel* and the Gothic Tradition." *Wordsworth Circle* 13 (1982): 221–28.

Durant, David. "Ann Radcliffe and the Conservative Gothic." *Studies in English Literature, 1500–1900* 22 (1982): 519–30.

Dussinger, John A. "Kinship and Guilt in Mary Shelley's *Frankenstein.*" *Studies in the Novel* 8 (1976): 38–55.

Dutt, Sukumar. *The Supernatural in English Romantic Poetry: Being a Critical Scrutiny of Supernaturalism: Its Growth and Phases of Development in English Poetry during 1780–1830.* 1938. N.p.: Folcroft Library Editions, 1972.

Edwards, Paul, and Macdonald Emslie. "The Limitations of Langdale: A Reading of *Christabel.*" *Essays in Criticism* 20 (1970): 57–67.

——. " 'Thoughts all so unlike each other': The Paradoxical in *Christabel.*" *English Studies* 52 (1971): 236–46.

Ellis, Kate Ferguson. "Monsters in the Garden: Mary Shelley and the Bourgeois Family." Levine and Knoepflmacher 123–42.

Ende, Stuart A. *Keats and the Sublime.* New Haven: Yale UP, 1976.

Enscoe, Gerald. *Eros and the Romantics: Sexual Love as a Theme in Coleridge, Shelley, and Keats.* The Hague: Mouton, 1967.

Evert, Walter H. *Aesthetic and Myth in the Poetry of Keats.* Princeton: Princeton UP, 1965.

Fass, Barbara. *La Belle Dame sans Merci and the Aesthetics of Romanticism.* Detroit: Wayne State UP, 1974.

Ferry, David. *The Limits of Mortality: An Essay on Wordsworth's Major Poems.* Middletown: Wesleyan UP, 1959.

Florescu, Radu. *In Search of Frankenstein.* Boston: New York Graphic Society, 1975.

Fogle, Richard Harter. "Art and Illusion: Coleridgean Assumptions in Hawthorne's Tales and Sketches." *Ruined Eden of the Present.* Ed. Thompson and Lokke. 109–27.

——. "The Great English Romantics in Hawthorne's Major Romances." *Nathaniel Hawthorne Journal* 6 (1976): 62–68.

——. "Nathaniel Hawthorne and the Great English Romantic Poets." *Keats-Shelley Journal* 21–22 (1972–73): 219–35.

Frank, Frederick Stilson. "Perverse Pilgrimage: The Role of the Gothic in the Works of Charles Brockden Brown, Edgar Allan Poe, and Nathaniel Hawthorne." Diss. Rutgers U, 1968.

Fruman, Norman. *Coleridge, the Damaged Archangel.* New York: George Braziller, 1971.

Frye, Northrop. *A Study of English Romanticism.* Chicago: U of Chicago P, 1968.

Gittings, Robert. *John Keats.* Boston: Little, Brown, 1968.

Gleckner, Robert F. *Byron and the Ruins of Paradise.* Baltimore: Johns Hopkins UP, 1967.

Haggerty, George. *Gothic Fiction/Gothic Form.* University Park: Pennsylvania State UP, 1989.

Halliburton, David. *Edgar Allan Poe: A Phenomenological View.* Princeton: Princeton UP, 1973.

Hartman, Geoffrey H. "Wordsworth, *The Borderers,* and 'Intellectual Murder.' " *JEGP* 62 (1963): 761–68.

———. *Wordsworth's Poetry, 1787–1814.* 1964. New Haven: Yale UP, 1977.

Harvey, Karen J. "The Trouble about Merlin: The Theme of Enchantment in 'The Eve of St. Agnes.' " *Keats-Shelley Journal* 34 (1985): 83–94.

Hawthorne, Nathaniel. *Centenary Edition.* Ed. William Charvat, Roy Harvey Pearce, Claude M. Simpson, et al. Columbus: Ohio State UP, 1962–1988. 20 vols.

Heller, Terry. *The Delights of Terror: An Aesthetic of the Tale of Terror.* Urbana: U of Illinois P, 1987.

Hertz, Neil. *The End of the Line: Essays in Psychoanalysis and the Sublime.* New York: Columbia UP, 1985.

Hipple, Walter John, Jr. *The Beautiful, the Sublime, and the Picturesque in Eighteenth-Century British Aesthetic Theory.* Carbondale: Southern Illinois UP, 1957.

Hobsbawm, E. J. *The Age of Revolution, 1789–1848.* New York: New American Library, 1962.

Hoffman, Daniel. *Poe Poe Poe Poe Poe Poe Poe.* Garden City: Doubleday, 1972.

Holstein, Michael E. "Coleridge's *Christabel* as Psychodrama: Five Perspectives on the Intruder." *Wordsworth Circle* 7 (1976): 119–28.

Hume, Robert D. "Exuberant Gloom, Existential Agony, and Heroic Despair: Three Varieties of Negative Romanticism." *The Gothic Imagination: Essays in Dark Romanticism.* Ed. G. R. Thompson. [Pullman]: Washington State UP, 1974. 109–27.

———. "Gothic versus Romantic: A Revaluation of the Gothic Novel." *PMLA* 84 (1969): 282–90.

Jackson, Rosemary. *Fantasy: The Literature of Subversion.* New York: Methuen, 1983.

Jacobus, Mary. *Tradition and Experiment in Wordsworth's Lyrical Ballads (1798).* Oxford: Clarendon, 1976.

Janowitz, Anne. "Coleridge's 1816 Volume: Fragment as Rubric." *Studies in Romanticism* 24 (1985): 21–39.

Jones, Daryl E. "Poe's Siren: Character and Meaning in 'Ligeia.' " *Studies in Short Fiction* 20 (1983): 33–37.

Jones, John. *The Egotistical Sublime: A History of Wordsworth's Imagination.* London: Chatto and Windus, 1960.

Jordan, J. E. "Wordsworth's Humor." *PMLA* 73 (1958): 81–93.

Joseph, M. K., ed. Introduction and Appendix. *Frankenstein, or The Modern Prometheus.* By Mary Shelley. 1818. New York: Oxford UP, 1969.

Kant, Immanuel. *Critique of Judgement.* 1790. Trans. J. H. Bernard. 1892. New York: Hafner, 1951.

Keats, John. *Complete Poems.* Ed. Jack Stillinger. Cambridge: Belknap-Harvard, 1982.

———. *The Letters of John Keats.* Ed. Hyder E. Rollins. 2 vols. Cambridge: Harvard UP, 1958.

Kendall, Lyle H., Jr. "The Vampire Motif in 'The Fall of the House of Usher.' " *College English* 24 (1963): 450–53.

Kennedy, J. Gerald. "Phantasms of Death in Poe's Fiction." *The Haunted Dusk: American Supernatural Fiction, 1820–1920.* Ed. Howard Kerr, John W. Crowley, and Charles L. Crow. Athens: U of Georgia P, 1983. 37–65.

Kern, Robert. "Keats and the Problem of Romance." *Philological Quarterly* 58 (1979): 171–91.

Ketterer, David. *Frankenstein's Creation: The Book, the Monster, and Human Reality.* Victoria, B.C.: U of Victoria P, 1979.

———. *The Rationale of Deception in Poe.* Baton Rouge: Lousiana State UP, 1979.

Knight, Richard Payne. *An Analytical Inquiry into the Principles of Taste.* 4th ed., 1808. Westmead, England: Gregg, 1972.

Kramer, Lawrence. "That Other Will: The Daemonic in Coleridge and Wordsworth." *Philological Quarterly* 58 (1979): 298–320.

Kramnick, Isaac. *The Rage of Edmund Burke—Portrait of an Ambivalent Conservative.* New York: Basic, 1977.

Krause, Sidney J. "Romanticism in *Wieland*: Brown and the Reconciliation of Opposites." *Artful Thunder: Versions of the Romantic Tradition in American Literature in Honor of Howard P. Vincent.* Ed. Robert J. DeMott and Sanford E. Marovitz. Kent: Kent State UP, 1975. 13–24.

Laurence, David. "William Bradford's American Sublime." *PMLA* 102 (1987): 55–65.

Lea, Sydney L. W. *Gothic to Fantastic: Readings in Supernatural Fiction.* New York: Arno, 1980.

Leighton, Angela. *Shelley and the Sublime: An Interpretation of the Major Poems.* Cambridge: Cambridge UP, 1984.

Levin, Harry. *The Power of Blackness.* New York: Alfred A. Knopf, 1958.

Levine, George. "The Ambiguous Heritage of *Frankenstein.*" Levine and Knoepflmacher 3–30.

Levine, George, and U. C. Knoepflmacher, eds. *The Endurance of Frankenstein: Essays on Mary Shelley's Novel.* Berkeley: U of California P, 1979.

Levine, Stuart, and Susan Levine. *The Short Fiction of Edgar Allan Poe: An Annotated Edition.* Indianapolis: Bobbs-Merrill, 1976.

Levinson, Marjorie. *The Romantic Fragment Poem: A Critique of a Form.* Chapel Hill: U of North Carolina P, 1986.

Lewis, Matthew G. *The Monk.* 1795. Ed. Howard Anderson. New York: Oxford UP, 1981.

Lewis, Paul. "Mysterious Laughter: Humor and Fear in Gothic Fiction." *Genre* 14 (1981): 309–27.

Liggins, Elizabeth M. "Folklore and the Supernatural in 'Christabel.' " *Folklore* 88 (1977): 91–104.

Lipking, Lawrence. "The Marginal Gloss." *Critical Inquiry* 3 (1977): 609–56.

Lipski, John M. "The Literature of the Unknowable." Collins and Pearce. 113–21.

Lovell, Ernest J., Jr., ed. *His Very Self and Voice: Collected Conversations of Lord Byron.* New York: Macmillan, 1954.

Lundblad, Jane. *Hawthorne and the Tradition of Gothic Romance.* 1946. New York: Haskell House, 1964.

———. *Nathaniel Hawthorne and European Literary Tradition.* 1947. New York: Russell and Russell, 1965.

Mabbott, Thomas Ollive, ed. *Collected Works of Edgar Allan Poe.* 3 vol. Cambridge: Harvard UP, 1969–1978.

MacAndrew, Elizabeth. *The Gothic Tradition in Fiction.* New York: Columbia UP, 1979.

McGann, Jerome J. *The Romantic Ideology: A Critical Investigation.* Chicago: U of Chicago P, 1983.

McKeithan, D. M. "Poe and the Second Edition of Hawthorne's *Twice-Told Tales.*" *Nathaniel Hawthorne Journal* 4 (1974): 257–69.

MacKinnon, D. M. "Coleridge and Kant." *Coleridge's Variety: Bicentenary Studies.* Ed. John Beer. Pittsburgh: U of Pittsburgh P, 1974. 183–203.

Magnuson, Paul. *Coleridge's Nightmare Poetry.* Charlottesville: UP of Virginia, 1974.

Maier, Rosemarie. "The Bitch and the Bloodhound: Generic Similarity in 'Christabel' and 'The Eve of St. Agnes.' " *JEGP* 70 (1971): 62–75.

Marchand, Leslie A. *Byron: A Portrait.* Chicago: U of Chicago P, 1970.

Marshall, William H. *The Structure of Byron's Major Poems.* Philadelphia: U of Pennsylvania P, 1962.

Martin, Terence. *The Instructed Vision: Scottish Common Sense Philosophy and the Origins of American Fiction.* 1961. New York: Kraus Reprint, 1969.

———. "The Method of Hawthorne's Tales." *Hawthorne Centenary Essays.* Ed. Roy Harvey Pearce. Columbus: Ohio State UP, 1964. 7–30.

Marx, Leo. *The Machine in the Garden: Technology and the Pastoral Ideal in America.* New York: Oxford UP, 1964.

Mellor, Anne K. *Mary Shelley: Her Life, Her Fiction, Her Monsters.* New York: Methuen, 1988.

———. *Romanticism and Gender.* New York: Routledge, 1993.

Miller, J. Hillis. *The Disappearance of God: Five Nineteenth-Century Writers.* Cambridge: Belknap-Harvard, 1963.

Mitchell, W. J. T. *Iconology: Image, Text, Ideology.* Chicago: U of Chicago P, 1986.

Modiano, Raimonda. *Coleridge and the Concept of Nature.* Tallahassee: Florida State UP, 1985.

———. "The Kantian Seduction: Wordsworth on the Sublime." *Deutsche Romantik and English Romanticism.* Ed. Theodore G. Gish and Sandra G. Frieden. Munich: Wilhelm Fink Verlag, 1984. 17–26.

Mogen, David. "Frontier Myth and American Gothic." *Genre* 14 (1981): 329–46.

Monk, Samuel H. *The Sublime: A Study of Critical Theories in XVIII-Century England.* New York: MLA, 1935.

Morris, David B. "Gothic Sublimity." *New Literary History* 16 (1985): 299–319.

———. *The Religious Sublime: Christian Poetry and Critical Tradition in 18th-Century England.* Lexington: UP of Kentucky, 1972.

Morse, David. *Romanticism: A Structural Analysis.* Totowa: Barnes and Noble, 1982.

Murphy, John V. *The Dark Angel: Gothic Elements in Shelley's Works.* Lewisburg, Pa.: Bucknell UP, 1975.

Nethercot, Arthur. *The Road to Tryermaine: A Study of the History, Background, and Purposes of Coleridge's "Christabel."* Chicago: U of Chicago P, 1939.

Nicholson, Marjorie Hope. *Mountain Gloom and Mountain Glory: The Development of the Aesthetics of the Infinite.* Ithaca: Cornell UP, 1959.

O'Connor, Robert H. "Keats' 'The Eve of St. Agnes' and Ballad Gothicism." *Lamar Journal of the Humanities* 9 (1983): 17–27.

Otto, Rudolph. *The Idea of the Holy: An Inquiry into the Non-Rational Factor in the Idea of the Divine and Its Relation to the Rational.* 1917. Trans. John W. Harvey. 2nd ed. New York: Oxford UP, 1957.

Owen, W. J. B. "The Charm More Superficial." *Wordsworth Circle* 13 (1982): 8–16.

———. "The Sublime and the Beautiful in *The Prelude.*" *Wordsworth Circle* 4 (1973): 67–86.

———. " 'The Thorn' and the Poet's Intention." *Wordsworth Circle* 8 (1977): 3–17.

———. "Wordsworth's Aesthetics of Landscape." *Wordsworth Circle* 7 (1976): 70–82.

Paley, Morton D. *The Apocalyptic Sublime.* New Haven: Yale UP, 1986.

Pandeya, Prabhat K. "The Drama of Evil in 'The Hollow of the Three Hills.' " *Nathaniel Hawthorne Journal* 5 (1975): 177–81.

Parrish, Stephen Maxfield. "Dramatic Technique in the *Lyrical Ballads.*" *PMLA* 74 (1959): 85–97.

Patterson, Charles I., Jr. "The Daemonic in *Kubla Khan:* Toward Interpretation." *PMLA* 89 (1974): 1033–42.

———. "The Daemonic in *Peter Bell.*" *Wordsworth Circle* 8 (1977): 139–46.

———. *The Daemonic in the Poetry of John Keats.* Urbana: U of Illinois P, 1970.

Paulson, Ronald. "Gothic Fiction and the French Revolution." *English Literary History* 48 (1981): 532–54.

———. *Representations of Revolution.* New Haven: Yale UP, 1983.

Pearce, Roy Harvey. *The Continuity of American Poetry.* 1961. Rev. ed. Princeton: Princeton UP, 1965.

———. "Hawthorne and the Sense of the Past." *ELH: A Journal of English Literary History* 21 (1954): 327–49.

Peckham, Morse. "Toward a Theory of Romanticism." *PMLA* 66 (1951): 5–23.

Perkins, David. *The Quest for Permanence: The Symbolism of Wordsworth, Shelley and Keats.* Cambridge: Harvard UP, 1959.

Peterfreund, Stuart. "Keats's Debt to Maturin." *Wordsworth Circle* 13 (1982): 45–49.

Poe, Edgar Allan. *Collected Works of Edgar Allan Poe.* 3 vols. Ed. Thomas Ollive Mabbott. Cambridge: Harvard UP, 1969–1978.

———. *Essays and Reviews.* Ed. G. R. Thompson. New York: Library of America, 1984.

Porte, Joel. "In the Hands of an Angry God: Religious Terror in Gothic Fiction." *The Gothic Imagination: Essays in Dark Romanticism.* Ed. G. R. Thompson. [Pullman]: Washington State UP, 1974. 42–64.

———. *The Romance in America: Studies in Cooper, Poe, Hawthorne, Melville, and James.* Middletown: Wesleyan UP, 1969.

Prescott, F. C. "Wieland and *Frankenstein*." *American Literature* 2 (1930): 172–73.

Price, Martin. "The Sublime Poem: Pictures and Powers." *Yale Review* 58 (1968): 194–213.

Punter, David. *The Literature of Terror: A History of Gothic Fictions from 1765 to the Present Day.* London: Longman, 1980.

Radcliffe, Ann. *The Mysteries of Udolpho: A Romance.* 1794. Ed. Bonamy Dobrée. New York: Oxford UP, 1966.

———. "On the Supernatural in Poetry." *New Monthly Magazine and Literary Journal* 16 (1826): 145–52.

Railo, Eino. *The Haunted Castle: A Study of the Elements of English Romanticism.* 1927. New York: Humanities Press, 1964.

Randel, Fred V. "*Frankenstein,* Feminism, and the Intertextuality of Mountains." *Studies in Romanticism* 23 (1984): 515–32.

———. "The Mountaintops of English Romanticism." *Texas Studies in Literature and Language* 23 (1981): 294–323.

———. "Wordsworth's Homecoming." *Studies in English Literature, 1500–1900* 17 (1977): 575–91.

Reeve, Clara. *The Old English Baron: A Gothic Story.* 1778. Ed. James Trainer. New York: Oxford UP, 1967.

———. *The Progress of Romance through Times, Countries, and Manners.* 1785. New York: Garland, 1970.

Richmond, Lee J. "Edgar Allan Poe's 'Morella': Vampire of Volition." *Studies in Short Fiction* 9 (1972): 93–94.

Ridley, M. R. *Keats's Craftsmanship.* Oxford: Clarendon, 1933. 96–190.

Rieger, James. "Dr. Polidori and the Genesis of *Frankenstein*." *Studies in English Literature* 3 (1963): 461–72.

———. *The Mutiny Within: The Heresies of Percy Bysshe Shelley.* New York: George Braziller, 1967.

Ringe, Donald A. *American Gothic: Imagination and Reason in Nineteenth-Century Fiction.* Lexington: UP of Kentucky, 1982.

———. *Charles Brockden Brown.* New York: Twayne, 1966.

Ronald, Ann. "Terror-Gothic: Nightmare and Dream in Ann Radcliffe and Charlotte Brontë." *The Female Gothic.* Ed. Juliann E. Fleenor. Montreal: Eden, 1983. 176–86.

Rosenthal, Bernard. "The Voices of *Wieland.*" *Critical Essays on Charles Brockden Brown.* Ed. Bernard Rosenthal. Boston: G. K. Hall, 1981. 87–103.

Schiller, Friedrich. "The Sublime." *Essays Aesthetical and Philosophical.* London: George Bell, 1875.

Scoggins, James. *Imagination and Fancy: Complementary Modes in the Poetry of Wordsworth.* Lincoln: U of Nebraska P, 1966. 139–90.

Scott, Peter Dale. "Vital Artifice: Mary, Percy, and the Psychopolitical Integrity of *Frankenstein.*" Levine and Knoepflmacher. 172–202.

Scott, Walter. "On the Supernatural in Fictitious Composition." *Foreign Quarterly Review* 1 (1827): 60–98.

Shackleford, Martha Hale. " 'The Eve of St. Agnes' and *The Mysteries of Udolpho.*" *PMLA* 31 (1921): 76–94.

Shapiro, Barbara A. *The Romantic Mother: Narcissistic Patterns in Romantic Poetry.* Baltimore: Johns Hopkins UP, 1983.

Shaver, Chester L., and Alice C. Shaver. *Wordsworth's Library: A Catalogue.* New York: Garland, 1979.

Shelden, Pamela J. " 'True Originality': Poe's Manipulation of the Gothic Tradition." *American Transcendental Quarterly* 29 (1976): 75–80.

Shelley, Mary Wollstonecraft Godwin. *Frankenstein, or the Modern Prometheus.* Ed. M. K. Joseph. New York: Oxford UP, 1969.

———. *Mary Shelley's Journal.* Ed. Frederick L. Jones. Norman: U of Oklahoma P, 1947.

Shelley, Percy Bysshe. *The Complete Works of Percy Bysshe Shelley.* 10 vols. Ed. Roger Ingpen and Walter E. Peck. New York: Gordian, 1965.

———. *Shelley's Poetry and Prose.* Ed. Donald H. Reiman and Sharon B. Powers. New York: Norton, 1977.

———. *Zastrozzi and St. Irvyne.* Ed. Stephen C. Behrendt. 1810–1811. New York: Oxford UP, 1986.

Shurr, William H. "Montresor's Audience in 'The Cask of Amontillado.' " *Poe Studies* 10 (1977): 28–29.

Sickels, Eleanor. "Shelley and Charles Brockden Brown." *PMLA* 45 (1930): 1116–28.

Siebers, Tobin. *The Romantic Fantastic.* Ithaca: Cornell UP, 1984.

Simon, John. "Coleridge and the Sublime." *Charles Lamb Bulletin* 56 (1986): 260–63.

Siskin, Clifford. "Wordsworth's Gothic Endeavor: From Esthwaite to the Great Decade." *Wordsworth Circle* 10 (1979): 161–73.

Slote, Bernice. *Keats and the Dramatic Principle.* Lincoln: U of Nebraska P, 1958.

Small, Christopher. *Ariel Like a Harpy: Shelley, Mary, and Frankenstein.* London: Victor Gollancz, 1972.

Smith, Charles J. "Wordsworth and Coleridge: The Growth of a Theme." *Studies in Philology* 54 (1957): 53–64.

Smith, Louise Z. "The Material Sublime: Keats and *Isabella.*" *Studies in Romanticism* 13 (1974): 299–311.

Smith, Nelson C. "Sense, Sensibility, and Ann Radcliffe." *Studies in English Literature, 1500–1900* 13 (1973): 577–90.

Solve, Mervin T. "Shelley and the Novels of Brown." *Fred Newton Scott Anniversary Papers.* Chicago: Chicago UP, 1929. 141–56.

Spacks, Patricia Meyer. *The Insistence of Horror: Aspects of the Supernatural in Eighteenth-Century Poetry.* Cambridge: Harvard UP, 1962.

Spatz, Jonas. "The Mystery of Eros: Sexual Initiation in Coleridge's 'Christabel.' " *PMLA* 90 (1975): 107–16.

Sperry, Stuart. *Keats the Poet.* Princeton: Princeton UP, 1973.

Sterrenburg, Lee. "Mary Shelley's Monster: Politics and Psyche in *Frankenstein.*" Levine and Knoepflmacher. 143–71.

Stevenson, Warren. "Lamia: A Stab at the Gordian Knot." *Studies in Romanticism* 11 (1972): 241–52.

Stewart, Dugald. *Philosophical Essays.* 1810. Vol. 5 of *The Collected Works of Dugald Stewart.* 10 vols. 1855. Ed. Sir William Hamilton. Westmead, England: Gregg, 1971.

Stillinger, Jack. *The Hoodwinking of Madeline and Other Essays on Keats's Poems.* Urbana: U of Illinois P, 1971.

Stock, Ely. "Witchcraft in 'The Hollow of the Three Hills.' " *American Transcendental Quarterly* 14 (1972): 31–33.

Stoddard, Eve Walsh. "Flashes of the Invisible World: *The Prelude* in the Context of the Kantian Sublime." *Wordsworth Circle* 16 (1985): 32–37.

Storch, R. F. "Wordsworth's Experimental Ballads: The Radical Uses of Intelligence and Comedy." *Studies in English Literature, 1500–1900* 11 (1971): 621–39.

Strunk, W., Jr. "Some Related Poems of Wordsworth and Coleridge." *Modern Language Notes* 29 (1914): 201–5.

Sweet, Charles A., Jr. "Retapping Poe's 'Cask of Amontillado.' " *Poe Studies* 8 (1975): 10–12.

Tetreault, Ronald. "Shelley and Byron Encounter the Sublime: Switzerland, 1816." *Revue des Langues Vivantes* 41 (1975): 145–55.

Thompson, G. Richard. "The Apparition of This World: Transcendentalism and the American 'Ghost' Story." *Bridges to Fantasy.* Ed. George E. Slusser, Eric S. Rabkin, and Robert Scholes. Carbondale: Southern Illinois UP, 1982. 90–107, 207–9.

———. "Poe and the Paradox of Terror: Structures of Heightened Consciousness in 'The Fall of the House of Usher.' " *Ruined Eden of the Present: Hawthorne, Melville, and Poe: Critical Essays in Honor of Darrel Abel.* Ed. G. R. Thompson and Virgil L. Locke. West Lafayette: Purdue UP, 1981. 313–40.

———. *Poe's Fiction: Romantic Irony in the Gothic Tales.* Madison: U of Wisconsin P, 1973.

———, ed. "Introduction: Gothic Fiction of the Romantic Age: Context and Mode." *Romantic Gothic Tales 1790–1840.* New York: Harper and Row, 1979.

Thorpe, Clarence DeWitt. "Coleridge on the Sublime." *Wordsworth and Coleridge: Studies in Honor of George MacLean Harper.* Ed. Earl Leslie Griggs. 1939. New York: Russell and Russell, 1962. 192–219.

Todorov, Tzvetan. *The Fantastic: A Structural Approach to a Literary Genre.* 1970. Tr. Richard Howard. Cleveland: Case Western Reserve UP, 1973.

Tuttle, Donald Reuel. "*Christabel*'s Sources in Percy's *Reliques* and the Gothic Romance." *PMLA* 53 (1938): 445–74.

Tuveson, Ernest. "Space, Deity, and the 'Natural Sublime.' " *Modern Language Quarterly* 12 (1951): 20–38.

Twitchell, James B. *The Living Dead: A Study of the Vampire in Romantic Literature.* Durham: Duke UP, 1981.

———. *Romantic Horizons: Aspects of the Sublime in English Poetry and Painting, 1770–1850.* Columbia: U of Missouri P, 1983.

Usher, James. *Clio: or, A Discourse on Taste.* 2nd ed. 1769. New York: Garland, 1970.

Varnado, S. L. *Haunted Presence: The Numinous in Gothic Fiction.* Tuscaloosa: U of Alabama P, 1987.

———. "The Idea of the Numinous in Gothic Literature." *The Gothic Imagination: Essays in Dark Romanticism.* Ed. G. R. Thompson. [Pullman]: Washington State UP, 1974. 11–21.

Varma, Devendra P. *The Gothic Flame: Being a History of the Gothic Novel in England: Its Origins, Efflorescence, Disintegration and Residuary Influences.* London: Arthur Baker, 1957.

Voller, Jack G. "The Power of Terror: Burke and Kant in the House of Usher." *Poe Studies* 21 (1988): 27–35.

Waldoff, Leon. *Keats and the Silent Work of the Imagination.* Chicago: U of Illinois P, 1985.

Walpole, Horace. *The Castle of Otranto. Three Gothic Novels.* Ed. E. F. Bleiler. New York: Dover, 1966.

Walter, James. "A Metaphysical Vision of History in Hawthorne's Fiction." *Nathaniel Hawthorne Journal* 6 (1976): 276–85.

Ware, Malcolm. *Sublimity in the Novels of Ann Radcliffe: A Study of the Influence upon Her Craft of Edmund Burke's Enquiry into the Origin of our Ideas of the Sublime and Beautiful.* Copenhagen: Ejnar Munksgaard, 1963.

Wasserman, Earl R. *The Finer Tone: Keats' Major Odes*. Baltimore: Johns Hopkins UP, 1953.

——. *The Subtler Language: Critical Readings of Neoclassic and Romantic Poems*. Baltimore: Johns Hopkins UP, 1959.

Watson, J. R. *Wordsworth's Vital Soul: The Sacred and the Profane in Wordsworth's Poetry*. London: Macmillan, 1982.

Webb, Timothy. *Shelley: A Voice Not Understood*. Manchester: Manchester UP, 1977.

Weiskel, Thomas. *The Romantic Sublime: Studies in the Structure and Psychology of Transcendence*. Baltimore: Johns Hopkins UP, 1976.

Weissman, Judith. " 'Language Strange': 'La Belle Dame sans Merci' and the Language of Nature." *Colby Library Quarterly* 16 (1980): 91–105.

Wellek, René. *Immanuel Kant in England, 1793–1838*. Princeton: Princeton UP, 1931.

Wiener, David. "The Secularization of the Fortunate Fall in Keats's 'The Eve of St. Agnes.' " *Keats-Shelley Journal* 29 (1980): 120–30.

Wilt, Judith. *Ghosts of the Gothic: Austen, Eliot, and Lawrence*. Princeton: Princeton UP, 1981.

Wlecke, Albert O. *Wordsworth and the Sublime*. Berkeley: U of California P, 1973.

Woodring, Carl. "The Mariner's Return." *Studies in Romanticism* 11 (1972): 375–80.

Wordsworth, William. *The Poems*. Ed. John O. Hayden. 2 vols. New Haven: Yale UP, 1981.

——. *The Prelude: A Parallel Text*. Ed. J. C. Maxwell. New Haven: Yale UP, 1981.

——. *The Prose Works of William Wordsworth*. Ed. W. J. B Owen and Jane Worthington Smyser. 3 vols. Oxford: Clarendon, 1974.

Ziegler, James D. "Primitive, Newtonian, and Einsteinian Fantasies: Three Worldviews." Collins and Pearce, 69–75.

Index

House, The," 211; "Ethan
Brand," 218; "Feathertop,"
213–15; "Graves and Goblins,"
216; "Grey Champion, The,"
213; "Hall of Fantasy, The,"
214; "Haunted Mind, The,"
212; "Hollow of the Three Hills,
The," 213, 214, 215–16; *House
of the Seven Gables, The*, 211,
215, 234; "Legends of the Prov-
ince House," 213; *Marble Faun,
The*, 83, 209; *Mosses from an
Old Manse*, 221; "My Kinsman,
Major Molineaux," 213; "New
Adam and Eve, The," 218; "P.'s
Correspondence," 214; "Rap-
pacini's Daughter," 218; "Select
Party, A," 214; "Snow-Image,
The," 213, 219, 222; *Twice-
Told Tales,* 221; "Visit to the
Clerk of the Weather, A," 214;
"Young Goodman Brown,"
216–18, 222
Hegel, Georg Wilhelm Friedrich, 225
Heller, Terry, 241, 242, 241n.4
Hertz, Neil, 241n.1
Hipple, Walter, 16
Hobhouse, John Cam, 179
Hobsbawm, E. J., 226
Hoffman, Daniel, 222, 247, 247n.8
Hogg, Thomas, 169
Holstein, Michael, 119, 125
Hume, Robert, 32, 39, 87, 88, 162, 184

Irving, Washington, 210, 212, 223

Jackson, Rosemary, 220, 223, 224, 238, 241n.4
Jacobus, Mary, 145, 146, 244, 244n.3
James, Henry, 235
Janowitz, Anne, 112

Jones, Daryl E., 247n.6
Jones, John, 133
Jordan, J. E., 244n.3
Joseph, M. K., 245n.6, 244n.1

Kafka, Franz, 235
Kant, Immanuel, 127, 164, 180; sublime: influence on Coleridge,
Samuel Taylor, 98–99, 101;
———, dynamical, 100–1;
———mathematical 99–101,
243n.2; ———, theory of, 97–
100. Works: "Analytic of the
Aesthetical Judgement," 98; *Critique of Judgement*, 98; *Observations on the Feeling of the
Beautiful and the Sublime,* 97
Keats, John, 49, 126, 134; lamia, use
of compared to Coleridge, Samuel Taylor, 124; supernaturalism, 185–87, 192, 197; ———,
understanding of, 185; ———,
understanding of compared to
Coleridge, Samuel Taylor, 185;
———, understanding of compared to Shelley, Percy Bysshe,
186; sublime: relationship to
negative capability, 187; ———,
supernatural, 199, 204, 206;
———, understanding of, 185–
86, 188, 203; ———, under-
standing of compared to
Coleridge, Samuel Taylor, 185;
———, understanding of compared to Shelley, Percy Bysshe,
186; ———, understanding of
compared to Wordsworth, William, 185. Works: "Eve of St.
Agnes, The," 187, 191–97, 199,
245nn.1–3, 246n.5; "Isabella,"
187–191, 245n.2; "La Belle
Dame sans Merci," 187, 191,
196–98, 246nn.6–7; "Lamia,"

www.ingramcontent.com/pod-product-compliance
Lightning Source LLC
Chambersburg PA
CBHW030259100426
42812CB00002B/507